CO-AMH-193

C
I
N
E
M
LANDSCAPES
T
I
C

OBSERVATIONS ON THE
VISUAL ARTS AND CINEMA
OF CHINA AND JAPAN
Edited by
LINDA C. EHRLICH
AND DAVID DESSER

LANDSCAPES

CINEMATIC

University of Texas Press
Austin

FIRST EDITION, 1994

Requests for permission to reproduce
material from this work should be sent to
Permissions, University of Texas Press,
Box 7819, Austin, TX 78713-7819.

⊗ The paper used in this publication meets
the minimum requirements of American
National Standard for Information
Sciences—Permanence of Paper for Printed
Library Materials, ANSI Z39.48-1984.

LIBRARY OF CONGRESS

CATALOGING-IN-PUBLICATION DATA
Cinematic landscapes : observations on the
visual arts and cinema of China and Japan /
edited by Linda C. Ehrlich and
David Desser. — 1st ed.
p.   cm.
Filmography: p.
Includes bibliographical references
and index.
ISBN 0-292-72086-6 (alk. paper). —
ISBN 0-292-72087-4 (pbk. : alk. paper)
1. Art and motion pictures—China.
2. Art and motion pictures—
Japan.   I. Ehrlich, Linda C. (Linda
Channah), date.   II. Desser, David.
N72.M6C55   1994
791.43'01—dc20   93-43041

COLORPLATES

FIGURES

ACKNOWLEDGMENTS

We would like to thank the following persons for their assistance and encouragement: Lisa Atkinson of the Canadian Consulate in Beijing, Nadine Covert and the Program for Art on Film, Nancy Grossman and Kelly Baumer-Braun of the Cleveland Museum of Art, Robert Harrist of Oberlin College, Hayashi Kanako and other staff members of the Kawakita Memorial Film Library (Tokyo), the staff of the Audio-Visual Division of the Japan Foundation (Tokyo), Sumie Jones of Indiana University, Don Kirihara of the University of Arizona, Chuck Maland, Chris Holmlund, and Stan Lusby of the University of Tennessee/Knoxville, and David Soren of the University of Arizona/Tucson.

Generous publication-assistance grants from the Japan Foundation and the University of Illinois/Urbana-Champaign facilitated the production of this anthology. A special thanks to Douglas Wilkerson for assisting with many aspects of the editing of the essays on Chinese cinema and art. His sense of scholarly excellence and his impressive knowledge of both Chinese and Japanese culture have helped shape this anthology.

We are indebted to our editors, Joanna Hitchcock and Frankie Westbrook of the University of Texas Press, for their openness to this topic and their careful guidance through the many steps required to produce an anthology of this scope. The comments of copy editor Bob Fullilove also helped foster an overall sense of unity in the manuscript.

Celine Bassetti's summary and translations of Jacques Aumont's writings were especially insightful. Additional thanks go to Fukuda Yūko for her help with final details involving Japanese terms and to Jane Lewis and Jennifer

Vasil for their insightful assistance with the placement of the illustrations and with the index.

We are grateful to the Department of Romance Languages and Asian Languages and Literatures of the University of Tennessee/Knoxville for their assistance in the publication of this anthology and to the many museums, film studios, and individuals who helped locate and reproduce the illustrations which add so much to the written text. Thanks also to friends and colleagues in the Unit for Cinema Studies, University of Illinois, especially Lyn Petrie and Debbie Drake.

Finally, special thanks are extended to Ira and Phyllis Ehrlich for their support and enthusiasm, to Cathleen and Madeline Desser for their patience, and to the essayists and translators in *Cinematic Landscapes,* whose work has been an inspiration to us in the molding of this anthology.

INTRODUCTORY
REMARKS

After viewing a film from another culture, we might silently ask ourselves: What makes such a film *look* so different? The film ends, the lights come on; we blink our eyes and try to readjust to the boxlike dimensions of the theatre, and to the sense of quotidian time returning. We know we have seen something special, something that cannot be explained solely by the fascination of the story or the excellence of the acting. Certain scenes might remind us of a landscape painting once seen hanging on a museum wall, or a woodblock print in a book on a shelf at home. Yet we are almost afraid to trust these impressions, for surely a painting is a painting, and a film a film—two different art forms, created with different techniques, perhaps even for different audiences.

But are these art forms really so disparate? Drawing on precedents set by writers in the fields of cinema studies and art history, this volume attempts to identify some of the bridges that link both worlds. Filmmaking is a relatively recent, collaborative art form;

Because classical Chinese and Japanese painting both come from the same source, their spatial consciousness, compositional techniques, and construction of images have much in common. . . . Our understanding of Asian films should be deepened through comparative and comprehensive study. (NÍ ZHÈN)

many of the visual art forms discussed in *Cinematic Landscapes* date back centuries. The exciting history of the interplay between these various art forms has been too little studied in the case of East Asian films.

In her editor's statement to a special issue of *Art Journal* entitled "Art History and the Study of Film," Diane Kirkpatrick notes that "curiously, although the primarily visual nature of films is widely acknowledged, art historians are relative latecomers to its study."[1] In subtle ways, however, the two fields have been linked; for example, both art historians and scholars of cinema studies employ common terminology in discussions of the use of space and depth in compositions, the ability of lighting to alter an object, the psychological effects of color, the masking effects of the frame, the problem of distortion caused by reproduction of the original, and so on.

Both filmmakers and visual artists have long perceived the influence on the cinema of the pictorial and graphic arts—from the early avant-gardes in Europe, which saw artists like Salvador Dali, Fernand Léger, Man Ray, and Hans Richter, among others, and art movements like surrealism, expressionism, dadaism, futurism and constructivism finding their way into the cinema—just as the cinema influenced many of the pictorial arts themselves throughout the twentieth century.

In the history of Western cinema, famous examples of the influence of the visual arts on film are D. W. Griffith's *Corner in Wheat* (1909), inspired by Millet's *Sower* (and Griffith's integration of shots into *Birth of a Nation* [1915] which were in response to paintings), Jean-Luc Godard's *Passion*, with its recreation of Rembrandt's *Night Watch*, and the famous freeze-frame in Luis Buñuel's *Viridiana* (1961) which transposes a beggars' feast into Leonardo da Vinci's *Last Supper*. This concern with the "painterly" style of film, or with the appearance of paintings within the diegetic structure of a film, corresponds to the intent of this anthology to point out how some films cite the visual arts as a reference point or as a relevant basis for comparison.

What makes a film distinct from a painting or print, however, is precisely that it *moves*, that it is concerned with issues of continuity, a fact highlighted by Anne Hollander in *Moving Pictures*, one of the sources of inspiration for this volume. Hollander, an art historian by training, observes that films are closer to prints and paintings than to theatrical performances, in the sense that both films and the visual arts remain as lasting artifacts, while a stage performance is ephemeral. Drawing her examples primarily from Northern European and American art from the fifteenth to the twentieth centuries, Hollander calls certain pictures which reflect a concern with the "instability" of sight "proto-cinematic."

Among French writers this theme of the relationship between the visual arts and cinema has been explored by critics like Pascal Bonitzer in his *Décadrages: Peinture et cinéma* and, more recently, by Jacques Aumont in his *L'Oeil interminable: Cinéma et Peinture.* As Lynne Kirby points out in her review of Bonitzer's book, that writer's concern is with "shared techniques and premises" between cinema and painting.[2] Aumont's densely written exploration into cinema's links with the other arts, including painting, owes much to the inspiration of André Bazin, while it is also in keeping with, even to differentiate itself from, the influential ideologically based theories of French poststructuralism as represented by Jean-Louis Comolli and Jean-Louis Baudry.[3] The foundation of this ideologically based criticism which arose in France in the 1970s may be found in the interpretation of the function of Renaissance perspective. For these critics, and writers in English who followed in their wake (e.g., Stephen Heath), the basic apparatus of cinema (i.e., the camera as a mechanical means of reproduction) reproduces the principles of linear perspective perfected by the Renaissance painters.

Aumont is loath to reproduce some of this thinking in terms of the cinema's relation to painting. While sympathetic to the idea that film, and other forms of art, have an ideological dimension, Aumont feels that "it is within stylistic standards, rather than in the apparatus, that the effects of ideology emerge" (literally "the effects of ideology are inscribed": "que s'inscrivent les effets idéologiques").[4]

More significantly, he questions the direct correlation between the *dispositif* ("setup," or arrangement as spectacle) of cinema and painting. As Alan Williams notes in a review of Aumont's book: "Aumont argues that the setup of the cinematic show is in fact much more variable and difficult to define than the *dispositif* of painting . . . [and he feels] that the 'all-seeing' subject, long recognized as the subject of cinema, is a *dated* subject, historically dated by modernity, its [nature] anything but 'technical.' "[5] This is to say that while "the subject of cinema initially conformed and adapted itself to the demands of an *oeil variable,* or 'mutable eye,' which had previously manifested itself in painting and later in photography,"[6] the contemporary film subject is not so easily formed.

Western critics may, in fact, reject any notion of the ideologically based reading of perspective, or reject that cinema in any meaningful sense simply reproduces Renaissance perspective. Such is the tack taken by Noël Carroll in his attempt to reject much current French-derived psychoanalytically based film theory.[7] The idea of subject construction in the Lacanian sense, which is an effect of the basic apparatus and is aided by the "system of the suture," is similarly rejected in favor of alternate models of perception and image recognition.

We need not rehearse Aumont's complex arguments here, nor Carroll's either, for we may be struck already by the fact that in no significant sense does traditional Asian art rely upon Renaissance perspective. The essays in this anthology discuss alternatives to the one-point perspective and the *horror vacui* (fear of empty space) of Renaissance art, and the impact of those alternatives on the cinemas of China and Japan. The "framelessness" and greater contextuality of Japanese and Chinese scroll painting, and the concerns for variations on a theme found in the printmaking of those countries, are among the topics discussed in detail by the authors represented in this anthology.

While often drawing on the conventions of mainstream Hollywood cinema and on other Western models, such as Soviet social realism, the cinemas of China and Japan have nevertheless displayed unique styles that can be successfully examined in terms of indigenous traditions. The organization of the classical Hollywood narrative is marked by a linear and closed continuum of time and space in which all efforts are made to preserve this illusion of strict continuity. The classical Hollywood narrative presents psychologically defined individuals who struggle to solve a problem within this cause/effect chain. In order to preserve this illusion of continuity, editing techniques feature establishing shots, shot/reverse shots, and eyeline matches in dialogue scenes. As the essays that follow will illustrate, such concerns do not necessarily correspond to the overriding aesthetics of many films from China and Japan.

Considerable research has already been carried out on the possible relationships between the narrative structures of non-Western cinemas and traditional forms of theatre and literature. Despite the enthusiastic response in the West to the visually stunning work of many Chinese and Japanese film directors, considerably less has been written on the "similarity of purpose between [visual] artist and filmmaker" (Richie) in these cultures. Hollander and Aumont each devote only a few pages to the possible influence of the Asian arts on cinema. Clearly there exists a need for that kind of detailed analysis.

In 1989–1990, we placed a general call for papers in professional journals devoted to art history, cinema studies, and Asian studies. The responses to this call revealed considerable interest in the topic, and encouraged us to continue developing our ideas about the anthology. Subsequent correspondence with individuals who might serve as contributors helped us assemble a varied collection of essay topics, reflecting the diversity of scholarship in these fields.

Working closely with each contributor on editorial details, we then selected what we considered to be the best of the essays. The work of integrating the drafts into a single volume occupied the following two years.

The question still remained: Why combine a discussion of China and Japan into one volume? Although the term "East Asia" is an artificial construct, the ties between the two cultures are both profound and dynamic. Our decision was based on the awareness, shared by our contributors, that although the filmic cultures of the two countries display considerable differences, the shared art-historical background offers fertile ground for consideration of both Chinese and Japanese films in this context. Many of the essays point specifically to this shared background. The question of whether there is a fundamentally different sense of mimesis in the aesthetic traditions of countries like China and Japan—both compared to each other and compared to those of the West—serves as a motivating force behind a number of the essays in *Cinematic Landscapes*.

A cursory view of early Japanese history reveals that contact with Chinese culture may have occurred in Japan as early as the third century B.C., but it is certainly known that there were influential interchanges from the seventh century when Prince Shōtoku sent scholars to China to study Buddhism and Chinese culture. From those times to the contemporary period with its co-productions between Chinese Fifth Generation film directors and Japanese producers, the movement of artists back and forth between these two related, yet autonomous, geographical regions cannot be denied.[8] In particular, Japan's selective borrowings from China invite comparison and contrast between these two cultures.

As Robert Treat Paine writes in *The Art and Architecture of Japan,* "In the wide potentialities of hair brush and Chinese ink it [Japanese painting] indubitably derived from the art of China."[9] But he also immediately precedes this statement with the assertion that "the debt of Japan to the culture of China has often been stated in such a manner that the indigenous character of the art of the Island Empire has been depreciated or underestimated."

The perceptive reader will note similar terminology appearing in essays in both the Chinese and the Japanese sections of this volume—the "ambulatory, panoramic point of view and freely expandable frame" of handscrolls (Ní Zhèn, Richie), the equation of cinematography with brushwork (Berry/Farquhar, Satō), the use of "emptiness" as "a positive compositional element" (Ān Jǐngfū, Geist), and so on. These concepts point to variations in the way characters can be connected with setting, and narrative developed, in the cinema. The combining of essays on these various art forms into one volume illuminates the interrelated nature of these artistic discourses, with their shared assumptions about artistic experience and style, in a way that would prove impossible under another format.

As Wilkerson points out, the combination of "Eastern spirit with Western form" and technology serves as an underlying theme of many of the essays. The writers in this anthology comment on the ways many Chinese and Japanese films have incorporated an aesthetic based on Taoist and Chán (Zen) Buddhist principles, following the traditional emphasis on calligraphic line, pattern and design, and "flat" lighting, rather than on the use of chiaroscuro to create mood and a sculptural sense of three-dimensional form. The writers describe the "visual grammar" (Rimer) created by the use of these indigenous aesthetic traditions in the composition, lighting, and editing of films as diverse as Hou Hsiao-hsien's (Hóu Xiàoxián's) *A City of Sadness* (*Bēiqíng chéngshì*, 1988), Chén Kǎigē's *Yellow Earth* (*Huáng tǔdì*, 1984), Fèi Mù's *Spring in a Small Town* (*Xiǎochéng zhī chūn*, 1948), Ozu Yasujirō's *The End of Summer* (*Kohayagawake no aki*, 1961), and Suzuki Seijun's *Gate of Flesh* (*Nikutai no mon*, 1964).

Traditions of portraiture and of color, based on folk art and a sense of playfulness, figure into the discussion of the unique visual quality of films like Zhāng Yìmóu's *Judou* (*Júdòu*, 1990), Ozu's *Ohayō* (*Ohayō*, 1959), and Ichikawa Kon's *An Actor's Revenge* (*Yukinojō henge*, 1963). Color is used in these films for both realistic and deliberately decorative purposes, thus linking the films to traditions as diverse as those of *nóng cǎi huà* (rich color painting), both Chinese and Japanese "bird and flower paintings," and the *sōsaku hanga* (contemporary woodblock print). This is contrasted to what Desser describes as the "invisibility of classical Hollywood film style in which color should be attached to a specific meaning."

Davis introduces the reader to a particularly Japanese way of seeing in relation to the *kare sansui* (dry rock and sand) garden, echoed in the dynamics of the opening tracking shot of Mizoguchi's *The Loyal Rōnin of the Genroku Era* (*Genroku chūshingura*, 1941–42). Looking at what he calls the "concealed geometry" of many of the shots in this film, Davis discusses how this quality "domesticates the irrational . . . through the displacement of narrative by perceptual, aesthetic, and religious contemplation."

In contrast, Berry and Farquhar's discussion of a film like *Black Cannon Incident* (*Hēipào shìjiàn*, 1985) highlights both the film's freedom from "the aesthetic stranglehold of socialist realism on the cinema" and the incorporation of a modernist sense of alienation and disorientation, in which the dwarfing of the human form assumes a vastly different signification than it did in landscape painting. This trend marks a movement from a universal point of view transcending the individual and momentary toward a sense of entrapment. On the more positive side, the modern trend to bring back "the artist's vision as a creative, cohesive force in artistic production" (Berry/Farquhar) is examined through works by directors like Kobayashi Masaki, Huáng Jiànxīn, and Kurosawa Akira. Discussions of the artistic implications of political constraints placed on directors of mainstream Chinese cinema before the small "window of opportunity" provided directors in the early eighties, and of similar constraints imposed during the prewar and wartime periods in Japan, remind us that art never operates in a vacuum, and that traditional motifs can sometimes be used as a kind of camouflage for an underlying revolutionary discourse.

Discussions of the backgrounds of several East Asian film artists (notably Mizoguchi, Zhāng Yìmóu, Ichikawa, Miyagawa Kazuo), and of general exposure to, and training in, the visual arts among the general public in China and Japan, provide clues to why the visual arts have been so influential in the work of these directors and cinematographers. This in turn ties in to the issue of audience reception of the films, and to the question raised by Rimer: How do the expectations of traditional viewers and those of modern ones differ in terms of their ability to "read" a film or work of art based on these traditional aesthetics? And how do these differences in audience preparedness affect the artistic visions of the film directors as they conceive their work?

Because of its scope, the general organization of this book provided difficult editorial challenges. In the end, we chose a basic plan in which both the Chinese and the Japanese sections open with an introductory discussion by a scholar whose main research area is that of literary studies. The cogent overviews by Douglas Wilkerson and J. Thomas Rimer serve as guides to aid readers from a variety of backgrounds through the essays that follow, and to offer points for further contemplation.

The first essays in each section (Hǎo, Ní Zhèn, Richie, Satō) open vistas onto the theoretical issues that underlie this kind of intertextual investigation. The subsequent essays are arranged in a roughly chronological order in terms of the subject matter presented in the films. This is clearest in the Japanese section where the films discussed range from a depiction of the Tokugawa period (1615–1868) to films which reflect a more contemporary, even avant-garde, perspective. In the Chinese section, the scholars analyze some early mainstream films but choose to focus on films of the so-called Fifth Generation directors, which lend themselves so readily to analogies with the visual arts.

The original intent of the anthology was to balance the length of the Chinese and Japanese sections; for several reasons, an imbalance in the number of essays in the two parts has occurred. Western scholarship on Japanese cinema has been more plentiful than that on Chinese cinema, partially due to greater access to film texts from Japan. This anthology reflects this current situation. Although we were fortunate to receive several important essays from scholars at the Beijing Film Academy, such contacts were more difficult to develop and maintain, particularly in light of changing political conditions in China. A special thanks is due Douglas Wilkerson and Ann Sherif for their sensitive English translations of essays submitted in Chinese and Japanese.

The variety of writing styles in the individual essays reflects the variety of disciplines—film studies, art history, Chinese literature, Japanese literature—and several nationalities—the People's Republic of China, Japan, Hong Kong, Australia, the United States—of the contributors. One contributor, Hǎo Dàzhēng, now resides in Germany and draws from European scholarship. Many of the Western writers have spent extensive periods of study in East Asia. The variety of approaches and styles is, in itself, an important aspect of this investigation, providing some of the interdisciplinary fervor that gave rise to film studies in the first place, and capturing some of the international flavor that makes art history and film studies exciting areas of inquiry.

Sherman Lee's essay "Contrasts in Chinese and Japanese Art" was included in the anthology to remind readers of what he calls "the most prevalent and characteristic modes of Chinese or Japanese art." Dr. Lee's essay offers extremely lucid examples of the tendency of Japanese art toward realistic detail, exaggeration, and a depiction based on intuition and emotion, while Chinese art, in his view, tends toward the logical, the idealistic, and the restrained. We thank Dr. Lee for his permission to reprint his essay.

Care was taken to select frame enlargements, production stills, and reproductions of relevant art objects. Although color illustrations would have been preferable in many cases, their number had to be limited to examples which dealt specifically with issues related to color, in order to keep the cost of the volume within reasonable limits. The Selected Works lists books and articles that consider the interplay of film and art; it is not intended as a comprehensive bibliography, nor does it include every work cited in the individual essays.

No attempt was made to assign specific topics to the essayists. In any anthology, omissions are bound to occur, and this anthology is no exception. Most notably, no one who responded to the call for papers or to our individual letters decided to write at length about the work of a Chinese or Japanese woman director, or on the even more direct connection between the visual arts and animation, video art, or nontheatrical/experimental film. Several of the articles (Lau, Andrew, Ehrlich, Desser) do address gender issues in their examination of specific films. (For example, note the observations about erotic prints [*shunga*] and "Roman porn" films in Satō's essay, and Andrew's discussion of "the scandal of the female body within the economy of artistic production and consumption.") After consulting several scholars, we were reminded that there has been little analysis of a woman's visual style in either Chinese or Japanese art, let alone in the newer field of Asian cinema studies.[10] It is our hope that subsequent articles and books on this topic will speak to these, and other, related issues.

Gathering together essays from specialists in the areas of Asian art history and cinema studies, we have attempted to provide a series of observations on the relationships between these fields as expressed in films from China and Japan. In no way is this intended as an exhaustive study; rather, it is a beginning to what is hoped will be a continuing, now-necessary discussion, and an end to what sometimes appears to be a segregation of film from art history, and art history from film. It is our further hope that the essays in this anthology raise key questions regarding the influence of the visual arts on the cinemas of these two major Asian art and film cultures, and in so doing may provide models for the continued study of the influence of the visual arts on cinema around the world.

The lines between the visual arts and cinema are both intriguing and elusive. Nevertheless, as Mario Praz expressed in his A. W. Mellon Lectures in the Fine Arts, "The idea of the sister arts has been so rooted in men's minds since times of remote antiquity, that there must be in it something deeper than an idle speculation, something tantalizing and refusing to be lightly dismissed, like all problems of origins. One might say that by probing into those mysterious relationships men think to come closer to the whole phenomenon of artistic inspiration."[11]

Now we invite the reader to explore the essays that follow and to ponder with the essayists the direct, and the more subtle, relationships between these vital art forms, between painting with ink and brush and "painting with light."

Notes

1. Diane Kirkpatrick, "Editor's Statement: Art History and the Study of Film," *Art Journal* 43, no. 3 (Fall 1983): p. 221.

2. Lynne Kirby, "Painting and Cinema: The Frames of Discourse," *Camera Obscura* 18 (1989): p. 95.

3. Jean-Louis Baudry, "Ideological Effects of the Basic Cinematographic Apparatus," *Film Quarterly* 28, no. 2 (1974–1975): pp. 39–47.

4. Jacques Aumont, *L'Oeil Interminable: Cinéma et Peinture* (Paris: Librairie Séguier, 1989), p. 140.

5. Alan Williams, review of *L'Oeil Interminable: Cinéma et Peinture* by Jacques Aumont, *Screen* 32, no. 2 (Summer 1991): p. 236 (emphasis in original).

6. Ibid.

7. Noël Carroll, *Mystifying Movies: Fads and Fallacies in Contemporary Film Theory* (New York: Columbia University Press, 1988).

8. The Fifth Generation of Chinese filmmakers graduated in 1982 from the Beijing Film Academy. (Note the essay by Berry and Farquhar for further description of these filmmakers.)

Examples of Chinese-Japanese coproductions are *The Go Masters* (*Mikan no taikyoku*, 1982) and *Raise the Red Lantern* (*Dàhóng dēnglóng gāogāo guà*, 1992).

9. Robert Treat Paine and Alexander Soper, *The Art and Architecture of Japan* (Penguin Books, 1981), p. 21.

10. Recent work on this subject can be seen in Marsha Weidner, ed., *Flowering in the Shadows: Women in the History of Chinese and Japanese Painting* (Honolulu: University of Hawaii Press, 1990), and in two exhibition catalogues: *Japanese Women Artists, 1600–1900* (curated by Patricia Fister for the Spencer Museum of Art, University of Kansas, 1988) and *Views from Jade Terrace: Chinese Women Artists, 1300–1912* (curated by Ellen Johnston Laing and Marsha Weidner for the Indianapolis Museum of Art, 1988).

Weidner points out in her Introduction to *Flowering in the Shadows* that "in comparison to scholars working in other areas of Asian Studies, specialists of East Asian painting have been slow to reconsider women's contributions" (7).

Women active as film directors in Chinese and Japanese artistic circles include such directors as Zhāng Nuǎnxīn, Péng Xiǎolián, Hú Méi, Huáng Shǔqín, Ann Hui, Clara Law, Haneda Sumiko, Kurisaki Midori, Sekiguchi Noriko, and Hidari Sachiko, among others.

11. Mario Praz, *Mnemosyne: The Parallel between Literature and the Visual Arts* (Princeton: Princeton University Press, 1970): p. 3.

TABLE: MAJOR HISTORICAL PERIODS

China	Approximate Dates
HAN DYNASTY	206 B.C.–220 A.D.
THREE KINGDOMS	221–265
SIX DYNASTIES	265–581
SUI DYNASTY	581–618
TANG DYNASTY	618–906
FIVE DYNASTIES	907–960
SONG DYNASTY	960–1279
NORTHERN SONG	960–1126
SOUTHERN SONG	1127–1279
YUAN DYNASTY	1279–1368
MING DYNASTY	1368–1644
QING DYNASTY	1644–1912
REPUBLIC OF CHINA	1912–1949
PEOPLE'S REPUBLIC OF CHINA	1949–PRESENT
CULTURAL REVOLUTION	1966–1976

Japan	*Approximate Dates*
NARA	710–794
HEIAN	794–1185
KAMAKURA	1185–1333
MUROMACHI	1333–1573
MOMOYAMA	1573–1614
TOKUGAWA/EDO	1615–1868
MEIJI	1868–1912
TAISHŌ	1912–1926
SHŌWA	1926–1989
HEISEI	1989–PRESENT

CONTRASTS IN CHINESE
AND JAPANESE ART

BY SHERMAN LEE

Art historians and art critics are spinners of
webs. Often we are guilty of torturing material to fit a concept we find particularly exciting or illuminating. Within reasonable limits
this is a valid thing to do if one remembers
that the materials are temporarily deformed
by this activity and that after one has explored the pattern, the material is suitable for
yet another pattern, for another spinner to
find something perhaps similar or even quite
different.

One of the questions asked most often
about Chinese and Japanese art is: What is
the difference between Chinese and Japanese
art? How does one tell a Chinese painting
from a Japanese painting? Or, as the question
is more often put: Isn't it true that Japanese
art is but a pale and weak imitation of Chinese art, the only difference being one of quality? There are periods in Japanese art where
the artist is either copying, or is heavily influenced by, Chinese art. At such times it can be
said that Japanese art is a strong reflection of
Chinese art. But other works show the most

Note: This article first appeared in *Journal of Aesthetics and Art Criticism*
21, no. 1 (Fall 1962).

original contributions of the island culture. In these we see the small differences magnified to such an extent that they become fully developed and original styles.

At the outset we must remember, and admit, that the substance of this essay is intended to apply only to the most prevalent and characteristic modes of Chinese or Japanese art. It would be easy to find works, even periods, of Japanese art that are more like dominant Chinese styles than other Japanese examples. There are secondary styles or fashions in Chinese art that are quite at variance with the main stream. The appearance and occasional revival of a Western-influenced technique of modelling painted figures in light and shade would be one case in point. There are others. But in general, and for the most typical art styles of China and Japan, I think these comparisons are meaningful. A colossal head and torso of a Buddhist deity, the *Eleven-faced Guānyīn* dating from about 820,[1] can be compared with a small Japanese wood sculpture of a seated *Shakyamuni*[2] dating from about the same time. The style of the head is one that developed in China in the eighth and ninth centuries and is characterized by a fleshy but elegant, rather sensuous attitude. The style goes back for its inspiration ultimately to India, and was transmitted to Japan by Chinese sculptors, sculptures, and copy books, where it became the fundamental style for Buddhist sculpture in the Jogan period. This period and the Chinese mid-Tang style produced works which are roughly comparable: large, rotund facial types; emphasis upon the geometric and even curves of the chin, throat, and eyebrows. There is a definite emphasis on representational mass even to the point of corpulence, like that found in the West in the works of Rubens, Jordaens, or even Michelangelo. The representation of a large figure is the simplest method of conveying the impression of weight and mass. Such appearances may not conform to our local traditions of beauty but they evidently do to others.

The general point to be observed in the first thread of this particular web is that the Japanese artist tends to exaggerate the style or technique of the Chinese artist, even where he follows it most closely. He emphasizes the corpulence of the figure even more. He heightens the rather geometric character of the drapery. Such exaggeration, often expressed in almost wild variations at extremes, seems to most sociologists and anthropologists rather characteristic of Japanese culture. One remembers the restrained grace and elegance of the tea ceremony and the uninhibited wild and noisy activities of some festivals; or the ritual "politesse" of domestic entertainment and the thoughtless rudeness evidenced in public transportation. On the other hand, we think of the golden mean when we recall the philosophy of Confucius and of the Neo-

Confucian tradition. I would, then, call attention to exaggeration as being typically Japanese and moderation as being characteristically Chinese.

Numerous works illustrate this point within seemingly identical styles. A detail of a handscroll by the great Southern Song artist of the thirteenth century, Xià Guī, in the Palace Collection, can be put beside two panels of a screen by the great fifteenth-century Japanese monochrome master, Shūbun, and reveal that on certain occasions it is virtually impossible to put one's finger on the precise difference between a Chinese work and a Japanese work in the same style (figures 1.1, 1.2). In these rare cases, the individual Japanese artist will so completely convince himself of the validity of the Chinese style and so absorb it into himself, that he will produce a work which is a re-creation of the work of the Chinese master of an earlier time. This is seen most strongly in the work of Shūbun, one of the founders of the monochrome school of painting in Japan. There may be a trace of exaggeration in the brushwork of the rocks in the lower left foreground of the screen; there may be also a trifling exaggeration in the compositional display of these great mountain heights, reaching up beyond the edge of the border of the painting; but fundamentally this is a faithful and creative re-creation of the earlier style.

However, if we look at the same detail of the painting by Xià Guī and at a detail of a handscroll by the pupil of Shūbun, the more famous Sesshū, we see, within the same stylistic framework, two fundamental differences. One is this matter of exaggeration: the axelike brush strokes that form the rock of the painting by Xià Guī on the upper right or the staccato accents of brushwork that make the bridge and the man walking on it are exaggerated in the scroll by Sesshū to a point where the brush strokes are no longer really functional in a representational sense. The brush strokes in the painting by Xià Guī seem to be a part of the representation. The brushwork and rock are identified and exist together. In the work by Sesshū certain elements of the brushwork have become an end in themselves. He has exaggerated the importance of the brushwork to a point where it becomes an aesthetic good somewhat divorced from its ends, and this, in a Chinese evaluation of this particular style, is a violation of the unity that must exist between representation and brushwork. This analysis does not say that the Chinese work is, in itself, greater, merely that there is a difference between them. It can also be pointed out that the space in the Japanese work tends to be more sharply divided: there is much more contrast between near and far, where in the Chinese work subtle gradations define the recession of space. Once again, then, in two rather similar works there is a contrast between exaggeration and

1.1 Xià Guī, *Pure and Remote View of Streams and Mountains,* China, Song dynasty, detail (courtesy of the National Palace Museum, Republic of China).

1.2 Shūbun, Abbot of Shokoku-ji, Kyoto (ca. 1390–ca. 1464), *Winter and Spring Landscape,* Japan, Muromachi period, six-fold screen, ink and slight color on paper (courtesy of The Cleveland Museum of Art, Gift of Mrs. R. Henry Norweb, 58.476).

SHERMAN LEE

moderation, and a Japanese emphasis upon the decorative development of brushwork—of great significance for the future.

Other comparisons may be in order. Another work by Sesshū,[3] the Japanese master who died in 1506, compared with a painting in Japan by the great Chinese artist Lǐ Táng, which can be dated effectively to 1135 or 1137,[4] confirms all that has been said before. If one looks at the massive rocklike structure behind the two small men, one is hardly aware of the differentiation of brushwork and representation, while in the Sesshū representation is clearly separate and there is a concurrent play with the brush which becomes a kinetic and aesthetic end in itself.

Now let us examine two particularly Oriental beasts, first, two tigers in the Cleveland Museum. The one is attributed to the Late Song Chinese artist Mùqī and was once in the collection of the fifteenth-century Japanese Ashikaga *shōgun* Yoshimitsu and Yoshimasa. The other is from a pair of screens by Sesson, the follower of Sesshū (figures 1.3, 1.4). Again we sense the difference between the representation of the Chinese tiger in rain from that of the Japanese work. The brushwork is assimilated into the structure of the tiger; the fur presents the baggy, shapeless character that the tiger presents when relaxed, with the folds of skin literally hanging from its frame. This keen observation is combined with brushwork which supports it, while the Japanese work presents a more playful handling. The same distinctions are true of the psychology of representation. The Chinese tiger gives the impression of reality, of power, of a presence that seems to emanate from the representation. Sesson's tiger exhibits a certain playfulness, passing almost into caricature, and this is of considerable significance for some facets of other Japanese works as we will see.

The other of the paintings by Mùqī represents a dragon and it is matched by Sesson's other screen (figures 1.5, 1.6). The Chinese dragon rests quietly but with an inner breathing power; he throbs with capability. The Japanese dragon by Sesson moves with great rapidity—strides, thrusts, turns, twists his way through the air. The waves in the Chinese painting occupy a subsidiary position and operate primarily as representations of water with foam. In the Japanese painting these have become a strong and decorative pattern, a major counterpart to the representation. Now it is entirely likely that Sesson saw such paintings and we may be witnessing a true case of direct influence. If one looks at details, these opposing qualities become clearer. The brushwork representing the stripes of Sesson's tiger are curling and playful. The expression of the beast—one fang protruding, bulging eyes, rather sharp and exaggerated delineation of the nose—is in contrast to the Chinese represen-

1.3 *Tiger,* China, attributed to Mùqī (Fǎcháng), active second half of thirteenth century, hanging scroll, ink on silk (courtesy of The Cleveland Museum of Art, Purchase from the J. H. Wade Fund, 58.428).

SHERMAN LEE

1.4 Sesson (ca. 1504–ca. 1589), *Tiger,* Japan, Muromachi period, six-fold screen, ink on paper (courtesy of The Cleveland Museum of Art, Purchase from the J. H. Wade Fund, 59.137).

tation, where the dominant quality is not of humor or exaggeration but of restraint and quiet power. Even the brushwork in the reeds and the bamboo shows less of the exaggerated, almost self-conscious art of Sesson. Details of the dragons reveal these qualities both in terms of brushwork and the psychology of representation.

A final comparison of two works of a rather similar nature will precede our examination of more striking contrasts between Chinese and Japanese art. One is a painting of *Two Peacocks* by the fifteenth-century academic Chinese master Lín Liáng;[5] the other is one of the famous sliding screens by Kanō Motonobu[6] in the Reiun-in in Kyoto. Certainly the Chinese considered the peacock painting a decorative painting, and it is decorative, rather in the sense of a French eighteenth-century tapestry—the artist tends to fill most of the space achieving an allover pattern. Beware the old cliché that the essence of Chinese painting is to be found in a large expanse of silk with a small tree or figure in the corner. The great majority of Chinese pictures show a quite different pattern: the artist attempts to fill the space, to achieve a complex and rational arrangement. The decorative pattern in the Lín Liáng *Peacocks* is carefully organized and rather formal, supported by an X which crosses in the center of the picture. The relatively balanced composition includes the presentation of bamboo against the other peacock, bamboo against bamboo,

1.5 *Dragon*, China, attributed to Mùqī (Fǎcháng), active second half of thirteenth century, hanging scroll, ink on silk (courtesy of The Cleveland Museum of Art, Purchase from the J. H. Wade Fund, 58.427).

SHERMAN LEE

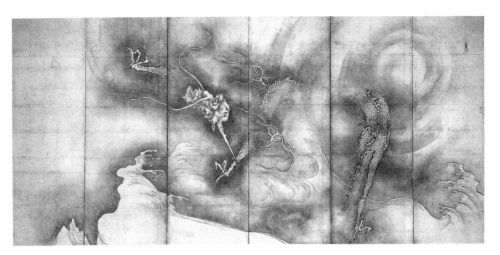

1.6 Sesson (ca. 1504–ca. 1589), *Dragon*, Japan, Muromachi period, six-fold screen, ink on paper (courtesy of The Cleveland Museum of Art, Purchase from the J. H. Wade Fund, 59.136).

and the peacock's tail balanced against the long sprig of bamboo in the upper left. The other example, a painting by Motonobu, is in the Chinese style of the fifteenth century but was executed in the sixteenth century, and shows one of the typical Japanese approaches to decoration. This is a tendency to force large blank areas against complex areas which usually include complex silhouettes, in this case the crane and the pine tree against the open space behind. The effect of this mode of decoration is allied to that often to be found in Braque, Matisse, or in other contemporary painters, founded on asymmetrical pattern, and depending upon a dynamic tension between nothing and something.

Some of these differences that exist in nuances on a very small scale take on a far more exaggerated character in more independent and creative works of Japanese art. One of these differences is that between an idealist approach, reconciling opposites, more or less to be equated with China, and a Japanese tendency to oscillate between either a decorative style and one which is realistic, even to the point of caricature. The anonymous portrait of the Zen Priest Wúzhǔn [7] is one of the most beautiful of Chinese Song portraits; while equally masterful is the contemporary portrait of Priest Jugen, kept at Tōdaiji in Nara, and dating from about 1210–1220.[8] The Chinese concept of portraiture makes us aware of a noble individual. But despite the fact the two men have similar facial structures, we are aware of the Chinese individual in a sympathetic but slightly removed way, as an ideal portrait. While he does not possess all the paraphernalia of old age, he gives the impression of ancient wisdom. The Japanese work emphasizes precisely those things that the Chinese artist de-emphasizes—the wrinkles of the face, the set of the jaw, the vast cavern of the ear, the sunken sockets of the eyes. Almost to the point of caricature it mercilessly exposes the realistic detail that marks both the character and the appearance of the individual.

These same divergent qualities are to be seen in the narrative scrolls which were painted both in China and Japan. In general, the narrative scroll in China was a secondary category. There were scrolls showing famous historical or literary events of the past, but usually the narrative content was restrained; and an interest in narration is one aspect of realism. On the other hand, the Japanese absorbed the handscroll format and made of it a great narrative tool in the late twelfth and thirteenth centuries. A Chinese painting of the twelfth or thirteenth century now in the museum in Beijing, represents the various activities in a Chinese town on a river during the spring festival.[9] Another, even more famous, but Japanese handscroll in the Boston Museum is *Scroll with Depictions of the Night Attack on the Sanjō Palace*, the first roll of three from the story of the Heiji uprising (figure 1.7).[10] In the Chinese scroll, despite the bustling activity to be inferred from the numerous figures represented before the shop-fronts, the little servant boys, the bales being unloaded, the little boy pointing out the way to a stranger, an ideal environment dominates. All this, and more, is present but it is not obtrusive. The emphasis is rather upon the figures as a part of the whole setting of nature, including civilization.

In the Japanese work, on the other hand, despite its roughly comparable scale, we are aware of violent activity. As a spinner of webs I must admit the juxtaposition is a purposely exaggerated one. One could show numerous other Japanese handscrolls where the representation is more comparable to that on the Chinese painting—a village scene with local activity—but you would still find the exaggeration which we see to a magnified degree in the *Heiji Monogatari*. When the Japanese represent a village there is almost always a repeated mise-en-scène: a gnarled and bent old woman staggering along the street, a boy fighting with another boy, an exaggerated caricature of a diseased and ugly person. There is a tremendous interest in a coldly rational, even satirical, realism, represented by the movement, the vigor and strife of this Heiji scroll. One must repeat that the Chinese work emphasizes rationality—everything in its place and nothing to excess. In this sense much of Chinese painting shares the serene and noble quality that we find in most Greek work before Hellenistic times.

SHERMAN LEE

1.7 *Scroll with Depictions of the Night Attack on the Sanjō Palace,* detail; from the *Illustrated Scrolls of the Events of the Heiji Era,* Japan, Kamakura period, second half of thirteenth century, handscroll, ink and colors on paper (courtesy of the Museum of Fine Arts, Boston, Fenellosa-Weld Collection, 11.4000).

Contrariwise, the Japanese work has a strong emotional quality. A revealing experience happened when I went to the cinema with some friends who had not been to Japan. They saw for the first time the Japanese work *Rashomon,* now a recognized classic of film art, and were horrified at the expression of emotion, the wildly exaggerated movements of the bandit, his snarling face, his spitting, and all the significant detail we remember so well. They were equally horrified by the music derived from Ravel, somehow so "unoriental"—not quiet and calm with a thin piping reed. But this wild, emotional quality is a basic part of much Japanese art. These people vacillate between the extremes of repression, or, if you will, self-control, and wild, emotional release. This latter is the quality that makes their narrative handscrolls one of the greatest contributions to Far Eastern painting. Even with two plates, the one a Chinese Imperial porcelain in the Tokyo National Museum made for the Qiánlóng Emperor some time about 1750–1760 (figure 1.8), the other a Japanese plate from the Kutani kilns and dating perhaps a half century earlier (figure 1.9), one finds a perfect "unloaded" example on the widest possible scale of these essential differences. The Chinese is interested in rationality and restraint combined with the observation of nature, the welding of brushwork to nature, and a strong interest in the written word

1.8 *Dish with Two Cocks in a Landscape,* China, Qing dynasty, semi-eggshell porcelain with famille rose enamels on white ground (courtesy of The Cleveland Museum of Art, Severance and Greta Millikin Collection).

1.9 Kutani ware plate with phoenix, Japan, Edo period (private collection, Tokyo).

SHERMAN LEE

combined with these things. The other and larger plate is one of the boldest and most original of all Japanese porcelains, a work in which I think we can use the term caricature in the best sense of the word. The phoenix struts, his enormous tail flung up, his head tilted, pushing to proud and masculine extremes quite in contrast to the Chinese style of porcelain decoration. One of the reasons that the old Kutani pieces have reached such astronomical prices is that the Japanese fully realize that these are their most original and creative porcelains of the later periods.

Even when one considers a Chinese expression of deep emotion, the comparative Japanese expression will "tear a passion to tatters, to very rags." The fragments of a handscroll in the Boston Museum tell the story of Wénjī's captivity in China (figure 1.10). One scene is of the highest emotional significance. These figures holding their sleeved hands to their eyes and noses are weeping because Wénjī, a captive who has lived long years of exile in Mongolia, must now be returned to China and so must leave her adopted Mongolian family. The situation contains deep elements of tragedy, yet the figures of the drama stand quietly, even stiffly erect and are subordinated to the setting. The whole has the effect of a *tableau vivant*, the figures frozen in space. The other detail is a scene from one of the greatest of all narrative paintings, *Ban Dainagon ekotoba* (note colorplate 1). It tells a story of intrigue and rebellion leading to a fire in the palace, with an accompanying "crowd scene." Wildly writhing and turning, the crowd is made up of faces with their wide-open mouths expressing extremes of panic and fear. The profiles of the various plebes are represented with terribly exaggerated jaws and noses;

1.10 *Eighteen Songs of the Nomad Flute: Wénjī parting from her children and the Han chieftain (thirteenth song)*, artist unknown, China, Song dynasty, twelfth century, album leaf; ink, color, and gold on silk (courtesy of the Museum of Fine Arts, Boston, Denman Waldo Ross Collection, 28.64).

there is great distortion in the size of the heads in relation to the body. The whole is a throbbing and dramatic presentation of a dramatic moment; contrariwise the Wénjī fragment is a quiet representation recalling Wordsworth's "emotion recollected in tranquility."

Even in the later scholarly painting of China and Japan, where painters painted for other painters, for only the gentleman-scholar was considered to be an original and creative artist, the same quality of idealism versus exaggeration is to be found; witness a painting by a great seventeenth-century individualist in China, Dàojì,[11] and an eighteenth-century Japanese man much influenced by what Dàojì represented, Ike-no Taiga.[12] In Dàojì's album leaf there is a wonderful play upon the idea of a beard: a bearded old man and his attendant are half hidden in the mist under a cave with beardlike hanging reeds and grasses, while above that is a waterfall, a magnified and fluid representation of a beard. The opportunity is presented to make a smashing belly-laugh; instead a quiet, restrained private joke is gently urged. In Taiga's album leaf the representation involves another visual pun: a man looks like a mountain. Which is the mountain, which is the man? And here the pun is presented with force, exaggeration, and evident humor. One seldom laughs at Chinese painting, but in Japanese painting numerous representations are humorous in the best sense of the word.

Another major contrast in the arts of the mainland and the islands is that between Chinese rationality and the intuitive quality of Japanese art with particular regard to the domination of, or surrender to, nature. One of the few hanging scrolls by, or close to, an eleventh-century master, Jùrán, is a monumental landscape in Cleveland where the Chinese artist has expressed perfectly the concept of rational principle in nature, or as the Chinese term it, lǐ.[13] In this hanging scroll we find a unified combination of rationality and observation which is neither a surrender to the material, nature, nor a domination of it. A Japanese painting, *Kumano Mandala: The Three Famous Temples,* also in the Cleveland Museum,[14] dates from the thirteenth century, and in its overall organization can be contrasted to the Chinese painting as an evident domination of nature. The geometric pattern of the temples, in plain view, is superimposed on nature so that one is more conscious of design than of nature. But when one looks at a detail of each painting, no matter how far into the Chinese painting one goes, one finds again a balance, a measured representation of principle by means of the brush, which is not only brushwork but also representation; while in the Japanese painting we sense a surrender to the loveliness of nature's forms—the seductive colors of blossoming nature, of pear and prunus, of moss and lichen. These different representations, rather than the brushwork, comprise the detail of the paint-

SHERMAN LEE

ing and produce a lovely and decorative effect quite removed from the consistent rationality of the Chinese painting.

Another side of the domination of, and surrender to, nature on the part of the Japanese, and of the middle position of the Chinese, is to be found in ceramic art. The Chinese combine an effective representation with a sure realization of technique and of the material. A seated figurine of the Han dynasty, perhaps of the third century,[15] can be juxtaposed with a *haniwa* in the National Museum in Tokyo.[16] The Japanese representation of the sixth century is dominated by its material, a dominance expressed in its name— *haniwa*, circle of clay. The artist leaves it rough and uses the circular form to produce an almost abstract symbol for a figure.

Before the rise of Abstract Expressionism, *haniwa* were the proverbial dime a dozen. But now the demand exceeds the genuine supply, with predictable results. In the Chinese figurine, the artist allowed the representation to meet the material halfway and the result is a representationally satisfactory substitute for reality. The same with the representation of horses in these burial figurines. The Chinese horse of the sixth century and the Japanese *haniwa* horse are contemporaneous (figures 1.11, 1.12). True to its name, a circle of clay, the legs of the Japanese sculpture are simply cylinders of clay; the body is almost a cylinder; the head is clearly based on a cylinder. These given shapes are combined to produce an equation, 3c equals horse. The Chinese burial substitute is the very living spirit of the horse expressed with attention to observed detail, yet with complete control of the clay medium.

These contrasts are even more evident in useful ceramics. In general, the Chinese pot is a cunning blend of material, body and glaze, with a logical near-geometric shape, usually a circle or a near-perfect circle, a cone, or ovoid shape. The Japanese bowl, later in time to be sure, developed from an art appealing particularly to recent modern taste, a style emphasizing asymmetry and which paradoxically dominates the material to a point where it makes the material look more natural. The English phrase, "studied nonchalance," perhaps expresses most nearly in Western terms what the Japanese tea-taste aims for, by indirection naturally. In the Chinese wares, there is little self-consciousness, no studied nonchalance. Rather one finds a devil-may-care directness in folk or peasant wares, or the utmost of rational and sensuous sophistication in the Imperial wares. One of these latter, one of sixteen Song Imperial pieces in Cleveland, displays a complex development of crackle deriving from an almost magical, if experimental, control of glaze enabling the kiln master to produce this perfect deep crackle, deep color, regulation of surface and of the flow of the glaze. There is an added fillip of an intellectual content implying a historical, even archaeological, interest: the

1.11 Mortuary Horse, China, Northern Wei dynasty (A.D. 386–535), pottery (courtesy of The Cleveland Museum of Art, The Norweb Collection, 72.82).

1.12 Horse, Japan, *haniwa*, third–fourth centuries, terra cotta (courtesy of The Cleveland Museum of Art, The Norweb Collection, 57.27).

SHERMAN LEE

use of archaistic shapes. The *lú* incense burner type reaches back over a thousand years, and yet it was consciously revived in the thirteenth century as homage to the past, a historical footnote. On the other hand, one of the most beautiful of Japanese tea-ceremony pieces, a Shino waterpot in a private collection in Japan, is a prime example of beautifully studied nonchalance— asymmetric treatment of the seemingly barely formed shape, no perfect circle, no perfect straight line, rather a subtly rough and ready, natural-looking piece eminently appropriate for use in the tea ceremony (figure 1.13).

In one medium the roles assigned by the web-spinner seem reversed. The garden art of China seems visually extreme and grotesque when compared with the quiet serenity and naturalness of the usual Japanese garden. And yet this may be the result of the contrasts we have assumed. The Chinese travel far to select the ancient and remarkable elements for the garden; but their respect for *lǐ* in nature may prevent them from controlling the untidy tendencies of untended nature. Thus one of the gardens in the Summer Palace outside Peking, when compared with perhaps the most famous of all Japanese gardens, the tiny jewel within the Daisen-in in Kyoto, brings out one part of the Chinese character which the Japanese also possess but seem able to control. Here, at least, the Chinese lets himself go—his love for old forms, for the spirit of antiquity, old rocks, especially twisted, gnarled, and perforated rocks, things that express the grandeur of old age. This basically Confucian idea of wise old age is most prominent in the gardens of the ancient mainland. The Japanese garden, like the tea-ceremony wares, takes the forms of nature and, with studied nonchalance, places them about in space so that they seem to create a painting. This is a reversal of the painting process. The Chinese painter takes a brush, looks at other paintings, observes nature, and paints a landscape. The Japanese garden designer, often a famous landscape painter, observes paintings, looks at nature, takes its elements, and makes them look like a painting.

Our last selection of contrasting works is selected to demonstrate the difference between the logical and descriptive style of most Chinese painting, even Chinese decoration, and the more intuitive and boldly decorative qualities of Japanese decorative style. One of the most interesting comparisons is that between the Chinese painting of *Hán Xīzài's Night Banquet,* a handscroll now in Beijing[17] (note colorplate 3), and a scene from one section of a Japanese scroll, illustrating the famous *Tale of Genji,*[18] readily available in the enchanting translation by Arthur Waley. *Hán Xīzài's Night Banquet* illustrates a particularly, as Chinese taste goes, wild party. The scroll is supposed to have been painted by Gù Hóngzhōng at the demand of an Emperor of the Southern Tang dynasty so that he might vicariously expe-

1.13 Shino ware cold water jar (*mizusashi*), with flowers and grasses, Japan, Momoyama period, sixteenth century, stoneware with glaze over painted iron oxide decoration (courtesy of the Seattle Art Museum, Eugene Fuller Memorial Collection, 51.208).

rience one of the reportedly licentious parties given by one of his ministers, Hán Xīzài. As Emperor he couldn't possibly attend and so he requested the painter to bring back the party alive. It is a masterpiece of logical organization, of space-setting in the Chinese system of perspective, of a rational representation of a group of men and women drinking, conversing, and listening to music on the lute. Only the most subtle hints of impropriety are to be found—rumpled bedclothes, indiscreet glances. In the scene from the *Genji monogatari*, as in the novel, everything is said by indirection. The human

SHERMAN LEE

figure is a decorative unit with a tiny head protruding from a pile of drapery. The interior is a cunning grid of lines that make a decorative pattern, and a space broken by large planes, almost in the manner of a contemporary painter dividing his picture space. In contrast to the rationality of the space in the Chinese painting is the irrational and intuitive quality of the Japanese space; and in contrast to the sober and descriptive quality of the Chinese painting is the arbitrarily asymmetrical, decorative quality of the Japanese painting.

Even the arbitrary and decorative fan shape provides evidence for these differences of style, as in a fan by Wén Zhēngmíng painted in the mid-sixteenth century, and a fan painting from a group by the seventeenth-century Japanese decorative master, Sōtatsu. The Japanese painting shows a completely arbitrary division of the fan shape with direct implications of objects in space continuing off the edge of the fan. But the Chinese painter has carefully bent his landscape, as Columbus crushed the egg, to logically fit the given format. He has allowed very little to project beyond the frame, which in turn contains the landscape. This is a combination of logic and description, while the Japanese artist has implied more, has intuitively placed his things in a balance that is asymmetrical and dynamic, and has, in a sense, denied the shape of the fan or, at least, used it for something more than the frame provides.

Or compare the Chinese fan of an *Early Spring Landscape* by the seventeenth-century master, Yùn Shòupíng,[19] and a pair of fans by Sōtatsu.[20] Again in the Chinese painting, nature is made to conform to the shape of the fan. We find the same type of composition in both Chinese and Japanese works—water, a point of land with a pavilion which reaches out into a bay fed by a stream. The Japanese painter makes his water and land conform to a decorative pattern emphasizing the rhythmical repetition of the larger but similar shapes of the spit of land. Above all, the composition is dominated by heavy layers of pure color: malachite green, azurite blue, and silver. Worse still, from a Chinese point of view, is what the Japanese artist did with the fan. To the Chinese, a fan was a personal gift, a token, a memento which one artist painted and gave to a friend. To the Japanese, the fan became a part of a gorgeous pair of screens in which the fans were distributed over a gold surface to produce an asymmetric, overall pattern. The fans are twisted and turned alternately, sometimes slightly overlapped, as in the two on the far right and far left. Thus we have a double decorative play, an overall pattern on a larger scale and daring variations within the smaller fan shapes.

When a Chinese did make a screen, as in the well-known Coromandel types,[21] they emphasized the frame with a border, even a series of borders, being careful to see that the whole scene was contained. Then he produced a logical and balanced development: one spray of flowers or leaves to each panel. The landscape is largely descriptive. A Japanese master such as Kōrin also had to contend with a border in his screens of red and white plum,[22] but the plum branch comes from outside the picture, reaches in past the low point, then sweeps up and out of the picture. The stream of water fixed on the surface by rhythmically repeated ripple whorls flows in from the outside right and reaches across the ground. The asymmetrical organization is achieved by balancing a large area of gold, controlled by the silhouette placed upon it, against a more dominant but smaller area of black made interesting by the patterning of the waves. If one looks at a detail of the Coromandel screen and at the second screen by Kōrin, there is the same contrast of descriptive quality with a rather simple use of color against the Japanese patterning of water and branch, perhaps even more prominent and even more decorative in this member of the pair.

These same differential qualities are to be found in porcelain. Made at almost the same time in the seventeenth century, the Imperial Kāngxī bowl[23] and the Kutani plate[24] are images from different worlds. For the Chinese the decorative quest was to find a way to use the peonies in three different colors, and to contain them, carefully balanced, within the circle of the bowl, while maintaining perfection of technique and purity of color. The designer and potter of the Lord of Kaga made a daring use of a string of mere eggplants on a rope diagonally across the center of the large plate, with a background of waves and whorls not unlike that motif in the Kōrin screens. There is no difference of aesthetic quality here, only one of style.

Or consider the Chinese lacquer, an Imperial example of Middle Ming in the sixteenth century,[25] and a remarkable Japanese writing box of the early seventeenth century owned by the Seattle Art Museum.[26] The Chinese lacquer has the same qualities already studied in the Coromandel screen; the border is self-contained; the representation is of a fairly naturalistic landscape; the presented image is rational and descriptive. For the box designed by Kōrin one finds the same style as that in his screens: overall decorative patterning in an asymmetrical way; tensions, suggestions of movements beyond the surface; de-emphasis of the frame to imply continuity beyond. All of this is part of the Japanese decorative taste including the ability and imagination to use exotic or mundane materials in a decorative way. The gold lacquer is familiar, but some of the other cranes are done in two different metals, pewter and lead, and the textures of these different metals subtly differentiate the birds from an aesthetic viewpoint. Of course the Chinese have used pewter and lead, but seldom if ever in so sophisticated a context, or juxtaposed with precious gold.

Finally, observe two almost exactly contemporaneous paintings, the one a landscape after the great Northern Song master, Guō Zhōngshù, by the seventeenth-century individualist priest-painter, Zhū Dā,[27] the other a hanging scroll by the Japanese scholar-painter Gyokudō.[28] Zhū Dā's construction, though based upon a style like that of the monumental landscape by Jùrán which we saw much earlier, is a personal re-creation by an individualist of the seventeenth century; but wild as they were we are aware of something here that can be sensed only in general terms—a certain rational remove. The landscape seems to be distant from the spectator, he views it from afar. The use of cold, blue-black ink heightens the quality of icy rationality. The way the mountain twists while leading the eye up to the mist that suddenly appears and separates the viewer from the higher peak, this whole construction is one of a strong will but an equally strong mind. On the contrary, while the Japanese painter is equally willful—notice the way he has turned many of the rocks and points of land into little round "pancakes" tilted up toward the spectator—still this landscape seems to come toward you, somehow you seem a direct participant in the landscape, you are intuitively involved. Despite the exaggeration of the Japanese style—the little pancakes, the fluffy trees, the overall warmth of the mist, the softness of the whole—it is all part of an intuitive and decorative approach which plays counterpoint to the logical and descriptive approach of the Chinese artist.

One could pursue these webs endlessly. Japan has long been famous for the wealth of its collections of Chinese art. But what did they collect? To the Chinese they are equally notorious for their usual selection of just those products of the Chinese artist which fail to meet general acceptance among artists and critics of the mainland—the asymmetric compositions of the Southern Song Painting Academy, Tang realistic pottery figurines, the rough tea bowls of Fukien [Fùjiàn], the wild and humorous blue and white wares of South China in the Late Ming period, or the products of that aberrant form of Buddhism, Chán or Zen.

Such is the web I have tried to spin. In general many of the principles hold true and may serve as a useful framework to understand something of the differences of style between Japanese and Chinese art.

Notes

1. Sherman E. Lee and Wai-kam Ho, "A Colossal Eleven-Faced Guānyīn of the Tang Dynasty," *Artibus Asiae* 22, pp. 123–124.
2. Kitagawa Momō, *Murō-ji* (Tokyo: Bijutsu shuppan-sha, 1954), pl. 35.

3. *Chinese Art Treasures* (Geneva: Skira, 1961), pls. 36, 37.

4. *Sesshū* (Tokyo: Tokyo National Museum, 1956), pl. 10.

5. *1000 Jahre Chinesische Malerei* (Munich: Haus der Kunst, 1959), pl. 79.

6. *Pageant of Japanese Art* (Tokyo: Tokyo National Museum and Tōtō bunka, 1952), vol. 2, pl. 64.

7. James Cahill, *Chinese Painting* (Geneva and Cleveland: Skira and World, 1960), p. 48.

8. *Pageant of Japanese Art*, vol. 3, pl. 44.

9. Chen-to Cheng, *Qīngmíng shànghé tú* (*Ch'ing-Ming Festival along the River Pien*) (Beijing: Cultural Objects Press, 1958).

10. Robert Treat Paine and Alexander Soper, *The Art and Architecture of Japan* (Harmondsworth, England, and Baltimore: Penguin Books, 1955), pl. 69.

11. *Sekitō meiga-fu* (*A Catalogue of Shíhtāo Paintings*) (Tokyo: Shurakusha, 1937), "Album of Landscape Painting 1, Kōzanhasshō-gasatsu."

12. Suzuki Susumu et al., *Ike-no Taiga sakuhinshu* (*The Works of Ike-no Taiga*) (Tokyo: Chūō-kōron bijutsu shuppan, 1960), pl. 483.

13. Sherman E. Lee, *Chinese Landscape Painting*, rev. ed. (Cleveland and New York: The Cleveland Museum of Art and Abrams, 1962), p. 21.

14. Sherman E. Lee, *Japanese Decorative Style* (Cleveland and New York: The Cleveland Museum of Art and Abrams, 1961), p. 35.

15. Koyama Fujio et al., *Sekai tōji zenshu* (*Ceramic Art of the World*) (Tokyo: Zauho Press and Kawade shobō, 1955), vol. 8, pl. 101.

16. Miki Fumio and Roy Andrew Miller, *Haniwa, the Clay Sculpture of Proto-Historic Japan* (Rutland, Vt., and Tokyo: Charles E. Tuttle and Kodansha, 1958 and 1960), pl. 30.

17. Osvald Sirén, *Chinese Painting: Leading Masters and Principles* (London and New York: Lund Humphries and Ronald Press, 1956), part 1, vol. 3, pls. 120–123.

18. *Japanese Decorative Style*, p. 29.

19. Suzuki Kei, *Nántián Yùn* (*Famous Chinese Paintings*) (Tokyo, Heibonsha, 1957), ser. 1, p. 9.

20. Kodama Kōta, *Zusetsu Nippon bunka-shi taikei* (*An Illustrated Cultural History of Japan*) (Tokyo: Shogakkan, 1956–1958), vol. 8, pl. 4.

21. Edward F. Strange, *Chinese Lacquer* (New York: Scribner's, 1926), pls. 50, 51.

22. Yashiro Yukio, *2000 Years of Japanese Art*, ed. Peter C. Swann (London: Thames & Hudson, 1958), pls. 155, 156.

23. *Chinese Art Treasures*, p. 263.

24. *Sekai tōji zenshu*, vol. 6, pl. 20.

25. Fritz Low-Beer, "Chinese Lacquer of the Middle and Late Ming Period," *Bulletin of the Museum of Far Eastern Antiquities*, vol. 14, pl. 137.

26. *Japanese Decorative Style*, pl. 127.

27. *Chinese Landscape Painting*, p. 116.

28. *Nihon nanga-shū* (*Japanese Southern School Paintings*) (Tokyo: Tokyo National Museum, 1951), p. 40, lower right.

1 *(above) Illustrated Stories of the Courtier Ban Dainagon,* artist unknown, Heian period, ink and color on paper, National Treasury (courtesy of the Idemitsu Museum of Arts, Tokyo).

2 *(below)* Zhāng Zéduān, *Qīngmíng Festival on the Canal*, detail, China, twelfth century, light watercolor on silk (collection of the Palace Museum, Beijing). An illustration of a scroll as a horizontally moving long take.

3 Gù Hóngzhōng, *Hán Xīzài's Night Banquet,* details, tenth century. Watercolor on silk (Collection of the Palace Museum, Beijing). The same host appears five times within a time-space continuum *(viewing right to left).*

5 Qǐ Bǎishí (1863–1957), *The Three Autumns,* China, 1934, ink and color on paper hanging scroll: (91-1/4" × 23-3/4") 231.8 × 60.3 cm. (courtesy of the Arthur M. Sackler Gallery, Smithsonian Institution, Washington, D.C., accession no. S1987.217). Note the contrast of thick dark ink with bright colors.

4 *(opposite)* Zhāo Zhènchuān, *Shǎnběi Plateau* (courtesy of the Hong Kong Gallery Centre Collection). Typical coloring, composition, and brushwork of the Chang'an school's depiction of the Shanbei plateau.

6 Zhāng Yìmóu, *Judou* (*Júdòu,* 1990) (courtesy of Miramax Films). Golden images.

7 *(below)* Zhāng Yìmóu, *Judou* (courtesy of Miramax Films). An expressionistic use of bright red and yellow.

8 Ay-O, *Hair-B* (courtesy of the Mitzie Verne Collection of Japanese Art).

9 *(above)* Ohayo *(Ohayō)* (courtesy of Shochiku Co., Ltd.). The archetypal Ozu *tatami*-level view finds a red bowl in the center of the frame.

10 *(below)* Cha Li, *Untitled*, 1981, industrial paint on canvas (courtesy of Cha Li and Joan Lebold Cohen).

FILM AND THE VISUAL
ARTS IN CHINA:
An Introduction

FILM AND THE VISUAL ARTS IN CHINA:

An Introduction

BY DOUGLAS WILKERSON

In the last few years Chinese movies have become more easily accessible to a wider nonresident population. After many years of severely curtailed film production and effective cultural isolation, a number of recent Chinese films were submitted to Cannes, Berlin, and other international film juries from which they received unprecedented acclaim and attention. But unlike the few Chinese films shown in Europe and America during the 1960s and 1970s, it is not the political content but the innovative cinematic characteristics of these films which have startled the critics and captivated audiences around the world.

The year 1984 is notable because of the appearance of Chén Kǎigē and Zhāng Yìmóu's *Yellow Earth* (*Huáng tǔdì*), an international success which established the Chinese cinema as a serious art form and announced the triumph of the Fifth Generation of Chinese film directors, those trained after the end of the Cultural Revolution. In their article on "Post-Socialist Strategies," Chris Berry and Mary Farquhar use the painting traditions consciously adopted by *Yellow Earth* and *Black Cannon Incident* (*Hēipào shìjiàn*) as a gauge to determine what, if anything, distinguishes the films of the Fifth Generation from those of earlier generations. In brief, they conclude that it is the use of classical traditions not found in the earlier films of socialist realism that sets many of the new films apart from their predecessors. The classical tradition to which many of the recent films turn is that of landscape painting—to be more specific, landscapes in the tradition of what has been called, since the end of the Ming dynasty, the Southern School (*nánzōng*).

Most of the essayists represented in this collection agree that this Southern

School is the most remarkable and characteristically Chinese of the various styles of painting. Hǎo Dàzhēng takes it as representative in his attempts to explain the visual peculiarities and distinctiveness of Chinese films in terms of the qualities unique to Chinese painting; these he first elucidates according to underlying cultural predilections which characterize Chinese civilization and distinguish it from Western forms. Ān Jǐngfū sees this landscape tradition as the embodiment of Taoist influence in art, and finds this same Taoist influence in both the narrative and visual expression of Chén Kǎigē's *King of the Children* (*Háizi wáng*). Ní Zhèn's article makes mention of the contributions of Chán Buddhism to this style, and asserts the intimate connection between the aesthetic system of this tradition and the ideology which produced it and which it incorporates.

Ní goes on to detail the way in which the aesthetics and technology of Western cinema also embody an ideology, but one which is different from, and opposed to, that which gave rise to the classical Chinese landscape tradition. What happens when the two are combined? Hǎo, Ní, and Berry/Farquhar all assert that both the foreign medium and the native tradition are necessarily transformed in the process. Jenny Lau, though discussing a different painting tradition, the highly colored alternative to monochrome ink landscapes, affirms that the combination must result in radically new meanings for all elements included.

Anyone familiar with modern Chinese history will immediately recognize a variation on an old and troubling theme, perhaps the most persistent problematique of the last century and a half: the problem of combining Eastern spirit with Western form (*Zhōngxué wéi tǐ, Xīxué wéi yòng,* and other formulations). Ever since the days when China first began to realize that the Western nations aggressively refused to fit into the traditional Chinese world order, she has struggled with the problem of how to meet the West on its terms without sacrificing her unique and treasured cultural heritage. From the early failures to establish a modern navy and military arsenals to the recent calls for developing a native form of socialism with Chinese characteristics, this nation has sought to adopt the science, technology, art forms, and other aspects of Western culture while resisting many elements of the ideology which spawned them. In the present case, the question becomes: How can the cinema—an institution developed entirely within the ideological framework of Western technology, capitalism, and consumer-oriented economy—and in particular, its visual aspects, be "Sinicized?" Can Western modes of cinematography, linked to the very mechanism of the camera through the dominant postmedieval perspective system, be replaced by modes which are linked to traditional Chinese aesthetics?

The debate over the "nationalization" of the cinema has received a great deal of attention in China since 1978, expanding to include every aspect of cinematic art. When discussing visual systems, the tendency is to point to those films which have most successfully integrated the new technology with the style of visual art which appears to be most distinct from that of the West, and therefore most distinctively Chinese. This, all seem to agree, is the Southern School of landscape, with its multiple perspectives, relative flatness, use of blank spaces, elastic framing, lack of chiaroscuro and sculptural shading, and emphasis on expressive, calligraphic contour lines. The striking visual styles of *Yellow Earth* and *King of the Children* are masterful examples of synthesis which seem to overcome the apparent contradictions underlying the aesthetic system and the technical medium of expression.

Lau takes it upon herself to balance this approach with a more inclusive account of the history of Chinese painting. She points out other reasons for the apparent dominance of the Southern School and introduces other styles into the discussion. She analyzes one of Zhāng Yìmóu's more recent films, *Judou* (*Júdòu*), in terms of the tradition of brilliant colorists, perhaps not as distinctively Chinese as monochrome painting, but nonetheless an important style, the history of which extends back many centuries earlier than that of the monochrome landscape. The folk art tradition also receives passing notice for its use of flat colors inside heavy borders, resulting from traditional brush-painting techniques and the printing technology peculiar to this genre.

The distinctiveness of the classical Chinese painting tradition raises the question of compatibility between the ideological background of Taoist-inspired landscape and the nature of cinema. Hǎo, Ní, Lau, and Berry/Farquhar all maintain the possibility, and even desirability, of combining the monocular perspective of the camera with the multiple perspectives of Chinese painting (and indeed virtually all figural art except that of post-Renaissance Europe). But philosophical Taoism was an introspective, eremitic philosophy which exhibited a marked distrust of all technological innovation; the artistic tradition engendered by it was very personal and individualistic in nature, stressing momentary inspiration and immediate reaction, and limited in appeal and currency to a tiny portion of Chinese society. Is it possible for such an art to participate in a form whose very existence is entirely dependent on highly sophisticated technology, is meant for mass consumption, and requires the concerted, long-term cooperation of a well-regulated, hierarchically organized group? Can such a mode of production, inimical to the spirit and practice of Taoism, be said to embody Taoist ideology or incorporate Taoist-inspired aesthetics? Ān Jìngfū perhaps comes closest to attempting an answer to this dilemma. He discovers Taoist influence not only in the composition and prevalence of scenic shots, dwarfing of human figures by natural background, still and silent tone, and use of mist and clouds to evoke the pregnant voids of paintings, but in the moral, philosophical, and political implications of the narrative as well. Suggestively he has entitled his essay "The Pain of a Half Taoist," for any evidences of Taoist philosophy and life-style the protagonist may at times exhibit are undercut and frustrated by narrative demands for coherent, purposive action and the drama of conflict and thwarted purpose. Perhaps a film can never be more than half Taoist if it hopes for any public reception.

Though cinema in China, as in the West, relied heavily on the narrative techniques of drama and fiction for interest in its early days, other elements were occasionally allowed to encroach on their dominant position. Lyrical interludes of dance and music, part and parcel of all traditional Chinese drama, indiscriminately interrupt the narrative in many films. Ní, Lau, and Ān all make the point that the films they are analyzing have attenuated the narrative interest in favor of some aspect more closely associated with the Chinese painting tradition: non-narrative space and time, color, or the contemplation of nature. The contrast between the films of the Fifth Generation and those of the preceding thirty years in terms of narrative is certainly striking. The insistence of Marxist historiography on narrative significance made such films extremely unlikely during the earlier years, and freedom from this constraint is a significant component of Berry and Farquhar's "post-socialist" film aesthetic.

The misty monochrome landscape represents for many the culmination of hundreds of years of Chinese painting; but Ní points out very insightfully that its influence in the cinema is most evident in what he calls "lyrical" films. These films might be placed under the more general rubric of what in other countries are referred to as "art films." They are able to draw most directly on the refined classical Chinese traditions of landscape painting and poetry because, like them and in contrast to many dominant Western art forms, they stress lyrical evocation over narrative development. During the early phases of the debate over the nationalization of Chinese cinema, most attention was focused on the content of the narrative, with the assumption that this essential element of cinematic art could be used alone as a measure of the "Chineseness" of a film. In recent years the more adventurous Chinese directors have moved the debate into other areas, and raised the question of whether or not this preoccupation with narrative style and content might not itself be a betrayal of the Chinese heritage.

What then of the mainstream narrative films which constitute the bulk of production in China, Taiwan, and Hong Kong in every historical period?

Perhaps it would not be out of place to suggest that they too may be drawing on ancient Chinese traditions, but traditions that lack the pedigree and esoteric appeal of Tang poetry or Song landscapes. Similarities between popular (as distinct from the more monastic Chán) Buddhist art and sculpture, as well as the compositional techniques of folk art, and depiction in martial arts (gōngfu) films are readily apparent. Even the iconography of heroes and villains in films made under the Communist regime exhibit many traits in common with traditional Confucian hagiography.

It is interesting to note that the text of the Mòzi (Mo Tzu) shows a fairly sophisticated conception of light rays, apparent size and distance, and observation of the characteristics of the primitive camera obscura. Empirical experimentation was an important element of Mohist philosophy as well. But the Han imperial house promoted Confucian ideas over those of other schools, and the Mohist tradition languished. The Han critic Wáng Chóng took Mòzi to task for assuming that truth or falsehood could be determined by eye or ear alone, and insisted on the exercise of intellect in judging the meaning and importance of sense impressions. The Chuang Tzu recognized the relativity of all sensory perception and the reciprocal dependence on nonperception for their existence. Thus, both Confucianism and Taoism seriously called into question the epistemological status and ontological preeminence of the visual image.

A high degree of physical similarity between representation and the object represented was naturally important to the early portraiture of China. But as the depiction of natural scenes began to grow in importance, even while portraiture was the main concern of many painters, a distinct aesthetic quickly became apparent. Mountains and streams were not painted "from nature" but rather according to memories of them, and impressions made by them, in the mind of the painter. The great painter and theorist Zōng Bǐng traveled throughout the scenic regions of China, but painted the sights he had seen only after he returned to his home. Infused with religious and metaphysical significance, landscapes came to be conceived of more as a means of expression, a presentation of the inner being of the artist, than as a reflection or representation of what may have passed before the artist's eyes. The concept of xiěyì referred to in many of the essays points to the goal of communicating a feeling, idea, or state of mind with little concern for verisimilitude, except as the medium of this communication. As in Buddhist thought, in which color and form are understood to be illusory, the image itself has no independent status.

This is perhaps the most serious challenge to the adaptation of a Chinese aesthetic system to the technology of the cinema, which owes its invention to the privileged position of the image in Western thought and art. Although the objectivity of human vision was often called into question, the desire to literally "mirror" nature led to the development of Renaissance perspective, in which "light writing" eventually took the place of the more fallible human eye and hand. Challenges to the foundational concepts of Western positivism eroded faith in the image and encouraged Western artists to turn to other modes of representation. Berry and Farquhar see a similar progress in *Black Cannon Incident* and its use of modern art to portray a society in which the positivist assertions of socialist history are replaced by questioning, suspiciousness, and alienation. The mirror held up to reality reveals only illusions. These essays explore some of the ways in which these illusions can be understood to reveal deeper truths.

Note: The romanization system used in the articles on Chinese cinema is the *pinyin* system adopted by the People's Republic of China; however, the following words have been left in the older Wade-Giles system because of their familiarity to Western readers: Tao(-ism, -ist) [Dào], Lao Tzu [Lǎozi], and Chuang Tzu [Zhuāngzi].

CHINESE VISUAL
REPRESENTATION:
Painting and Cinema

BY HǍO DÀZHĒNG
Translation by Douglas Wilkerson

The visual peculiarities of Chinese film can
be explained in terms of the principles of
visual representation which have dominated
Chinese painting over the past two thousand
years. Chinese and Western systems of visual
representation are separated by differences as
great as those dividing Chinese and Western
culture, differences arising from the respective relationships between human beings and
their natural frame of reference.

The sources of Chinese culture are to be
found in a highly developed agricultural civilization. This ancient system of agriculture
relied solely on the blessings bestowed by
heaven, leaving no place for human beings
to oppose or remake nature. The primary
subject of social transmission, agricultural
knowledge, was an accumulation of generation upon generation of experience. The stan-
dardization of agricultural production demanded that people look upon nature from a
common point of view and maintain a unified
relationship to it. Utilitarianism encouraged
an intellectual ellipsis, a tendency to ignore

any aspect of nature not deemed useful to the agricultural enterprise. At the same time, humanity was not seen as opposed to nature, but embraced by it, and thus had no reason to investigate its more abstruse aspects. This produced a system of intuitive thought which made no distinction between awareness, emotion, and intentionality, or between subject and object. In terms of the Chinese worldview, it fostered utilitarianism at the expense of materialism; in terms of values, it fostered common utility at the expense of objective truth. Thus was born China's pragmatism. Concurrently, there was formed an agrarian life-rhythm consisting of generational cycles further articulated into years, the basic temporal unit. These are the ideological foundations of Chinese visual representation. While the subject provided the form of visual representation, the object provided its content, and thus were constituted the elements of Chinese vision.

Point of View

Traditional Chinese landscape painting (*shānshuǐ huà*) generally employs multiple perspectives, with objects on a smaller scale, such as buildings and gardens, represented in parallel perspective.[1] Both of these perspective systems, multiple and parallel, theoretically would require a viewing distance of infinity, but the clearly visible images of Chinese painting imply a finite viewing distance. Thus the perspective system of Chinese painting must be understood as a conceptual one, not dependent on biological mechanisms of the naked eye, as was the Renaissance system. The use of multiple perspectives in Chinese painting was not for the purpose of making a hologram, nor was the use of parallel perspectives for the purpose of retaining the true dimensions of the objects represented. What was desired was rather a point of view which transcended that of the individual. The apparent horizon and vanishing point employed by Renaissance perspective made the image seem concrete, but demanded substantial identification with a particular viewer. Such images were perceived as both individual and momentary, seen by a particular person at a particular time. Chinese painting strove for a timeless, communal impression, which could be perceived by anyone, and yet was not a scene viewed by anyone in particular. Thus the subjects of Chinese painting were no more than a medium for generalities. Furthermore, since medieval times Chinese intellectuals have looked upon painting as a kind of linguistic discourse. Their works, known as literati paintings (*wénrén huà*), employed both graphic and written codes.[2] According to classical Chinese art theory, all things have their own individual spirit (*shén*), the essence of their form. The highest aspiration of Chinese painting was to render a spiritual (*shénsì*), rather than a purely physical, likeness. Each painting had its own intellectual and philosophical world to which the viewer gained access by means of the imagination.

Classical Chinese painting bore no burden of realistic representation, and chose to achieve generality through abstraction rather than through the use of archetypal forms. One effective means of accomplishing this was to reduce the concreteness of the pictorial image, and classical Chinese painting adopted multiple perspectives and/or a perspective elevated well above the apparent horizon in order to avoid the visual concreteness which accompanies the use of a visual horizon and vanishing point (figure 2.1). A strict avoidance of any upwardly inclined perspective which would have introduced a second, vertical vanishing point may be considered an unbreakable rule in Chinese painting. The best example of this elimination of visual horizon in film is Fèi Mù's neorealist masterpiece, *Spring in a Small Town* (*Xiǎochéng zhī chūn*, 1948). The director skillfully set the heroine's daily walk on top of the city wall so that her point of view, and that of the audience which sees through her eyes, is constantly changing. This same device also serves to visually embellish the heroine's character. One can perceive the traditional bird's-eye view imbued with new meaning in a scene portraying the New Year's Dragon Dance in *Country Folks* (*Xiāngmín*, 1986 [figure 2.2]), the third film of Hú Bǐngliú's trilogy.[3]

When a visual horizon is unavoidable, objects are often ranged horizontally, and the background and midground forms, which might contribute to visual concreteness, are simplified in order to obscure the vanishing point and weaken the feeling of depth. When observing nature, the ancient Chinese were more interested in horizontal expanse than in depth. This also served, along with similitude, to overcome the discrepancies between a three-dimensional reality and the two-dimensional picture plane. Traditional Chinese drama made excellent use of this same principle, employing no background or props which would convey a sense of space, relying rather on a flat mise-en-scène and a suggestion of imaginary depth to conjure up any required space. Nationalistic (*mínzú pài*) films of the twenties and thirties, such as Zhèng Zhèngqiū's *Twin Sisters* (*Zǐmèi huā*, 1934), clearly exhibit this use of a flat mise-en-scène.[4]

Abstract realism is another principle of Chinese visual representation. Different from both realism and abstract painting, the Chinese refer to this as "representation of intention" (*xiěyì*); rather than transforming the objects

2.1 Zhōu Chén, landscape illustrating the multiple-viewpoint perspective, China, Ming dynasty, watercolor on silk (courtesy of the National Palace Museum, Republic of China).

HĂO DÁZHĒNG

2.2 Hú Bǐngliú, *Country Folks* (*Xiāngmín,* 1986) (courtesy of the director, Pearl River Film Studio, Canton).

of representation, they abstracted the elements of graphic discourse in order to represent a meaning which transcended form.

Framing and Shot

The ancient Chinese working in the field were accustomed to communing with nature, but not with each other. Seeing that their crops were the same as those raised by others, they believed they comprehended the world. This experience directed their interest toward communality and totality and away from individuality and particularity. A human being was defined as one participant in a relationship, rather than as a free and independent agent. Considering individuals as only a small part of humankind, there was no need for close-ups to view them. The scale of framing in Chinese paintings is clearly larger than that in Western paintings. In other words, the portion of space occupied by human figures in Chinese paintings is considerably smaller. The dominant theme of Chinese painting has always been nature,

Chinese Visual Representation   49

and the world of landscape painting was the utopia of the Chinese intellectual, who firmly believed that by means of an understanding of nature one could return to nature and find a resting place for one's spirit there. The frequent use of "empty shots" of nonhuman subjects (*kōng jìngtóu*) in traditional Chinese films conveyed the message that humanity could not be separated from Nature.[5] Contemporary films have endowed this technique with new meaning. In *Country Voice* (*Xiāngyīn*, 1984), the second film of Hú Bǐngliú's trilogy, and *Swansong* (*Juéxiǎng*, 1986 [figure 2.3]) by his student Zhāng Zémíng such shots have a spiritual power which connects past and present.

Human relations in ancient China were often indirectly reflected in the relationship between humans and nature. Even at the beginning of this century the Chinese did not come into physical contact when greeting one another, but made contact with nature instead. Striking the head on the earth when greeting a superior was known as the kowtow, and in conversation one evidenced respect by gazing at the ground, rather than directly at one's interlocutor. "In giving and receiving, male and female must not touch" (*Mencius*, "Lílóu," 1). Relationships of love were, of course, strictly private matters. Therefore Chinese portraiture never developed significantly. Ancient Chinese families paid respect to their ancestors in the form of memorial tablets, rather than to painted representations of them. Figure painting also remained quite weak. Many painters were skillful in rendering the folds of someone's garments, but quite inept at representing the face. The mechanical application of Western-style anatomical knowledge only served to destroy the harmony of the painting as a whole. In traditional Chinese films, human characters are primarily actors in a plot, and not the object of visual appreciation. Close-ups served only as a source of uneasiness in such films.[6] Medium shots, which clearly portrayed the activities of the characters without revealing much detail, were preferred. Moreover, traditional Chinese films avoided the sudden change of extreme shots (i.e., close-ups and far-distance shots) and the discontinuity of rapidly alternating shots, being unreceptive of the forceful rhythms which they engendered. A distinguishing feature of a great number of the nationalistic films, such as *Twin Sisters*, was the use of one primary shot for each scene, and a gradual transition between shots.[7]

The dimensions of Chinese paintings make it clear that framing was seen as a hindrance to the expression of nature's infinitude. These paintings often have a horizontal or vertical extension which exceeds any momentary field of vision. Because of their use of detail, these paintings must be viewed from close at hand; one cannot appreciate them from a distance, as one can a Western painting. The frame plays an essential role in the appreciation of the

2.3 Zhāng Zémíng, *Swansong* (*Juéxiǎng*, 1986) (courtesy of Hú Bǐngliú, Pearl River Film Studio, Canton).

latter, demarcating a definite area of spatial extension. Such a demarcation was studiously avoided by Chinese painters, who desired the viewer to ignore the borders and enter a world of infinitude, in the same way they entered the world of nature. But Chinese paintings did not portray reality; the world which the viewer entered was the realm of literature or philosophy, a realm

Chinese Visual Representation

which transcended nature. To enjoy a long tableau with small figures, one must shift one's line of sight left and right, or up and down, a necessary condition for the appreciation of Chinese visual representation. This reminds one of the tracking technique used in films. When viewing a 30 cm × 10 m scroll which can only be enjoyed with the help of two persons unrolling and rolling the scroll at opposite ends ("scrolling" it past the viewer), one is in fact viewing a lengthy lateral tracking shot. At such a time the viewer can easily appreciate the usefulness of multiple perspectives, as used, for example, in the widely reproduced Northern Song dynasty painting *Qīngmíng Festival on the Canal* (*Qīngmíng shànghé tú*) by Zhāng Zéduān (colorplate 2). The medium shots and medium close-ups most frequently employed in traditional Chinese movies are particularly suitable for this type of lateral tracking. Chinese moviegoers evidently take great pleasure in reenacting their experience with paintings. Chinese films before the forties, in complying with the convention of flat mise-en-scène, rarely revealed significant depth in their lateral tracking. A striking example of this is the sequence of five long takes at the climax of *Spring in a Small Town* (figure 2.4): following the development of the plot, tracking is used in the more and more complex mise-en-scène of the three protagonists, incisively revealing the subtle relationships between them.

Depth of space was a problem in Chinese visual representation. The Chinese were unaccustomed to watching a person intently or investigating affairs in depth. That the Chinese in their classical paintings did not employ perspective relations which effectively express a sense of depth—the optical system of the eye perceived from a single point—is proof of this. They chose instead other perspectives, which manifested flatness. Flatness and expansive scenes are typical of both Chinese painting and traditional films. Psychological tension produced by gradually increasing the concentration of image in a zoom-in is an experience completely foreign to the conventional Chinese way of life. In traditional Chinese visual activity, horizontal movement was substituted for narrowing of focus.

Unlike Western architecture, the traditional Chinese had no individual buildings worthy of prolonged appreciation because of their outward magnificence or inner complexity. Instead, classical Chinese architecture employed aggregates of relatively simple buildings to build up a total effect which could be perceived only by moving about within this architectural space. Highly stylized details allowed the viewers to concentrate their attention on the atmosphere created by delicately laid-out spatial relations. An important principle of classical Chinese garden landscaping was that "the scenery [should] change as one walks" (*jǐng suí bù yí*). The wooden columns

2.4 Fèi Mù, *Spring in a Small Town* (*Xiǎochéng zhī chūn*, 1948).

and carved crossbeams of walkways divided the scenery into a series of framed pictures which one could enjoy while strolling through the garden, a skillful combination of rigid frame with movement. It is interesting to note that the result is a standard dolly shot produced as the viewer moves forward through the scene; where the walkway leads is unimportant. The Five Dynasties (A.D. 907–960) painting *Hán Xīzài's Night Banquet* (*Hán Xīzài yèyàn tú*) by Gù Hóngzhōng employs this technique with remarkable effect (colorplate 3). The host, Hán Xīzài, appears no less than five separate times in a single space-time continuum. When faced with the problem of assumed depth posed by the camera, what response will the Chinese system of visual representation, with more than one thousand years of experience with horizontal motion, finally make?

Line, Light, Color

The most basic item of the Chinese visual vocabulary is line. In every highly developed culture, line is the basic semiotic element of the written word. The use of line in Chinese painting reveals the tendency to unify systems of graphic and literary signification. Classical Chinese art theory declared that "calligraphy and painting arise from the same source" (*shū huà tóng yuán*). The ancient Chinese did not consider the expression of an object's inherent qualities or character to be as important as the expression of its quality as referential object. Thus they found it necessary to abstract the symbolic codes inhering in form and to invest them with the character of an arbitrary code in order to employ them in larger systems of signification.

The rejection of chiaroscuro techniques in Chinese painting implies a rejection of Western principles of realism.[8] Light reveals the shape of objects, but objects exist even without light. Chinese painting sought to transcend light which reveals only a transitory existence, in order to express the forms of eternal existence. Surface and volume were transformed into line in order to use methods distinct from those of realism to represent the spirit hidden within form. The Chinese did not separate humanity from nature, but rather personified natural objects: not only could objects arouse human emotions, but they also possessed qualities which could be communicated, qualities like the intelligence of mountains and waters, or the aloofness of orchid and bamboo. Chinese paintings are able to express poetic content, as indicated in the expression "A painting in a poem, a poem in a painting" (*shī zhōng yǒu huà, huà zhōng yǒu shī*). Since medieval times images and poetry have coexisted in paintings, achieving a type of composite signification. The "empty shots" which characterized nationalistic films had a similar abstract expressiveness mediating between pictorial surface and caption. The Chinese cultural context provides some help in understanding this: the "cinematic pen" differs from the writing brush in that it employs only light and shadow in "writing." This serves as a stimulating challenge to the contemporary director who wants to utilize China's visual experience in the cinema.

The ancient Chinese did not make use of light in visual representation, or rather, more precisely, used light only in the most basic sense of flat light. Unwilling to allow anything such as perspective or chiaroscuro, which would express instantaneity, to intrude, they found a space-time structure without any hint of specific space or time most suitable for their endeavors. Classical Chinese drama represented all times and places in front of an unchanging curtain in natural or flat light, allowing each member of the audience to imagine the scene as seemed most fit. Until the forties, nationalistic directors, such as Zhèng Zhèngqiū, Zhāng Shíchuān, and Yáng Xiǎozhòng, employed flat lighting in their many films.[9] This nationalistic style reached maturity during the forties in such films as Sāng Hú's *Long Live Missus* (*Tàitai wàn-suì*, 1947) and *Miserable at Middle Age* (*Āi lè zhōngnián*, 1948). Over a

54   HǍO DÀZHĒNG

period of several centuries, China's theatrical arts evolved an integral system of visual representation in keeping with these same principles. Well versed in this dramatic tradition, Fèi Mù successfully applied it to the cinematic medium in his *Spring in a Small Town*.

The Chinese neorealist movement which emerged in the late forties was a high point in Chinese film history. The films of this period consolidated the achievements of all previous experiments in applying the principles of Chinese visual representation to the cinema. Some of the directors, such as Cài Chǔshēng (*A Spring River Flows East* [*Yī jiāng chūnshuǐ xiàngdōng liú*, 1947]) and Shěn Fú (*Myriads of Light* [*Wànjiā dēnghuǒ*, 1948]), came from the innovative branch of the nationalistic school; others, such as Fèi Mù, Sūn Yú (*The Life of Wǔ Xùn* [*Wǔ Xùn zhuàn*, 1950] [figure 2.5]), and Zhèng Jūnlǐ (*Crows and Sparrows* [*Wūyā yǔ máquè*, 1949] [figure 2.6] and *Between Husband and Wife* [*Wǒmen fūfù zhī jiān*, 1950] [figure 2.7]), came from the cinema art school, but all were well trained in the Chinese cultural tradition. The last neorealist director was the actor Shí Huī (*This Life of Mine* [*Wǒ zhèi yībèizi*, 1950] [figure 2.8] and *Lieutenant Guan* [*Guān liánzhǎng*, 1950]). The neorealist movement was cut short by the political turmoil of the late forties.

Traditional Chinese visual representation eliminated not only chiaroscuro, but also color, even though color can be perceived even in flat lighting. This also served the purpose of reducing the concreteness of the objects of representation. It may be helpful in understanding this to mention that in the course of the development of Chinese pictograms, all the elements of volume, surface, light, and color were discarded, leaving only line. The development of Chinese painting seems to have followed the same path. Classical Chinese art theory states that "India ink contains all colors" (*mò fēn wǔsè*), reminding us of the importance of the imagination in "reading" a painting. Under these conditions, the symbolic code was linked to the arbitrary code; the identity of implements (brush and ink) used by the two media made their unity complete.

Nevertheless a rudimentary tradition of coloring persisted in artisanal painting (*gōngbǐ huà*) and in the New Year's folk print (*nián huà*).[10] The former remained outside of the mainstream of literati painting, while the latter was to be found only in peasant homes. The color system of the New Year's prints consisted of solid, usually primary, colors within an outline (*dānxiàn píngtú*), a practical technique for woodblock prints, resulting in a simple, flat, decorative effect. Young directors of the Fifth Generation drew on this for their sense of color, applying it deftly to their evocations of peasant life. A representative example is Chén Kǎigē's *Yellow Earth* (*Huáng tǔdì*,

2.5 Sūn Yú, *The Life of Wǔ Xùn* (*Wǔ Xùn zhuàn,* 1948–1950) (courtesy of Lǐ Xùn, China Film Art Research Center, Beijing).

2.6 Zhèng Jūnlǐ, *Crows and Sparrows* (*Wūyā yǔ máquè,* 1949) (courtesy of Lǐ Xùn, China Film Art Research Center, Beijing).

HǍO DÀZHĒNG

2.7 Zhèng Jūnlǐ, *Between Husband and Wife* (*Wǒmen fūfù zhī jiān,* 1950) (courtesy of Lǐ Xùn, China Film Art Research Center, Beijing).

2.8 Shí Huī, *This Life of Mine* (*Wǒ zhèi yībèizi,* 1950) (courtesy of Lǐ Xùn, China Film Art Research Center, Beijing).

1984). Since this color system is incompatible with chiaroscuro, it cannot be applied widely; it is necessary to discover a new color system within the achromatic tradition of Chinese visual representation.

Begun by the Fourth Generation in the late seventies and continued by the Fifth Generation, China's New Cinema Movement lasted for more than ten years before it was cut short for political reasons. One clear objective of this movement was the renewal of China's cinematic language. The fruits of this exploration have yet to be consolidated, but the nearly fifty films of these two generations of directors did accomplish a return from a thematic classification of films to a stylistic one.

Illustration and Narration

Although movable type was invented in China in the eleventh century, woodblock printing remained the dominant technique employed by the publishing industry. Modern reprints of classic Chinese novels with illustrations from as early as the fourteenth century are still widely available. The monochrome line drawings of Chinese art were easily reproduced in woodcuts, so it is not surprising that these illustrations were Chinese paintings in miniature, though they now functioned more as narrative than as lyric. Each illustration covered the entire surface of a block and, in accordance with the principles of traditional visual representation, presented a complete scene from a bird's-eye view in parallel perspective. It is interesting to note that the illustrators preferred this means for showing interior scenes as well as exterior, allowing the "reader" to peer through an open door or window (figure 2.9). Neither conventional morals nor the visual tradition permitted a more convenient means of presentation. Confucius had once commanded, "Do not look upon that which is indecorous" (*Analects*, "Yányuān," 12). Psychological and ideological constraints lay in the way of a freer use of medium shots, medium close-ups, and close-ups. China's first pictorial, the *Pebble Studio Pictorial* (*Diǎnshízhāi huàbào*), was published in Shanghai at the end of the nineteenth century. Lithographically reproduced, it retained the traditional principles of visual representation enumerated above even in journalistic drawings. The lyric tradition of literati painting embraced all areas of visual representation.

Lithographic picture-story books made their appearance at the beginning of the twentieth century, with full-page drawings in uniform sexagesimo-quarto (64mo, ca. 3¾ in. × 5¼ in.) size. These small volumes often used more than one hundred pages to tell a single story, and experimented with

2.9 *The Nine Elders of the Mountain of Fragrance*, China, attributed to Xiè Húan, Ming dynasty, handscroll; ink and color on silk (intended gift to The Cleveland Museum of Art, Mr. and Mrs. A. Dean Perry). A voyeuristic glance into an interior scene.

full scenes in somewhat closer perspective viewed from a lower angle. Although the artists were careful in their selection of objects from the reproductions of Western paintings and drawings then available in China, the inclusion of some interior scenes was unavoidable. Nevertheless, they did avoid the use of portions of complete scenes, not wanting to see the bodies of their subjects abruptly cut off. At the same time they refused to employ a perspective with a definite vanishing point and rarely presented their subjects with a sense of visual depth.

Another characteristic which distinguished these books from modern comic books was the exclusion of written dialogue from the picture frame: explanations were always written underneath the illustrations. The Chinese did not hesitate to inscribe characters on the surface of pure art, but kept their narrative pictures free from the written word. They maintained that pure art is subjective, whereas narrative is objective. Moreover, they viewed the illustrations in picture-story books more as stock situations than as particular occasions, endowing them with more generality than concreteness. These books appeared at about the same time as China's first movies, and the intimate relationship between picture-story books and films can be seen in the exclusive use of full-scened compositions in the earliest two-reeler, *A Worker's Love; or The Romance of a Fruit Peddler* (*Láogōng zhī àiqíng; huò zhìguǒ yuán,* directed by Zhèng Zhèngqiū, 1922). Medium shots, medium close-ups, and close-ups irresistibly encroached upon Chinese films in the twenties, but at the cost of being adapted to the flat native mise-en-scène. The improvement of the concept of depth had to wait another ten years.

The Chinese narrative tradition, like the tradition of visual representation, derived its source from the ancient worldview and methods of observation. The classic Chinese novel was also composed of a number of disparate viewpoints. Events and characters in parallel, rather than sequential, relationship were combined into undramatic structures.[11] Chinese narrative, like visual representation, avoided descriptions of the inner world of its characters. These novels affected the reader mainly through plots sketched out at great length. Under this type of narrative influence, classical Chinese drama produced a number of serial works whose performance might run for half a month or more. Echoing this tendency, Zhāng Shíchuān's serial martial-arts film, *The Burning of Red Lotus Temple* (*Huǒshāo Hóngliánsì*), was filmed in eighteen episodes over a period of four years, from 1928 to 1931.

Accompanying this narrative rhythm was a rather relaxed attitude toward the act of viewing. Faced with disparate perspectives and a flat mise-en-scène, the viewer was not required to concentrate, but could give the imagination free rein as the eyes passed over the images on the screen, the mind meanwhile communicating freely with the narrative. These habits of audience reception, of course, were derived from ancient Chinese views of time and space. One response to them during the thirties was a hybrid genre, typified by *The Western Chamber* (*Xīxiāng jì,* directed by Zhāng Shíchuān, 1939 [figure 2.10]), containing seven, eight, or even more songs, yet without becoming a full-fledged musical; as a rule, the heroine performed the songs, thereby introducing periodic changes in the narrative rhythm. The source of this genre can be traced back to medieval Chinese novels which contained lyrical passages inserted into the body of the prose narrative to regulate the narrative rhythm.

2.10 Zhāng Shíchuān, *The Western Chamber* (*Xīxiāng jì*, 1939) (courtesy of Lǐ Xùn, China Film Art Research Center, Beijing).

We now live in a world of cultural plurality. In order for Chinese film to act as a medium of cross-cultural communication, it must employ a cinematic language comprehensible to the people of other cultures; otherwise communication is impossible. But it must use its own cinematic language, for otherwise communication is unnecessary.

Notes

I would like to thank Mr. Lǐ Xùn of the China Film Art Research Center in Beijing for his kind assistance during the preparation of this article.

References in this article are restricted to films shot in mainland China.

1. "Multiple" and "parallel" are terms used by the Chinese to distinguish their perspective systems from that of the Renaissance, which is characterized by two vanishing points formed by a fixed viewpoint. In a multiple perspective painting, viewers can feel a seemingly normal perspective relation among the objects when they concen-

trate on a limited area of the picture. Once they move their eyes to a neighboring area, however, they will get an impression of another perspective relationship which bears no relationship to the previous one, and so on. Multiple perspective is used in classical landscape paintings.

In paintings with rectangular or other regular-shaped objects like buildings and furniture, parallel perspective is used. The viewer can find a fixed viewpoint suggested by the imagery, but he or she can not estimate the distance between the viewpoint and the objects because all orientation lines are drawn parallel. This indicates that two vanishing points exist in infinity.

2. Editor's note: This term, *wénrén huà*, denotes the tradition and practice of painting as a fine art, largely limited to the leisure and aesthetic activities of the small, well-educated gentry class (the literati).

3. Editor's note: Hú Bǐngliú's trilogy consists of: *Country Affections* (*Xiāngqíng*, 1981), *Country Voice* (*Xiāngyīn*, 1984), and *Country Folks* (*Xiāngmín*, 1986).

4. In Chinese film history, the term "nationalistic school" is used to denote the work of directors whose screen imagery possesses the pictorial quality of classical Chinese painting, especially that of medieval woodcut illustrations whose narratives reveal the prototype of the loose structure of the classic Chinese novel. The "cinema art school" denotes the work of directors whose films show more of an international style.

5. "Traditional Chinese film" is a term used in Chinese film history in opposition to the "modern Chinese film." In China, the time demarcation is 1978–1979. "Traditional," in this case, is a synonym for "classical."

6. The early Chinese audience concerned itself merely with the characters in relation to a certain plot. They wanted to see human characters "in" a plot, rather than an isolated close-up without a visible plot background. They were so unaccustomed to photographic techniques that a close-up might make them think of a severed head. Almost all classical Chinese figure painting and portraits depicted the whole body.

7. Primary shots were used in early Chinese films according to the theatrical principle that each "act" of a film should have a dominating main shot.

8. Classical Chinese paintings showed the shapes of objects without any hint of the light source. The painters only used line drawings and eliminated all representations of shade and shadow. Thus, the perceivable time-space reference was reduced to a minimum.

9. "Flat lighting" is a term used among modern Chinese cinematographers. It indicates a way of lighting which avoids the creation of shadow and varying degrees of brightness.

10. Editor's note: Artisanal painting was the technical tradition and practice of painting as a craft and decorative art, practiced primarily by individuals who made their living by painting.

11. The structure of the classical Chinese novel was more like a record of events than a well-organized narrative.

CLASSICAL CHINESE
PAINTING AND
CINEMATOGRAPHIC
SIGNIFICATION

BY NÍ ZHÈN
Translation by
Douglas Wilkerson

Spatial Consciousness as Embodied in
Classical Chinese Painting

The inflexibility of the cinematographic
frame and the principles of optical image formation determine technologically that the
image on the silver screen will be a three-
dimensional illusion produced on a two-
dimensional screen according to the laws of
focal perspective. Although the sense of depth
and verisimilitude of the objective world of
cinematic representation are realized through
the function of mechanical duplication, the
means employed correspond to the laws
of plastic modeling which underlie realistic
Western painting. These laws are, namely, the
representation or recording of objects according to the principles of focal perspective with
a viewpoint in which the position of the
viewer, the line of sight, and the frame are all
fixed. This results in a horizontal depth, characterized by a vanishing point, which causes
objects further from the viewer to appear
smaller than closer objects.

Since the fifteenth century, European painting has supplemented these principles of focal perspective with increasingly skillful techniques of figuration and coloring, developing a richly varied pictorial space, and establishing a "discourse" of realistic painting. This is not only an aesthetic principle; it also has important ideological connotations.

> (1) Classical figurative painting is a discourse. This discourse is produced according to figurative codes. These codes are directly produced by ideology and are therefore subjected to historical transformations. (2) This discourse defines in advance the role of the subject, and therefore pre-determines the reading of the painting. . . . (3) This exploitation of the imaginary, this utilization of the subject is made possible by the presence of a system which Oudart calls "representation." This system englobes the painting, the subject, and their relationship upon which it exerts a tight control.[1]

That is to say, the language of classical painting embodies its ideological function by two characteristic means. One is the realistic nature of the painting techniques, which conceals the existence of the figurative codes. The other is the determinate nature of the point of view: the observed painting resembles one stage, while the viewer (subject) occupies a corresponding stage, the position of the subject being determined by focal perspective. This invisible second stage and its point of view show that the language of painting functions to control and assimilate. Furthermore, this system can be used as a premise in analyzing the "suture" theory of classical cinema and the "tutor-code."[2] However, the pictorial theories of classical Chinese painting, one of the important traditions of Asian art, are markedly different from those of Western painting. We can see this difference in that, in classical Chinese painting, neither the viewer's position, the line of sight, nor the frame are fixed. Classical Chinese landscapes and portraits are spread out on horizontal or vertical scrolls, not viewed as through a window frame. These extensions in the plane of the painted surface imply a mobile point of view and an open temporal ordering. In other words, it is an attempt to set up on a still, flat surface a spatial plan which contains a temporal dimension. The difference is that, in Western painting the temporal dimension extends in a plane perpendicular to that of the painted surface, while in Oriental painting it is embodied in horizontal or vertical extension within that plane. Thus, Oriental painting is a system of nonfocal, antifocal, and multifocal perspective.

> The Romantic landscapes of the nineteenth century submit nature to a remodeling which imposes on them a monocular perspective, transforming the land-

scape into that which is seen by a given subject. This type of landscape is very different from the Japanese landscape with its multiple perspective. The latter is *not* the visible part of a two-stage system.[3]

Since Japanese and Chinese painting belong to the same system, this quote may be understood as applying to Chinese painting as well.

The ambulatory, panoramic point of view and freely expandable frame of classical Chinese painting, together with the nonrealistic nature of its figuration and coloring, make up a symbolic code. This system not only fails to conceal the existence of this code, but rather intensifies and displays the manipulative function of the code and distances the viewer from it. Just as any painting uses the signifier of its "text" to make the viewer feel as though he or she were placed in a position determined by the painting, the unique manipulatory code of a Chinese landscape painting insinuates a floating, shifting point of view on the part of the viewer standing before it. Though this is vastly different from the way in which Western "window-frame painting" guides the viewer's line of sight, this movement of vision also has its own spatial consciousness controlled by a particular philosophical view.

Classical Chinese landscape painting is permeated with Taoist and Buddhist thought, which, in terms of spatial consciousness, are embodied in such terms as "vastness" (*bódà*) and the "Great Void" (*tàixū*). Compositions on horizontal or vertical scrolls are the codified embodiment of limitless spatial extension. Such aesthetic concepts as infinitude or magnificence were often debated in ancient texts. The *Tao Te Ching* says:

> There was something formless yet complete,
> That existed before heaven and earth;[4]
>
> . . . .
>
> Its true name we do not know;
> "Way" is the by-name that we give it.
> Were I forced to say to what class of things it belongs I should call it Great
> [*dà*].[5]

The *Tao Te Ching* also makes such propositions as

> Great music has the faintest (most rarified) notes;
> The Great Form is without shape;
> The largest square has no corners;[6]

thereby formulating a conception of space based on the Tao. Similar propositions can be found in the *Book of Changes* (*Yìjīng*):

Vast is the "great and originating (power)" indicated by [the hexagram] *Kh*ien [*qián*]! All things owe to it their beginning:—it contains all the meaning belonging to (the name) heaven.[7]

Complete is the "great and originating (capacity)" indicated by [the hexagram] Khwăn [*kūn*]! All things owe to it their birth;—it receives obediently the influences of Heaven.[8]

Other texts comment:

Ascending and descending with perfect freedom,
My mind roams the Great Void.[9]

Where Heaven meets Earth, there is no going away without return.[10]

Then, the spirit at full gallop reaches the eight limits of the cosmos,
And the mind, self-buoyant, will ever soar to new insurmountable heights.[11]

Quietly absorbed in contemplation, his thinking reaches back one thousand years; and with only the slightest movement of his countenance, his vision penetrates ten thousand *li*.[12]

All of these passages embody the ancient Chinese view of the universe. The Way (*Tao*) and Heaven (*tiān*) were concepts of absolute greatness and eternity, and underlay ancient Chinese thought and consciousness. "The greatness of the Way comes from that of Heaven; Heaven is unchanging, thus so is the Way." This directly influenced the cosmology and mythology of poetry, painting, and dramatic art. *Yǔ* (infinite space) and *zhòu* (all time) were understood as a giant sphere surrounding the earth in every direction. The infinitude of the cosmos and the minuteness of the individual, endless cycles and the unity of Heaven and humankind—all these produced a spatio-temporal relationship in which subject and object are not only opposed to, but also fused with, each other. "The cosmos is my mind; my mind is the cosmos." "Replete with all things, reaching across the Great Void." "Where Heaven meets Earth, there is no going away without return."

All of these passages embody this relationship between Heaven and humankind in which there is no barrier between the self and object, and the mind is free to roam throughout space. It was upon this understanding that the landscape compositions of vertical and horizontal scrolls, and the principles of multiple perspective employed in panoramic views, were constructed and developed. The temporal order of viewing a vertical scroll should be from top to center, then from center to bottom, thus proceeding from distant to near at hand.[13] The long horizontal scroll extends endlessly from left to right, expanding through unlimited movement back and forth, and theoretically forming a panoramic spatial world with the viewer at its center. It is in this sense that the ability to seek out the limits of vision in all directions and to see across myriad miles forms the essential core of Oriental painting and the fundamental principles of its perspective, putting it in a completely different framework from that of classical Western painting.

> Chinese and Westerners both have a fondness for limitless spaces (The Chinese like to refer to this as the Great Void, or Great Emptiness [*tàikōng*], "without end or boundary" [*wúqióng wúyá*]), but there is a great difference in the spiritual conception of the two. The Westerner stands in a particular spot, viewing spatial depth from a particular angle, the line of sight reaching out to, but then disappearing at, infinity. The attitude toward limitless space is one of searching, controlling, daring, exploring.
>
> But the Chinese attitude toward this limitless space is as set forth in the poem: "Gazing up at lofty mountains, / Strolling through a scene; / Though I cannot attain the summit / My heart continues on." Life in this world is like a shallow boat, tossed about between heaven and earth, engulfed in the current, carried off to the home of the gods, far beyond the horizon.[14]

When the Chinese encounter infinitude in finitude, or return from infinitude to finitude, their interest is not in unbounded movement, but in the cycle of reciprocal movement.

Chinese ink wash landscape, which rose to prominence in the middle of the Northern Song dynasty (eleventh century) and continued to develop through the subsequent Southern Song and Yuan dynasties (A.D. 1127–1368), embodies the profound influence which Chán (Zen) Buddhist thought exerted on Chinese literati and officials. Advocacy of the subtleties of India ink to the exclusion of colored pigments, and a sense of boundlessness transcending the limits of form, of unrestrained movement across the Great Void, became the hallmarks of Song and Yuan landscapes.

> We can see now that the principle of *sumiye* [ink wash] painting is derived from this Zen experience, and that directness, simplicity, movement, spirituality, completeness, and other qualities we observe in the *sumiye* class of Oriental paintings have an organic relationship to Zen.[15]

It was from the end of the Tang dynasty through the Northern Song (ninth to eleventh centuries) that Chán teachings grew in popularity, eventually occupying a very important position among the various sects of Buddhism and exerting far-reaching influence on the arts.

> In their attitudes toward nature there are many similarities between the tenets of Chán and the traditional Taoist philosophy of Lao Tzu and Chuang Tzu: they both take an intimate, quasipantheistic approach to nature, demand the union of humanity and nature, and hope to draw inspiration and enlightenment from nature in order to free the spirit from the shackles of human affairs.[16]

Such terms as "loftiness" (*gāoyuǎn*), "serenity" (*níngjìng*), "spiritual emptiness" (*kōnglíng*), and "Great Void" (*tàixū*) are in fact reflections of the psychological condition which results from the painter's experience of and union with nature, the realm of Chán enlightenment. By brush and ink, natural scenes are transformed into objects which convey the "emptiness" (*kōng*) and "spirit" (*líng*) of the painter; consequently, the employment of the subtle gradations of black and gray to the exclusion of color, and a predilection for the bleak and bare, characterize Song and Yuan landscapes. Another characteristic is the importance of large blank spaces as compositional elements in all the various formats of this period: both vertical and longer horizontal scrolls, as well as smaller Song album leaves. This is the result of reducing a large panorama, seen from a lofty vantage point, to fit onto a small surface; but, more importantly, "empty space" (*kōngbái*) embodies the ontological assumptions of Taoist and Chán philosophy. *Qì* (vital force), "emptiness," and "nothingness" (*wú*), while retaining a definite philosophical content, are transformed into various artistic images.

> "It is when peering into interstices that empty space gives birth to a blank." This blank white is not a spatial framework in the geometrical sense, a dead space, but rather the eternally creative Tao, producing everything in the phenomenal world. This "white" is the propitious light of the Tao.[17]

The Song dynasty poet Sū Dōngpō (A.D. 1037–1101) said: "Quiescence, thus all things can move; emptiness, thus all space is comprehended." This "emptiness" which comprehends all space is the Tao. It is by inscribing the composition and structure of paintings with "blank whiteness" that they become permeated with vital energy; form gives birth to void, void produces form in a process which transforms the Chinese landscape into a realm where "All things are of themselves produced and ordered, / The Great Void remains desolate," and "The myriad phenomena multiply to no avail; / In quietude the Great Void keeps its distance." In other words, the various mountains and streams, rivers and valleys, trees and forests, or undulations of mountain peaks and ranges all can become signifiers in the painting's "text," while "space" and "blanks" in the "text" connote and act as ambiguous symbols; brush and ink, line, blank space, and the interaction of form and void in traditional Chinese freehand brushwork imbue the completed work with the character of semiabstract painting.

A concrete reflection of this multifocal perspective and connotative space can be seen in the structure of horizontal landscape scrolls and their seemingly endless extension. Two Northern Song paintings, *Streams and Mountains without End* (figure 3.1) and *Qīngmíng Festival on the Canal* by Zhāng Zédūan (note colorplate 2), both embody a panoramic vision in which mountains and rivers overlap in vast horizontal extension. *Pure and Remote View of Streams and Mountains* (*Xīshān qīngyuǎn tú*) by the Southern Song painter Xià Guī is even more ethereal and understated, drawing the eye out across hundreds of miles, making use of large patches of blank space as structural elements of figural extension (note figure 1.1). The same compositional principles can be seen in smaller landscape formats, such as the round fan painting *After the Snow* (*Xuějì tú*, Northern Song). As the fifth-century theorist Zōng Bǐng said, "A three-inch stroke is a thousand-foot height, and a line of a few feet stretches ten thousand miles."

The above-mentioned principles are true not only for landscapes, but also for traditional Chinese portraiture. From the earliest Chinese depictions of human figures up to the time when Western oil painting began to exert its influence in China, almost all portraits, whether of individuals or groups, were painted as full-length figures; there are virtually none restricted to the head or bust. And these figures, whether alone or in groups, are placed in spacious surroundings, as in the Tang dynasty painting *Serving Girls with Flowers in Their Hair* (*Zānhuā shìnǚ tú*) by Zhōu Fǎng and the Song dynasty handscroll *Ladies Preparing Newly Woven Silk* attributed to Emperor Huīzōng (figure 3.2). *Hán Xīzài's Night Banquet* (*Hán Xīzài yèyàn tú*) by the Five Dynasties (A.D. 907–960) painter Gù Hóngzhōng represents a scene in which the host regales his honored guests with a feast complete with musical accompaniment (note colorplate 3). In this painting a temporal dimension extends horizontally across the flat surface, which presents successive stages of the feast's progress.

The spatial consciousness and composition of classical Chinese painting exerted a direct influence on the imagistic structure and organization of cinematographic language in early Chinese films, such as *Twin Sisters* (*Zǐmèi huā*, 1933), which features a flatness of composition, horizontal extension, and even lighting. At various stages in the development of Chinese cinema,

3.1 *Streams and Mountains without End*, China, Northern Song period, early twelfth century, detail (courtesy of The Cleveland Museum of Art, Gift of the Hanna Fund, 53.126).

3.2 *Ladies Preparing Newly Woven Silk*, China, attributed to Emperor Huīzōng (1082–1135), Northern Song period, early twelfth century, ink, colors, and gold on silk handscroll (Museum of Fine Arts, Boston, courtesy of the Chinese and Japanese Special Fund, 12.886).

especially during the exploratory and innovative periods, we can clearly see the progress of conflict between, and interpenetration of, Western principles of figuration and Chinese theories of scenic formation.

The "suture" theory of classical Western cinema arose out of a theoretical study of the "double-stage" system of classical Western painting, revealing the ideological function of the "tutor-code." The extent and nature of influence exerted by the codes of Oriental painting on its imagistic structure and cinematographic language system remains to be discussed.

Relationship between the Visual Signification of Cinema and the Tradition of Chinese Painting

The incompatibility between, on the one hand, the inflexible aspect ratio of the screen, the laws of focal perspective, and the mechanical representation of images in the Western tradition and, on the other hand, the multifocal perspective, horizontal-scroll compositions, and nonrealistic language of classical Chinese painting can clearly be seen in the composition, arrangement, selection of shots, and lighting of early Chinese movies. The contradiction with classical paintings, on the level of image formation, is a contradiction between the medium and tradition. Yet another contradiction can be found on the narrative level. The cinema demands a narrative structure in which conflicts intensify within a climactic pattern. But it is the poetic, the lyrical that constitutes the strongest tradition in Chinese literature. Though Chinese drama and prompt books (*huàběn xiǎoshuō*) are considered narrative literature, in structural form and the treatment of time and space they are quite distinct from Western drama.

The New Cinema Movement (Xīndiànyǐng yùndòng) of China and Taiwan during the 1980s was the most concentrated and radical transformation of cinematic language in the history of Chinese films, and once again brought to the fore this conflict between the medium and tradition. The most prominent feature of this period is that, in the representative works of the Fifth Generation and Taiwan's New Cinema, the spatial consciousness and compositional theories of classical Chinese painting have been transformed into a system of imagistic signification. In moving from one medium to the other, the code is transformed, thereby achieving a new visual "tutoring" function. Although this leads to unique results in each of the various films by such directors as Chén Kǎigē, Tián Zhuàngzhuàng, Zhāng Yìmóu, and Hou Hsiao-hsien (Hóu Xiàoxián), this text shall deal primarily with Chén Kǎigē's *Yellow Earth* (*Huáng tǔdì*, 1984), and Hou Hsiao-hsien's *The Time to Live and the Time to Die* (*Tóngnián wǎngshì*, 1985) and *A City of Sadness* (*Bēiqíng chéngshì*, 1988).

Yellow Earth is a symbolic allegory of history. Its meaning is comprised of signification on the level of both image and narrative, but it is the connotations of this imagistic signification and stylized understatement which are more prominent. Because the narrative has been enervated, the individual figures of the leading characters appear in codified form, and the marriage, waist-drum dance, and prayers for rain of the villagers are presented in a ritualized manner. The liberal symbolism of the overall narrative dimension lends a broader freedom to the iconic signification. The plateau, mighty river, yellow soil, and Yellow River (which symbolizes the birthplace of the people) act, on the narrative level, as the signifying code of the natural environment, uniting with the stylized actions of the villagers to deepen the connotations of *Yellow Earth* on the imagistic level.

One of the basic tasks of the iconic signification of *Yellow Earth* is to reveal the acute contradictions between humankind and nature, present and past, the primitive environment and the conditions of communal life. It also reveals a type of discontinuity between protohistory and current discourse. Of particular interest is the fact that these contradictions are more fully realized by means of a displacement of the code of classical Chinese painting by cinematic images.

The flattening of space and its boundless extension imbue blank space on the surface of a painting with a specific meaning. This feature, characteristic of classical Chinese painting, also becomes important in *Yellow Earth.* Here we can see the conflict between the principles of cinematography and traditional norms, as well as the transformation of the code of classical painting between two different media and two different systems of meaning. "Distance" is an important element in composing shots, and constitutes a unifying focus in *Yellow Earth:* the difference between distant shots and extreme long shots; the greater part of the screen occupied by space, with tiny human figures serving as accessories to the natural world; fixed camera position and static shots to show the eternity and solemnity of primeval nature; the flattening of space, lack of vertical camera movement (tilting), prevalence of high or low shots which fill the screen with earth (in many cases the sloping plateau or mountain sides) or sky, emphasized by this flattening of space; the use of slow panning or tracking to represent horizontal shifting of focus, and to realize the boundless extension of surrounding space, and so on. These stylistic and semantic codes unite the iconic signification of *Yellow Earth* with its narrative system, and transcend the narrative to produce a relatively independent signification and stylistic flavor. As pointed out above, the spatial consciousness and "blank" spaces of classical Chinese painting function both as a code and as specific ideological connotation, reflecting the ancient Chinese philosophical, as well as religious, consciousness. But in *Yellow Earth* it is through the duplicative function of the movie camera (i.e., the screen space in which the image is recreated) and through the combination of meanings on the narrative level that the specific codes mentioned above are able to create the meaning of the movie within the context of iconic signification. In other words, *it is only through the existence of the material space of cinematic re-presentation,* that "blank space" is imbued with new connotations. In his introduction to the work of Chén Kǎigē, Méng Yuè writes:

> As a film, what role does *Yellow Earth* play in contemporary culture? That is, what does it make you see? How does it make you see it? In the film it is a startlingly huge object which occupies the center of the frame, and of our vision. What we see is not "space," but rather objects that violate the ordinary sense of space—the earth, with no trace of human, sky, plant or anything else; the sky, having no point of contact with the human world; the river, boundless,

directionless. Humans are squeezed into a corner of the frame, tiny and helpless like ants. What is more, these objects do not belong to any dramatic space or time, to any narrative context; they do not form the particular background for human action or the occurrence of events; they are not circumstances or situations required by the narrative; nor are they fields civilized and cultivated by human hands. . . . These objects seem to be drifting outside of existing cultural codes. They are merely objects, which cannot be apprehended by any system of meaning, things-in-themselves which have nothing to do with human life.

Throughout this film, human and sky, human and earth or river, are grossly out of proportion. In ordinary movies things materialize about the characters; but here the insignificant existence of humans is like a distant mote of dust. The static camera brings out human subordination to things: the characters in the frame belong strictly to the objective world.

It is the chasm between the thing per se and discourse, between the world of reality and ideology that is so startling. In other words, *Yellow Earth*, through its own images, reveals that the truth of historical existence, like things-in-themselves, has been excluded from the field of discourse, and placed outside of ideology. But at the same time, *Yellow Earth* attempts to redeem this banished history. It reveals the continued existence of the unspoken, helpless, silent, meaninglessly extensive thing-in-itself which had been hidden by discourse, and completes the objectivization of the world of "things" by means of silent images, static camera position, and incomplete passage over the river. It makes of our unconscious history an object for contemplation, producing a complex, multilayered allegorical meaning.[18]

The cinematic text of *Yellow Earth* develops two qualitatively different types of discursive conflict and redemption. One is the conflict (or chasm) between things-in-themselves and the reality of existence on the one hand, and discourse and ideology on the other, as pointed out by Méng Yuè in the quotation above. One could even refer to it as the conflict between the camera and the redemption of banished history. The other type of conflict is that between the code of classical painting and its compositional language on the one hand, and the representational function and mechanical images of the camera on the other. By means of the coding strategies of *Yellow Earth*'s iconic signification, there is revealed within the frame of the silver screen the redemption or transformation of the connotations of classical painting discourse; and such terms as "emptiness," "nothingness," and "Great Void," which have specific philosophical connotations in horizontal scrolls, are transformed in the material reproduction of the imagistic world into extensions of things in the movie. This tendency in the filmic rhetoric of *Yellow Earth* naturally leads to a break with the forms of iconic signification found in mainstream Chinese movies. Interestingly enough, this new rupture is a

3.3 Hou Hsiao-hsien (Hóu Xiàoxián), *A City of Sadness* (*Bēiqíng chéngshì*, 1988),
Taiwan [Republic of China].

result of insight gained through sensitivity derived from a profound understanding and probing of the classical painting tradition.

If Chén Kǎigē's film develops its signification and implications from a spatial perspective, then Hou Hsiao-hsien's films, analyzed on the level of their
systems of iconic signification, express their meaning through codes of implicit and explicit signification by the manipulation of temporal "blanks"
and "empty shots." Chén Kǎigē's film attempts an inclusive historical reflection through allegory; Hou Hsiao-hsien's films are warm, intimate autobi-
ographies or family histories. Although the lyricized psychological portraits
are reminiscent of China's avant-garde director of the 1940s Fèi Mù,[19] Hou
Hsiao-hsien's systematic and highly stylized cinematic prose expresses very
incisively and vividly the ethical spirit of Confucian culture and the emotional attachment to one's native land typical of the Orient. The family is a
cohesive, highly symbolic unit of Confucian culture, the fundamental space
within which to view and examine the psychological world of the Chinese.
The iconic signification and rhetoric of Hou Hsiao-hsien's cinematic prose is
built onto the code of family space as defined by his camera shots (figure 3.3).

From the viewpoint of narratology, *The Time to Live and the Time to Die* and *A City of Sadness* both belong to a personal, intimate style of psychological portrayal. However, seen from a rhetorical perspective, Hou Hsiao-hsien's cinematographic grammar consistently maintains a certain distance from the objects portrayed. His cinematographic grammar does not belong to the "suture" syntax of classical film. (It does not use sutured declarations to make a consistent rhetorical grammar.) Its depth of field has a language system different from that proposed by Bazin, and often unfolds complete narrative statements in medium and long shots. "Sutured" declarations make each stated portion the signifier of its counterpart, often expressed by characters facing one another or in exchange with one another, thus breaking down dramatic space and rebuilding it. On the other hand, complete declarative statements emphasize the expression and depth of meaning in unified space. Examining the relationship between the spatial consciousness of films and that of paintings, this alienation between subject and object can be traced back to the compositional model adopted by the Chinese cinema:

> The selection of shots in Chinese movies is usually centered around the "medium shot system"; thus solid objects in space naturally appear positioned in the middle of the third dimension [midground]. This manifests the structure of Chinese shots, in which the midground acts as a fulcrum, and embodies the compositional principles of Chinese cinematic space expressed in the phrase "forming the image from a distance" [*yǐyuǎn qǔ xiàng*].
>
> This compositional space in which the midground acts as fulcrum may be described as a relatively broad space in which there is "symmetry in all directions, proportion in all dimensions."[20]

This conception of pictorial space described above—in the composition of traditional Chinese portraits, it can be seen in the scarcity of busts and half-length paintings, the lack of articulated space in compositions, the fact that individual or group portraits always present a complete scene with considerable space on all sides of the figure(s), and the extension of a temporal dimension in the plane of the painted surface—has influenced the cinema in many ways, from its earliest days down to the present. The code of classical cinema, whether through complete or partial, unconscious or completely conscious, transformation, has been able to reify cinematic declarations which maintain the distance between object and subject, and which, in unified space, concentrate on the unfolding of meaning in the temporal dimension. This is particularly true for Hou Hsiao-hsien's films.

As has been incisively pointed out:

Poetry is built not on conflict, but on mutual reflection and contrast. Because it does not use dramatic conflict to express pain, it cannot use the "redemption" of tragedy for catharsis. By reflecting the endless passage of time, poetry highlights the transient nature of the reality of human existence within time.[21]

The narratives of *The Time to Live and the Time to Die* and *A City of Sadness* push the concrete contradictions of historical violence, bloody conflict, and the vagaries of personal fate into the narrative background. Diegetic relationships, those between the characters in the film, emphasize emotional experiences resulting from the larger tragedies implied by the narrative background. Thus, on the level of iconic signification, Hou Hsiao-hsien often uses statements lacking in conflict but replete with emotion to describe the experiences and feelings of the protagonist oppressed by fate and profound melancholy—for example, in *The Time to Live and the Time to Die,* a long conversation between wife and daughter after a man's death, or the sudden, unnoticed death of a grandmother, and the subsequent bitter mourning of her grandsons. The unpredictable arrival of death, and the sprouting and unselfconscious maturing of youth realize their multivalent expression, not only in the unfolding of already enervated events and plot, but also in many other ways: on the level of iconic signification, in emotional connotations unrelated to the plot, in the "empty" screen, in the lives of passive characters, in the passing of time. These "blanks" in the temporal structure point toward unambiguous reading and interpretation, as well as toward experience and understanding. In the Western literary tradition, tragedy is often expressed as apotheosis and catharsis in the midst of conflict and destruction; but in the East, in Chinese literature, "fate is often a blank space, a blank image, a great, unending rhythm, sounding without human will, irresistible, transcending the individual."[22] Thus, "in contrast, poetry does not achieve catharsis through redemption, but rather ceaselessly prolongs its sighs, its musings, its silent meditations."[23] This is the tragic strength of *The Time to Live and the Time to Die* and *A City of Sadness.*

This article discusses the relationship between classical Chinese painting and filmic signification on a very small scale. In order to treat this topic more broadly, one must treat mainstream Chinese cinema—that is, one must examine the relationship between classical painting and the spatial consciousness and operation of codes in ordinary films with dramatic structures employing narrative techniques based on "sutured" propositions. Nevertheless, the lyrical Chinese movie is the most fruitful field of endeavor for those searching out the form and consciousness of the literati tradition, and, though outside the mainstream, is most replete with pioneering spirit. What is more, because classical Chinese and Japanese painting both come from the same source, their spatial consciousness, compositional techniques, and construction of images have much in common, a fact which is reflected in the compositions of many Japanese directors. Our understanding of the methods of image formation and signification characteristic of Asian films should be deepened through comparative and comprehensive study, but this must await future monographs for further discussion.

Notes

1. Daniel Dayan, "The Tutor-Code of Classical Cinema," in *Movies and Methods*, vol. 1, ed. Bill Nichols (Berkeley: University of California Press, 1976; Chinese translation in Lǐ Yòujiāo, ed., *Structuralism and Semiotics* [*Jiégòu zhǔyì hé fúhàoxué*; Beijing: Sānyǎ shūdiàn, 1987], p. 205), p. 444.

2. The suture is a system of discourse that is prevalent in classical cinema. It plays the role of a tutor-code by mediating between the story and the spectator.

Daniel Dayan discovers the function of "The Absent-One" in the process of enunciation of classical cinema. The shifting point of view of the Absent-One constitutes a system of codes that makes possible the continual unfolding of the story and thus brings about a shifting point of view on the part of the spectator. "Through the classical device of shot and reverse shot, the Absent-One becomes a character and the visual world of the film becomes transformed from enunciation into fiction, into a world that is not produced (by a filmmaker, by an ideological system) but is simply seen. . . . By this means classical cinema serves an ideological function even before we begin to examine it as fiction." This function is realized through the fusion of the different visual fields "of the spectator, who is robbed of his present and also placed in an imaginary relationship to the screen. It is the violence of an ideology that by seeming 'natural' goes unrecognized" (editor's introduction to Dayan, "The Tutor-Code," in *Movies and Methods*, pp. 438–439).

In Daniel Dayan's opinion, the system of the suture plays the role of tutor-code in the discursive process of a film.

3. According to Dayan, in J. Oudart's analysis of Velázquez's *Las Meninas*, Oudart argues that when the spectator is looking at the figures in the painting, the figures in the painting are also looking out at the spectator. "In theatrical terms, the painting represents the stage while the mirror represents its audience. Oudart concludes that the text of the painting must not be reduced to its visible part; it does not stop where the canvas stops. The text of the painting is a system which Oudart defines as a 'double-stage.' On one stage, the show is enacted; on the other, the spectator looks at it. In classical representation, the visible is only the first part of a system which always includes an invisible second part (the 'reverse shot')" (Dayan, "Tutor-Code," p. 445).

4. Arthur Waley, *The Way and its Power: A Study of the* Tao Tê Ching *and Its*

Place in Chinese Thought (London: George Allen & Unwin Ltd., 1934), p. 174.

5. Ibid.

6. Ibid., p. 193.

7. James Legge, trans., *I Ching: Book of Changes*, edited, with an introduction and study guide by Ch'u Chai, Library of Ancient and Modern Classics (New Hyde Park, New York: University Books, n.d.), p. 213.

8. Ibid., p. 214.

9. Jī Kāng, "Sending a Scholar Off to Join the Army" (Zèng xiùcái rùjūn), no. 4 of 5, in Uchida Sennosuke, ed., *Koshi gen*, vol. 1 (*Kanshi taikei*, no. 4; Tokyo: Shūeisha, 1964), p. 337.

10. Hexagram *tài*, "Treatise on the Symbolism of the Hexagrams" (*xiàng*), Ruán Yuán, ed., *Zhōuyì zhèngyì*, in *Shísān jīng zhùshū* (1816; reprint, Beijing: Zhōnghuá shūjú, 1979), p. 28 (fasc. 2, p. 16).

11. Lú Jī, "Essay on Literature" (*Wén fù*), trans. Chen Shih-hsiang, in *Anthology of Chinese Literature: From Early Times to the Fourteenth Century*, ed. Cyril Birch (New York: Grove Press, 1965), p. 205.

12. Liú Xié, *The Literary Mind and the Carving of Dragons* (*Wénxīn diàolóng*), Ch. 26, "Spiritual Thought or Imagination (*Shen-ssu*)," trans. Vincent Yu-chung Shih, Records of Civilization: Sources and Studies, no. 58 (New York: Columbia University Press, 1959), p. 154.

13. The Song dynasty painter Guō Xī proposes a theory of "three distances" in speaking of the creation of space:

> Mountains have three distances: looking up from the base of the mountain to the peak is called "high distance"; peering from the front of the mountain toward the back is called "deep distance"; gazing from near mountains to far is called "flat distance." The coloring of "high distance" is clear and bright; that of "deep distance," heavy and dim; that of "flat distance," both bright and dim. The form of "high distance" is sharp and jutting; "deep distance" presents a feeling of layer upon layer; and "flat distance," a sense of fading away into the distance. (Guō Xī, "Línquán gāoqí: shānshuǐ xùn," in *Huàlùn cóngkān* [Beijing: Běijīng rénmín yìshù chūbǎnshè, 1962], 1: p. 19)

14. Zōng Báihuá, "Zhōngguó shīhuàzhōng suǒ biǎoxiàn de kōngjiàn yìshì," in his *Měixué sànbù* (Shanghai: Shànghǎi rénmín chūbǎnshè, 1981), p. 94.

15. Daisetz T. Suzuki, *Zen and Japanese Culture*, Bollingen Series 64 (New York: Bollingen Foundation, 1959; rev. and enl. 2d ed. of *Zen Buddhism and Its Influence on Japanese Culture* [Ataka Buddhist Library, 9], Kyoto: Eastern Buddhist Society, 1938), p. 36.

16. Lǐ Zéhòu, *Měi de lìchéng* (Beijing: Wénwù chūbǎnshè, 1981), p. 169.

17. Zōng Báihuá, p. 95.

18. Méng Yuè, "Bāolù de yuánshēng shìjiè: Chén Kǎigē qiǎnlùn," *Diànyǐng yìshù*, no. 4 (1990), p. 25.

19. Fèi Mù (1906–1951) is known for such works as *City Nights* (*Chéngshì zhī yè*), *Sea of Fragrant Snow* (*Xiāngxuě hǎi*), *Natural Bonds* (*Tiānlún*), and *Confucius* (*Kǒng fūzi*). His film *Spring in a Small Town* (*Xiǎochéng zhī chūn*, 1948) with its psychological portrayal and long takes, was a forerunner of China's lyrical cinema; in the 1980s he received much attention from directors in both China and Taiwan.

20. Lín Niántóng, *Zhōngguó diànyǐng de kōngjiàn yìshì* (Hong Kong: Zhōngguó diànyǐng xuéhuì, 1984), p. 66.

21. Wú Niànzhēn and Zhū Tiānwén, *Bēiqíng chéngshì* (*A City of Sadness;* Taiwan: Sānsān shūfáng, 1989), pp. 15–16.

22. Lín Niántóng, p. 66.

23. Ibid.

POST-SOCIALIST
STRATEGIES:
An Analysis of Yellow Earth *and*
Black Cannon Incident

BY CHRIS BERRY AND
MARY ANN FARQUHAR

CHAPTER

4

Introduction

In 1982, the first class of cinematographers, directors, and art directors since the start of the "Cultural Revolution" in 1966 graduated from China's only film school, the Beijing Film Academy. Previous graduates might have had to work for twenty years in subsidiary, apprentice-like jobs before they had the opportunity to make their own films, but an unusual combination of circumstances enabled these young newcomers to make their first films within two years of graduation.[2] The films shocked the Chinese film world and the filmmakers became known as the Fifth Generation.

There is no question that the Fifth Generation were doing something different, and nearly all interviews with them attest to the fact that their effort to mark themselves out from their predecessors was self-conscious

Rodin said: "A real artist always expresses his own thoughts and is not afraid to break the existing rules." (HUÁNG JIÀNXĪN)[1]

and deliberate.[3] This differentiation occurs across all aspects of the films, from character types to plot structure, themes, and locations. In this article, we will consider what was new about the Fifth Generation by comparing the painting traditions they draw upon with those used by their predecessors.

This task is made complicated by the remarkable variety of Fifth Generation films. To take but a few brief examples, Tián Zhuàngzhuàng's film about life in Mongolia, *On the Hunting Ground* (*Lièchǎng zhásā*, 1984), adopts an almost cinema-verité style of ethnographic filmmaking, although it is a fiction film; Hú Méi's investigation of the personal sacrifices Chinese women make in exchange for participation in the public sphere, *Army Nurse* (*Nǚ-érlóu*, 1985), adopts stream-of-consciousness techniques with meandering voice-over and melancholic memories; and Chén Kǎigē's *Yellow Earth* (*Huáng tǔdì*, 1984) is frequently related to Chinese landscape painting techniques. However, although they have adopted a great range of different techniques, all these filmmakers are united in their effort to move away from what we will call here the socialist-realist model of Chinese filmmaking.[4]

In China this socialist-realist model was dominant from the fifties through the late seventies, and still exists today. Unlike the Fifth Generation films, it was relatively unified and constant. It was adapted from the classical Hollywood cinema and the Soviet socialist-realist cinema. (The latter was itself derived from the Hollywood model, prompting Jean-Luc Godard to refer to it as the "Hollywood-Mosfilm style.") The aesthetics of these two cinemas are founded on post-Renaissance realist painting techniques and, in the case of the Soviet films, agitprop poster art. Perspectival space is, of course, established, and illusionist editing techniques collaborate with this to ensure that a clear position is maintained for the viewer in relation to what is depicted. Mimesis is carefully constructed with close attention to authenticity of sets, costumes, acting, and so forth, and the humanist tradition operates in composition focusing on well-centered figures carefully displayed, full face and well lit, for inspection by the audience.[5] Narrative characteristics draw upon the nineteenth-century European novel, which complements the realist painting tradition with a linear structure whose absence of disjuncture helps to suture the viewer/reader into an illusion of reality, and a primary focus on human relations.[6]

After the break with the Soviet Union at the end of the 1950s, which occurred because the Chinese Communist Party was unwilling to join in the repudiation of Stalin, the socialist-realist tradition in the cinema was renamed as a combination of "socialist realism and revolutionary romanticism" and Chinese filmmakers were called upon to sinicize their films. Revolutionary romanticism was interpreted to mean the integration of an element of idealization, or "typicalization," whereby the revolutionary potential inherent in contemporary reality was supposed to be stressed.[7] For example, both heroes and villains were constructed as larger-than-life class types rather than psychologized individuals, a tendency which reached its apogee with the theory of the "Three Prominences" during the Cultural Revolution.[8] This technique might be referred back to Soviet poster art, but was also explicitly claimed as sinicized by reference to characteristics of traditional opera, but with proletarian figures replacing the emperors, generals, and courtesans of old.[9]

Sinicization was also applied to the image, with a certain aesthetic decorative style, where the basic socialist-realist style was stuccoed over with Chinese motifs. Catherine Yi-Yu Cho Woo has noted the appearance of symbols derived from ancient poetry and painting, and the construction of isolated shots to resemble classical painting, for example, by framing a shot with branches of blossoms in the "bird and flower" style or using natural metaphors such as flocks of geese to represent the character far from home or a pair of fish to imply sexual desire.[10] Other similarly isolated examples of a decorative sinicization might include the tendency to start a scene or a film with a lengthy pan of the landscape in which the story is set, referring to landscape scroll paintings, as in the opening of the 1963 film about Tibet, *Serfs* (*Nóngnú*). However, these flourishes hardly formed part of an integrated style, as in the use of landscape painting traditions in *Yellow Earth*.

The socialist-realist model we have described both adopted and adapted elements from Hollywood, Soviet socialist realism, and traditional opera, as well as from certain ancient painting and poetry traditions, but it did not do this simply to reproduce these elements. Rather, they were actively deployed to didactic ends. Similarly, the Fifth Generation directors have not drawn upon a wide range of different styles simply to distance themselves from the socialist-realist model. We could briefly gloss references to non-socialist-realist styles in a large number of films, but we do not wish to represent Fifth Generation films as sites where other styles are simply reproduced. Instead, we would emphasize the purposeful deployment of these styles as part of a larger project by way of extended discussion of two very different tendencies. One is a return to classical traditions not used extensively in the socialist-realist film, as represented by *Yellow Earth*. The other is the adoption of a style carrying connotations of Western modern art in Huáng Jiànxīn's political satire, *Black Cannon Incident* (*Hēipào shìjiàn*, 1985).

Before we enter this extended discussion, one further issue remains to be discussed: the nature of the shift away from the socialist realist style. As indicated by the sheer variety of Fifth Generation work, it cannot be argued that their work constitutes a unified paradigm. In this sense, it seems that either Marxist or modernist theories of historical change—which speak in terms of the completely new and different, the revolutionary, the radical rupture, and the paradigm shift—may be inappropriate. Even though Huáng Jiànxīn's *Black Cannon Incident* draws upon Western modernist art traditions and examines the Chinese discourse of modernization in the eighties, placed in reference to the Fifth Generation as a whole, it is only one instance in a network of different references which are drawn upon, pastiched together, played with, and transformed. Therefore, we would venture to suggest the term "post-socialist" to refer to the style and strategies of Fifth Generation films as worthy of further consideration.

This term, originated by Arif Dirlik in his discussion of Chinese politics, has already been adopted by Paul Pickowicz in his discussion of Huáng Jiànxīn's films.[11] Pickowicz's decision to use this term is highly suggestive, but he uses it mainly in reference to the plots of Huáng's films to suggest that they mark the death of socialism and the emergence of something different. What remains to be fully explored is the homology between this term and "postmodernist," from which it is clearly derived. Can postsocialism be seen as a complement to postmodernism? Is its pastiche of other styles, its ambiguity and play, part of an aesthetic parallel to postmodernism? And is its move away from socialist realism without establishing a new orthodoxy a "mutation" rather than a revolutionary break (to adopt Foucault's borrowing from Nietzsche)?[12] We hope that the discussion that follows can provide some ground for the elaboration of these questions.

Yellow Earth

> One may even suggest that Yellow Earth *is an "avant-gardist" attempt by young Chinese film-makers taking cover under the abstractionist ambiguities of classical Chinese painting.*   (ESTHER C. M. YAU)[13]

Yellow Earth, by director Chén Kǎigē and cinematographer Zhāng Yìmóu, is now regarded as the first major work in the exploratory cinema of Fifth Generation filmmakers in China. It redefined Chinese film language. Esther Yau calls it a "radical departure" from previous Chinese cinema.[14]

Numerous comments by film critics and, indeed, the filmmakers themselves suggest that the "radical departure" in *Yellow Earth*'s film language

CHRIS BERRY AND MARY ANN FARQUHAR

comes from classical Chinese aesthetics and particularly from the painting tradition. Like landscape painting, *Yellow Earth* emphasizes the natural over the human world, imagery over narrative, and symbolism over (socialist) realism. Tony Rayns claims that the film's work on "imagery and composition is central to [its] overall meaning and effect."[15] If we see the film's imagery as cinematography (or brushwork in the terminology of painting) and add color/lighting (ink) to composition, we have the three key principles in the theories of traditional Chinese painting and the precise references which Chén and Zhāng use to discuss the making of *Yellow Earth*: brushwork, ink, and composition.[16] Furthermore, Zhāng Yìmóu links these principles to the regional style of the Cháng'ān school of painting. Cháng'ān is the ancient name for Xī'ān, capital of Shǎnxī, and the School's style employs bold brushwork, warm tones, and high horizons to depict the loess plateau of the region. The filmmakers adapt this style to shoot the loess plateau which is the cinematic landscape of *Yellow Earth*.

BRUSHWORK

In Chinese painting, the highest form of brushwork delineates an idea (*yì*). Realistic rendering of form is not a primary consideration. Both Chén Kǎigē and Zhāng Yìmóu refer to the idea, or meaning, of the film as the determining factor in the way it was produced.

Zhāng Yìmóu states:

> In traditional Chinese aesthetics, a painting's value lies in its idea [*huà guì zài lì yì*] and this idea precedes the brush [*yì zài bǐ xiān*]. I think cinematography is just the same.[17]

In this way, Zhāng equates brushwork with cinematography and both Chén and Zhāng align their filmmaking with concepts at the heart of the painting tradition. Their method is to "express an idea" (*xiěyì*). *Xiěyì* is more than an abstract or symbolic approach to art, as some commentators on *Yellow Earth* have suggested; it includes a spiritual dimension. Chén Kǎigē wrote that he tried for "an inner truth based on outer reality,"[18] and it is this "truth" which decides the film's cinematography.

What is this "truth" or motivating idea in *Yellow Earth*? We have elsewhere called it "the hidden gender," or *yīn*, the female principle in traditional Chinese cosmology. In the film, this is realized in the story of Cuìqiǎo, the only major female character (figure 4.1), and in the images of the Yellow River (an addition to the original script) and the yellow earth. Visually and symbolically, both are key "characters" in the film which dwarf and decide the fates of the human characters. Water and earth are also symbols of the female in traditional China.[19]

The film also uses the associated symbols of *yīn*: darkness, death, and stillness. Rather than emphasize the surging power and movement (all male symbols) of the Yellow River, the filmmakers exploit its quietness.

> When you mention the Yellow River people think of its surging majesty. But when we stood beside the Yellow River in Jiā county in Shǎnběi [northern Shǎnxī], we were deeply moved by its quiet serenity . . . as it calmly flowed eastward. From afar, it seemed fixed in immobility among the ancient mountains.[20]

Similarly, Zhāng Yìmóu, a native of Shǎnxī, sees the plateau as "a vast stretch of land, securely blanketing the planet so that it seems very rich, deep, and serene . . . a stretch of tranquility."[21] The imagery of water and earth reflect this quietness; the camera rarely moves or changes focus because the idea behind the film means that stillness dominates the camerawork.[22]

A feature of the Cháng'ān school of painting[23] is the same sense of bold monumentality. While Southern Song painting reflects the lushness of the landscape, the Cháng'ān school captures the stark emptiness of the Shǎnběi loess plateau. Zhào Zhènchuān's 1944 painting *Shǎnběi Plateau* (colorplate 4) is typical. Like Zhāng Yìmóu's cinematography, his brushwork is strong, uncluttered, and almost "crude." The river really does seem to be as Chén Kǎigē first saw it: "fixed in immobility among the ancient mountains." The filmmakers emphasized this bareness by filming the yellow earth before its springtime growth. The landscape is thus reduced to a skeletal winter topography in keeping with the film's theme of drought and death, that is, dearth of *yīn* or water (see Fāng Jìzhòng's [1923–1987] comparison in the two plates from the album *Late Spring* [figures 4.2, 4.3]). Thus, the landscape itself partly prescribed its artistic expression, whether through brush- or camerawork.

How did Chén and Zhāng themselves understand the idea behind the film (*lì yì*)? As a film artist, Chén's understanding was visual and immediate. He said he was dissatisfied with the original script, which was too individually specific: a young girl's tragic death as she fights against feudal marriages in 1930s rural China.[24]

> In January, I came with my cinematographer and art director to Shǎnběi. There we saw the Yellow River . . . [which] in Shǎnběi is just like an image of our

4.1 Chén Kǎigē, *Yellow Earth* (*Huáng tǔdì*, 1984).

peoples. It is this part of the river which nurtured the splendors of China's ancient civilization. We faced this mother river, which both nurtures and destroys
our civilization, and were filled with emotion. Early one morning, we saw an
old man drawing a pail of water from the river. In that moment we knew how
the film would be and how to film it. . . . In the film, the person who embodies
this ideal of human endurance is the main female character, Cuìqiǎo. . . . The
river which drowns her is the same river which nurtures her.[25]

Chén added the Yellow River to the original script, in a region often called
the cradle of Chinese civilization, and so transposed the symbol of *yīn* to that
of Earth Mother of China itself. He links Cuìqiǎo's story to this "mother
river"; she is depicted again and again drawing water from the river, carrying
it home, and feeding the men who care for the land (her father and brother)
or who decide the fate of the nation (the Communist Party representative,

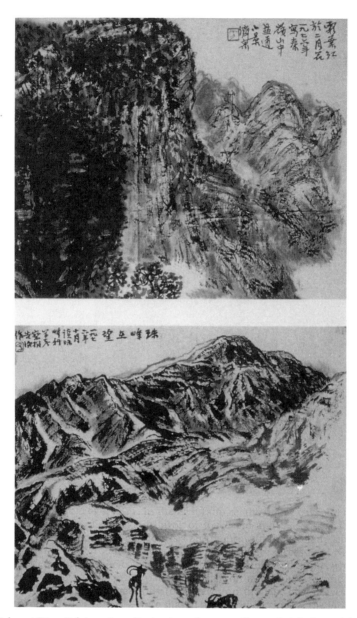

4.2 *(above)* Fāng Jìzhòng, *Late Spring* (two from an album of eight leaves) (courtesy of the Hong Kong Gallery Centre Collection). Cháng'ān school's depiction of the Shǎnběi plateau: Spring.

4.3 *(below)* Fāng Jìzhòng, *Late Spring* (two from an album of eight leaves) (courtesy of the Hong Kong Gallery Centre Collection). Cháng'ān school's depiction of the Shǎnběi plateau: Winter.

4.4 *Yellow Earth*.

Gù Qīng [figure 4.4]). The "radical departure" in *Yellow Earth* is the creative use of a centuries-old aesthetic and cultural code in the new film medium.

Chén's own account of this creative process is, again, akin to that of the traditional painter. William Willetts suggests that the painter's "idea" or "concept of composition" may utilize the eidetic faculty, which projects an image which is actually and vividly seen.[26] It is based on an aesthetic and emotional response. Because the materials of Chinese painting (brush and ink) necessitate swift execution, the painter did not work directly from external models as in the West but from "an image already fully and precisely formed in his mind's eye." This is Chén Kǎigē's moment of understanding.

While this image in painting theory follows the particular vision of the artist, it is also "generic," embodying every percept of a particular thing and reducing it to its essential nature. The artist uses the image to express "a oneness with the world of non-human realities and values."[27]

The cinematography relates the surface imagery to a coherent symbolic substructure. Scene 15, "Beside the Banks of the Yellow River at Dusk," is an example of the way the imagery links Cuìqiǎo's life to the river and, by implication, to centuries of Chinese rural life. The director notes in the script:

> It is enough to have the first two shots showing the full panorama of the Yellow River. The rest are partial, just of the water. Cuìqiǎo is linked to the river through a backdrop of yellow water which fills the frame. Too many panoramic shots would seem like a set of postcards. [This scene from shot 127 is repeated at the end of Scene 29. Drawing water is Cuìqiǎo's everyday ritual. The Yellow River must be filmed as her close friend, not as some distant deity.][28]

This scene strips the imagery of the river and Cuìqiǎo to bare essentials. Its eleven shots begin with a panoramic shot of the Yellow River, crimson in the setting sun (shot 123), and then shows the boatmen pulling a transport barge along the river bank (124). Cuìqiǎo stands watching the boat (125), her eyes drop to the water (126), which is shown close up (127). Shots 128 to 131 show Cuìqiǎo drawing water, and the only camera movement in this scene is the movement following the boat (125) and Cuìqiǎo filling the buckets (128, 131); that is, the motion of work. Cuìqiǎo herself gradually intrudes more and more into the frame: back-on watching the boat, side-on drawing water, and front-on—zooming from middle distance to close up—walking home with the water (132).

The images of Cuìqiǎo alternate with those of flowing water, ending with a close-up of "the surging, turbid water of the Yellow River."[29] This last shot and others like it are called "empty shots," but according to Zhāng Yìmóu, these shots and the constant backdrop of flowing water imperceptibly lead the audience to feel the Yellow River is indeed the "cradle of Chinese civilization" and also frees the viewer to concentrate on Cuìqiǎo's face, feelings, and movements. Thus, these shots are not "empty," but an active element in the aesthetics of the film. This notion of the power of emptiness comes from Taoist cosmology and is fundamental to painting theory; "the rules are embodied in the material parts and vitality is imparted through empty spaces so that emptiness materializes."[30] The river and humans are linked as friends in this scene and yet prefigure the drowning of Cuìqiǎo in this same torrent, shown in full majesty and surging close-up in the first and last shots respectively, as she tries to escape to Yán'ān later in the film. The river both nurtures and destroys.

This contrast, the serenity of the mother river in full panorama and a close-up of the power of water, is shown in two paintings by Fāng Jìzhòng: *The Dam* and *Stream from the Valley* (figures 4.5, 4.6). The beauty masks the

CHRIS BERRY AND MARY ANN FARQUHAR

4.5 Fāng Jìzhòng, *The Dam* (courtesy of the Hong Kong Gallery Centre Collection). Depictions of a river: panorama and close-up.

4.6 Fāng Jìzhòng, *Stream from the Valley* (courtesy of the Hong Kong Gallery Centre Collection). Depictions of a river: panorama and close-up.

potential destructive force of water or *yīn*, the female principle of Chinese cosmology.

In summary, the camerawork, shot content, or camera position and movement come from the idea behind the film (*lì yì*), as perceived by the filmmakers themselves. "The idea comes before the brush," or film in this case, and "the idea remains when the work is finished" (*huà jìn yì zài*). Certainly, the cinematography is stark and slow moving. It reflects not only the filmmakers' impression of the middle reaches of the Yellow River, but also Zhāng Yìmóu's feeling for the loess plateau beside it: bare, vast, elemental, and quiet.[31] It is this physical sense of the awesome, uncluttered beauty of the landscape that lingers after the film has finished.

INK

In Chinese painting, ink is as important as brushwork. A great artist must "have both brush and ink" (*yǒu bǐ yǒu mò*).[32] Although most traditional Chinese painting is in monochrome, various painting styles nevertheless influenced the lighting and color in *Yellow Earth*. The elite tradition, particularly the Cháng'ān school and the emphasis on *xiěyì*, led to the choice of the dominant yellow, which gives the film its name. The colors in the regional folk art, which favors red, white, and black, contrast with the basic yellow of the film, adding a local authenticity and a striking simplicity.

The film is about Shǎnběi's yellow earth, so yellow is, of course, the keynote color. But what shade of yellow? According to Zhāng Yìmóu, the actual color of the dry, barren earth in the sunlight is bleached almost white, which contrasts strongly with the bright blue sky. He worried that the film, if shot realistically, would look like an American Western's rugged landscape. This was inaccurate, according to their own idea (*lì yì*) of the film. They believed that the barren earth, as the cradle of Chinese civilization, was permeated with a "maternal warmth" and intimacy. The colors, therefore, should be rich and warm. By technical means and by shooting most exteriors in the soft light of dawn and dusk, the earth was filmed as a deep ochre color. The warmth matches the dim warmth of the colors in the peasants' cave home. This was so successful that when Chén Kǎigē saw the first rushes, he changed the film's name from *Silent Is the Ancient Plain* (*Gǔyuán wúshēng*) to *Yellow Earth*.[33]

The yellow earth in the film is actually depicted in a wide range of shades. Scenes 25 to 28 are of ploughing from early morning (25) to dusk (28). In the long shots of the topography or the close-ups of the earth, the color is a rich ochre yellow, merging into deeper shades in the ravines. At dusk, the land glows like burnished copper. In close-ups of the characters, however, the land fades, but the rich golden brown is echoed in the men's tanned skin and the color of the ox. The "mother" land is, indeed, warmly sensuous and austerely beautiful, and it is the color, much discussed by the filmmakers, which imparts this feeling.

It is the same feeling for the earth which is unique to the Cháng'ān school of painting. Painters, such as Zhào Wàngyún (1906–1965), the founder of the school, Zhào Zhènchuān, his son, Shí Lǔ (1919–1982), the school's most famous exponent, and Fāng Jìzhòng, who "reached out to life and back to tradition,"[34] often used a rich coffee ink to capture the color, akin to the copper tones of the land at dusk in *Yellow Earth*. The red in paintings, such as those by Zhào and Fāng included here, adds a late spring zest which is absent from the film. As we noted, the filmmakers consciously retained a winter austerity and added color in other ways.

Red, white, and black dominate against the golden background in *Yellow Earth*. These are favorite colors in the region's folk art, toys, and even clothes, according to Zhāng Yìmóu, who was a native of the region. These colors also found their way into Cháng'ān painting, which emerged out of revolutionary Yán'ān folk art during the war. In the film, black is found in the men's cotton clothes, and white in the fur clothes, white kerchiefs, and Gù Qīng's shirt. Red dominates the wedding scenes and is echoed in Cuìqiǎo's padded jacket. Thus, the minimalized palette is not strictly realistic but is again dictated by the content of the film and plays a crucial role in the color symbolism and narrative.[35]

Zhāng Yìmóu believes that color and lighting induce feelings but that these may be changed by the content. Red, for example, in the first wedding scene is positive, symbolizing excitement and freedom, although there is a hint of sadness in Cuìqiǎo's watchful fear as she sees her own fate. Red is repeated in Cuìqiǎo's own marriage scene, but the feelings of sadness and tension predominate. Two shots are "replete with red." One is of Cuìqiǎo dressed in red and covered with a veil as she sits immobile on the wedding bed. We hear the door open and close and entering footsteps. The next is a medium shot; a hand reaches out, lifts the veil, and Cuìqiǎo retreats in wordless, gasping fear. The Yán'ān Drum Dance in the next scene gives red back its positive, revolutionary connotations,[36] although it may be suggested that red, as a male (*yáng*) color in traditional cosmology, is positive for men and negative for women in this film.

In summary, color is a major visual and symbolic component of *Yellow Earth*, and lighting and shades of yellow were decided by the filmmakers' idea of the film. Although a different shade, the yellow echoes the rich coffee colors of the Cháng'ān school. Other colors, red, white, and black, came from the folk art of the region and were absorbed into the Cháng'ān school. These colors were shot in primarily "soft" (*róuhé*) lighting to give a feeling of warmth and intimacy for the land and among the four main characters.

COMPOSITION

In painting theory, composition is secondary to brush and ink, according to such writers as Huáng Bīnhóng.[37] To the makers of *Yellow Earth,* however, composition is primary and was much influenced in the film by the Cháng'ān school of painting. The unique composition of this style of painting was developed to give a feeling of the relationship between the region's land and its people. Zhào's painting of the Shǎnběi plateau is an ideal reference for links between this painting style and Zhāng Yìmóu's cinematographic composition.

In particular, the filmmakers adopted the high horizon of Cháng'ān landscapes so that the earth fills the frames just as it fills people's lives.[38] To further emphasize the ratio between land and peasants, many frames employ a wideangle shot with people as moving black (men) and red (women) dots within the landscape, a "decorative" device frequently found in paintings and poems of the region.[39] People do not enter or leave the frame from left to right; rather, they are often slowly swallowed by, or emerge from, the land itself. Thus, composition in the film reinforces the sense of maternal intimacy between land and people.[40]

The ploughing scenes in *Yellow Earth* are interspersed with such distant, empty shots. The first shows Gù Qīng arriving in the early morning to help the old man and his son plough the fields. He is shown as one black dot on the high left side of the frame while the ox and old man are two dots on the high right-hand side. Gù Qīng, the stranger, is separate from the everyday work of the family. The second such shot shows Gù Qīng as one of the dots on the right side; he is now working with the family. The third shows the ox, in miniature silhouette, resting at lunch, while the fourth depicts Gù Qīng and the entire family, including Cuìqiǎo, as dots against a vast panorama of earth, Yellow River, and distant shores. Finally, at dusk all three men and the ox move together on the distant horizon. The director notes:

> As the sun sets behind the mountain slope, the old man's "Yo!" to the ox reverberates, drawn out and sorrowful, around the land and sky. The line of dots on the high plateau moves slowly, ploughing, sowing, and scattering manure. It's like the long, difficult path our people have trodden throughout history.[41]

In this way, the composition of the frames powerfully depicts the ratio of land to people, their relationship, and the growing intimacy between the four main characters.

This growing intimacy is reinforced by the close-ups of the four main characters in these scenes. In the earlier scenes of the family and Gù Qīng in their cave home at night, the shots are of individuals. The family is wary of the strange official and uncommunicative. The director, however, notes in the script that the shots in these ploughing scenes mostly contain two or three people "to show the change in the characters' feelings for each other" as they work, eat, and talk together.[42]

In summary, the composition of the shots embodies the same idea (*yì*) of maternal warmth and intimacy which informed the camerawork, color, and lighting. This is deployed with an honest simplicity (*púshí*) which, Zhāng Yìmóu wrote, characterizes the peasants' lives and, in bold brushstrokes, the paintings of the Cháng'ān school.[43]

THE AESTHETICS OF PAINTING AND FILM

Yellow Earth, already recognized as China's major Fifth Generation film, launched a "new wave" in 1984.[44] Tián Zhuàngzhuàng, one of China's young film directors, said that it represented the future of Chinese cinema.[45] An important area of impact was in the debate on film aesthetics which followed its release in China and Hong Kong.[46]

Yellow Earth rejected the aesthetics of socialist realism by critiquing them through traditional aesthetic codes. It contains a limited range of set images: earth, water, sky, mountains, a tree, a boat (all from the classical landscape painting tradition), and peasants, an ox, a cave home, a Party cadre, and Liberation Army soldiers (all Maoist images). The single tree in *Yellow Earth*, for example, is very similar to Zhào Wàngyún's foreground tree in a painting called *In the Shade of the Tree* (figure 4.7). The ox in the film shelters beneath it just as the donkeys do in the painting. Zhāng Yìmóu comments that the peasant father in the film has frequently been likened to a famous Chinese oil painting, *Father* (*Fùqīn,* 1981) by Luo Zhongli.[47] Gù Qīng, frequently shot from below, has the handsome good looks and honesty of myriad depictions of Party heroes and martyrs. In classical Chinese aesthetics, however, the highest art is not to invent but to reinterpret:

> [T]he supreme art is to position, adjust and fit together . . . well-worn images in such a way that from this unexpected encounter a new life may spark.[48]

4.7 Zhào Wàngyún, *In the Shade of the Tree* (courtesy of the Hong Kong Gallery Centre Collection).

The "radical" departure in *Yellow Earth* was not a rupture; rather, it was a reordering of both traditional and socialist images in such a way as to de-mythologize the role of the Chinese Communist Party in its formative period. It questions, in particular, the rhetoric of intimacy between Party and people (figure 4.8), supposedly as close as fish and water, by returning that intimacy to the people and their environment. In the end, the land remains a solid, implacable presence in people's lives and Gù Qīng becomes an ambiguous, illusory passerby (figure 4.9).

This meaning is primarily achieved through imagery. While it is clear that painting styles influenced the specifics of *Yellow Earth*, the most important aspect of classical aesthetics in the film is the makers' idea of its meaning, which determined the mode of its production and unified the finished work: that is, writing the meaning of things (*xiěyì*) rather than describing their appearances. This is fundamental to classical aesthetics.

> Once more, the Chinese have analyzed more systematically and more deeply a phenomenon of which Western painters did not remain unaware: a painting must be invested with an inner cohesion that underlies forms and innervates the intervals between forms.[49]

This is Chén Kǎigē's "inner truth through outer reality." Most Chinese critics accept this as the filmmakers' method, although they differ as to its success.[50]

An interesting aspect of the relationship between Cháng'ān painting and film is that the "inner truth" or feeling about the landscape is similar in both instances. Essays on Chinese painting often emphasize the principles and abstractions at the heart of classical painting. This obscures the regionalism of the various styles, as we have discussed in the case of Cháng'ān paintings. What is important is that the artist "merges" with the actual subject matter to depict its "inner truth," not outward appearance only. This is called "communing with the essence of things" (*shénhuì*) in Chinese painting theory.[51] Chinese works abound with such stories. Wang Xia of the Tang dynasty roamed around the country, and whenever he wanted to paint,

> he would become dead drunk, 'loosen his clothes and sit cross-legged,' . . . then he would spontaneously create mountains and rocks or forests and stream according to their original shape.[52]

One millennium later, in the twentieth century, Shí Lǔ exhibited a similar untrammeled "communion with the essence of things." Huáng Miáozǐ, art

4.8 *Yellow Earth.*

historian, calligrapher, and familiar of Shí Lǔ, told Farquhar in an interview that Shí Lǔ was the outstanding painter of the Cháng'ān school.[53] He was also the teacher of Zhào Zhènchuān, whose paintings are included as representative of the style. Shí Lǔ loved to drink. He also loved to "commune" with his subject so that he became the subject itself. If he was painting a bird in a tree, he climbed the tree and sat in it like a bird. "He didn't even come down when his wife called him to dinner," Huáng recalled. He added thoughtfully that such eccentric individualism caused him much trauma during the Cultural Revolution.

Chén Kǎigē and Zhāng Yìmóu, albeit more soberly, share this centuries-old artistic praxis of communing with the specificity and feeling of a landscape. This involves emotion and sensuality in their *lǐ yì*. We could say that it is the yellow earth itself, and the mother river, which permeates the art of both the film and Cháng'ān paintings. Indeed, the landscape is so omnipresent in the film that Ní Zhèn wrote,

[T]he main characters are not just people, but the yellow earth itself from which the Chinese people emerge.[54]

In the final analysis, however, painting and film are different media. The visual impact of *Yellow Earth* is sustained by narrative and overlaid with song, sound, and silence. Perhaps, the real "departure" in *Yellow Earth* is a return to the artist's individual vision as a creative, cohesive force in artistic production. This is central to the painting tradition and anathema to Maoist literary policies which set up model works for collective imitation according

4.9 *Yellow Earth.* The revolutionary as passerby.

to set formulae. *Yellow Earth*, indeed, "played" with these formulae, albeit ambiguously. It was such a spectacular success that it widened the possibilities for other exploratory cinema in China in the eighties.

Black Cannon Incident

> *Picasso said: "An artist must know how to make people believe the true in the false."* (HUÁNG JIÀNXĪN) [55]

Among the films that emerged in the wake of *Yellow Earth* was *Black Cannon Incident*, completed one year later in 1985. When *Black Cannon Incident* first appeared, Chinese critics discussed the two films in the same breath as "stylized" films. This critical construction contrasted them to the "on-the-spot" (*dāngcháng*) trend toward documentary-style naturalism, which had dominated the early eighties following the publication of translations of works by Siegfried Kracauer and André Bazin lauding the realist possibilities of film. [56] These "on-the-spot" films included *Neighbors* (*Línjū*, 1981), *Yamaha Fish Stall* (*Yǎmǎhā yúdǎng*, 1984), *A Corner in the City* (*Dūshì de cūnzhuāng*, 1982), *Sunset Street* (*Xīzhào jiē*, 1982), and others back to *The Drive to Win* (*Shā'ōu*) in 1981. [57] Like the "stylized" films, the "on-the-spot" films saw themselves as moving away from the socialist-realist model, but their main drive was against what they saw as the theatrical and "false" elements of the socialist-realist model in favor of a truer and more naturalistic realism.

The stylized elements that bind *Black Cannon Incident* and *Yellow Earth* together include distanced, static camerawork in which the long shot is heavily favored; a limited palette of the same colors (red, white, yellow, and black predominate in each film); and a narrative structure distended with empty shots. Each of these features has been discussed in the preceding analysis of *Yellow Earth* under the respective rubrics of brushwork, ink, and composition. However, none of the writings on *Black Cannon Incident* surveyed for this piece consider the film in terms of classical painting. [58] This is perhaps unsurprising, because whereas *Yellow Earth* looks back to explore the roots of China's present dilemmas in its ancient cultural traditions, *Black Cannon Incident* resolutely situates itself within a problematic of the modern. In this context, these stylized elements take on the connotations of Western modern (and modernist) art rather than classical painting, and can be considered under the headings of alienation, expressionism/abstractionism, and distanciation rather than brushwork, ink, and composition. [59]

To understand how and with what effects these stylized elements take on connotations of Western modern art in *Black Cannon Incident,* it is necessary to examine what is meant by the "problematic of the modern" and "Western modern (and modernist) art" in the Chinese context in which the film was produced. It could be argued that since defeat in the Opium Wars of the nineteenth century, China has understood its relationship with the outside world in terms of a need to modernize. However, what "modern" means has been revised many times, and along with it the appropriate aesthetic of the modern. The socialist-realist aesthetic and its variations discussed in the introduction to this piece form one example.[60]

Black Cannon Incident, on the other hand, situates itself firmly with reference to the ideas constituting the modern established by Dèng Xiǎopíng in the 1980s. This is marked quite clearly by the narrative of the film, which invokes all the main constituents of that particular drive to modernization. The basic premise involves a Chinese company which hosts a West German engineer on two visits to help with the installation of some imported equipment mysteriously called the "WD." This premise refers to the Open Door policy (toward the West); the emphasis is on up-to-date (Western) technology and trade (with the West). This renewal of interest in the West is made visually explicit (if ironic) in the flashback to the preparations for translator-engineer Zhào Shūxīn's meeting with the German guest, Hans. Here, his bosses persuade Zhào into what they are convinced is an appropriate Western suit and tie they have borrowed from a song-and-dance troupe, although Hans himself never appears in such clothes throughout the film.[61]

In taking up all sorts of things with Western connotations as signifiers of the modern, *Black Cannon Incident* is no different from any number of other films made around this time. However, what does differentiate it is its construction of the modern not as an imminent utopia, but as dystopic. The conflict that develops out of the premise concerns the debilitating effects of disagreements within the Chinese company between the Party vice-secretary in charge of ideology and the manager of the company regarding the translator assigned to the German "expert." This conflict refers to obstacles to structural reform within Chinese work units designed to downgrade the role of the Party and encourage initiative and self-reliance; and unlike most other films that acknowledge these obstacles, *Black Cannon Incident* does not show them to be successfully overcome.

In fact, as those familiar with the plot of the film will know, it is this conflict that motivates the almost farcical (but certainly tragic) string of misunderstandings that make up the film. After Hans's second visit to China, Zhào discovers he has lost a Chinese chess piece called a "black cannon" in a hotel room and sends a telegram for it. His message is misunderstood as code, and the Party vice-secretary is convinced he is engaged in industrial espionage. She and her colleagues investigate the past in a search for clues, and keep Zhào away from the German expert, even though there is no other suitable translator available. The manager protests, but ineffectually, and by the time Zhào's innocence is proved to the vice-secretary, who is still incredulous that anyone would pay for a telegram to chase something as inexpensive as a chess piece, the damage has been done, and the "WD" has been incorrectly installed.

It is this unusual combination of dystopic and Western connotations around the modern that could be said to be the "idea that precedes the brush-work" of *Black Cannon Incident,* and which the film shares with certain tendencies in Western modern art. This combination therefore overdeter-mines the association of the film's aesthetic with Western modern art. The quotes from Rodin and Picasso that begin both the introduction and this section of this essay, although heroic in tone rather than dystopic, are clear instances of this invocation of Western modern art in relation to *Black Cannon Incident.*

The very use of a term like "Western modern art" to cover everything from cubism through abstractionism would be grossly reductionistic in a Western context. However, in a Chinese context, what appears, to the Western eye, as a historically and stylistically differentiated series of nonrealist movements and tendencies is more like one object. All these anti- and nonrealist move-ments were excluded from Chinese painting and art teaching during the pe-riod in which the socialist-realist cinema was dominant, and condemned as "bourgeois" and "decadent." It was only when China opened its fabled door to the world again after Dèng Xiǎopíng's ascent to power in late 1978 that these foreign tendencies arrived in China through books, art journals, and exhibitions. As such, they arrived all at the same time, and as one multi-faceted fine art tendency, contemporaneous with Dèng's reform movement. Articles in art journals on modernism, modern art, impressionism, surreal-ism, and Klimt appeared in 1980, and on German expressionism, Matisse, Millet, Picasso, and Munch in 1981, when an exhibition including abstract expressionist art was held in Beijing. German expressionist oil paintings were shown in 1982, as were works by Picasso and contemporary French painters. The following year, Shao Dazhen's *Traditional Art and Modernism (Chuán-tǒng měishù yǔ xiàndàipài)*, an influential book which treated modern art precisely as one multifaceted phenomenon, appeared.[62]

Given this history, it is not surprising that *Black Cannon Incident* builds associations with Western modern art in a much looser, more indiscriminate and less explicitly identified fashion than the way *Yellow Earth* draws upon the Chinese classical painting tradition. Nonetheless, those associations are easily drawn and contribute heavily to the highly original aesthetic of the film. To give a nonvisual but parallel example, the film uses various forms of music, all of which carry connotations of being Western and modern. The film opens with clashing, discordant music played on Western wind instruments over the title "Black Cannon Incident." In other places, "jazzy" saxophone music is used to suggest thoughtfulness and slight unease, for example in the Western food restaurant.[63] At lighter moments, Muzak-like synthesizer music is preferred. These three types of music, which might seem to have quite distinct and different connotations to many Westerners, are apparently considered sufficiently close and coherent in China today to be used together in this one film as an integrated set, all simultaneously signifying modernity, dystopia, and the West.

ALIENATION

Also contributing to the modern, Western, and dystopic aesthetic of *Black Cannon Incident* is a visually constructed double-alienation effect, whereby the viewer is refused an identification with the characters in the diegesis (the world of the film), while at the same time being given the sense that the characters have no control over their modern world. This corresponds to modern art techniques that have sought to draw attention to the subjugation of the individual in large-scale capitalism by refusing to employ the sovereign subject effect of traditional realism discussed in the introduction to this essay. Be it the abstractionist paintings of Jasper Johns or Picasso's cubism or the expressionist protest of the alienated soul, much antirealist modern art experiments with, and works to undermine or even reject, this subject position for the spectator, either refusing to provide any figure with which an identification might be possible, or else constructing such a figure as in extremis.

One of the most obvious ways in which this effect is achieved in *Black Cannon Incident* is through the manipulation of the supermodern setting of the film to dwarf the characters. This is quite different from both the warm, maternal dwarfing by nature described in *Yellow Earth*, and from the optimistic relationship to technology represented in various tendencies, including socialist-realist boy-loves-tractor optimism, the "Four Modernizations" proclaimed by Premier Zhōu Ēnlái in 1974 and upheld ever since, Western popular culture science fiction as exemplified by *Superman* and *Star Trek*, and by early twentieth-century futurism. In these latter instances, the modern appears mainly as a prosthesis for the human subject, empowering him (and it is usually him). Almost the only example of this relation to the modern in the entire film occurs after the industrial accident that results from the suspicious interference of the Party vice-secretary. In this scene, Zhào is called in to determine the cause of the accident, and is shown heroically riding to the scene on a huge, speeding earthmover—head up, face forward, and hair swept back in the wind.[64]

However, the more common relationship in *Black Cannon Incident* (as in, for example, German expressionist films, Neue Sachlichkeit paintings, and the cartoons of Georg Grosz) is the opposite: the modern is an exaggerated and distorted environment that dwarfs and threatens the human individual. Right at the very beginning of the film, when Zhào rushes into a post office, he bumps into two giants, and is thus both dwarfed and obstructed.[65] Huáng Jiànxīn discusses the appearance of these giants at the beginning of the film in fairly generalized terms as markers of the "absurd" (*huāngdàn*) and "stylized" (*fēnggéhuà*) character of the film, provoking the audience into conscious analysis and thought.[66] However, they also have a more specific function as the first example of dwarfing, a tendency generally taken on for the rest of the film by the huge machines and buildings that make up the plant where most of the film is set.

The best example of this dwarfing occurs where the Party vice-secretary and the manager are having yet another unproductive discussion of the translator problem. As they walk along, set against a towering heap of rocks, one of the enormous earthmovers that Zhào will later ride to the scene of the accident rushes past them. Its tires alone are twice the height of the men. Its engine noise drowns out their speech, and it kicks up a tremendous cloud of dust that obscures them almost completely.[67] Other examples in the film include the huge modern clock that dominates the two Party meeting scenes, ticking away relentlessly as the interminable discussions fail to resolve anything (figure 4.10).[68]

These meeting scenes, and especially the first meeting scene, typify another set of devices which adds to the dwarfing and "absurd" stylization to produce the double-alienation effect. This is a repeated combination of camera position and mise-en-scène which refuses the viewer an identification with the characters at the same time that it makes those characters appear trapped, squeezed between the set and the camera. In the first shot of the first Party meeting scene, the camera is set up at the end of a long, narrow table, down two sides of which are ranked the Party members, and at the head of which is Party Secretary Wú. The manager and the vice-secretary are on ei-

4.10 Huáng Jiànxīn, *Black Cannon Incident* (*Hēipào shìjiàn*, 1985).

ther side of him, and the clock towers over all of them. Because the walls and the clothes the characters are wearing are white, they appear suspended against a borderless expanse of white, which the camera confronts head-on. The effect of this is quite the opposite of the long shots of the landscape in *Yellow Earth*, where the characters appear out of and disappear back into the depths of the landscape itself. Rather, the limitless expanse of the pristine white wall and the head-on, confrontational angle of the camera refuse depth, and leave the characters with nowhere to go. This constricted effect is enhanced at the very end of the scene, when the meeting closes and the participants have to exit, moving in the small space between chairs and wall, and then squeezing past the camera on their way out.

Furthermore, the viewer is held at a distance from the scene by the use of the long shot. In the first Party meeting scene, the opening shot lasts several minutes, and although an argument breaks out between the various participants, we are not drawn in by use of shot/reverse-shot techniques, but kept outside by the interminable long shot. Even when this shot is abandoned and replaced by an exchange of shots between the manager and the vice-secretary, the characters are filmed from the side, and the viewer is still not afforded the full position of identification that shot/reverse-shot structures provide. To some extent, our position might be said to be similar to that of Zhào, who is also sidelined from the conflicts over the major decisions which affect his life throughout the film. However, whereas Zhào is not allowed in the Party meeting room and continues to trust his superiors, we are privy to the shenanigans that go on. As a result of being forcibly sidelined by the camera, we are more likely to be filled with anger and frustration than Zhào is, although we may tend to feel that Zhào should be angry, as many Chinese critics pointed out at the time.

This combination of devices producing a double-alienation effect is used repeatedly through the film. In one of the earliest scenes of fruitless discussion between the Party vice-secretary and the manager, they ride an enormous piece of orange red machinery as they argue. The camera is placed perpendicular to the machinery, which moves relentlessly ever closer to the camera, filling the frame, cutting the depth, and squeezing the characters between it and the camera. A long take is maintained throughout, and there is no shot/reverse-shot sequence to draw the viewer into an involvement with the argument, which, once again, gets nowhere.[69]

Another scene which foreshadows the Party meeting scenes occurs in a Western food restaurant, where Zhào has an argument with Hans. Here, the dominant color is an orange red, and Hans and Zhào sit across from each other at a red table, against a boundless orange red wall. As in the Party meeting scenes, the camera is placed at the other end of the table, head-on to the wall. No shot/reverse shot takes place during the exchange, and instead a long take is used (shot 72), until Zhào smashes a bottle of beer on the floor. At this point, Hans stands up (dwarfing Zhào), and the film cuts between the two of them; but as in the Party meeting scene, the camera is side-on to them, not taking their positions. Maybe this time we want to stop the argument, but once again we are held at a distance, and certainly not in a position to release our emotions by being positioned to identify with one or the other of the warring parties.[70]

EXPRESSIONISM/ABSTRACTIONISM

The strong presence of certain colors has been mentioned a number of times in the preceding discussion. The palette of yellow, red, white, and black in

Black Cannon Incident is the same as *Yellow Earth,* but although both films use these colors in stylized ways toward expressive ends, in *Black Cannon Incident* they do not call to mind classical painting so much as Western modern art, or Chinese modern art based on the Western model (colorplate 10). Whereas in *Yellow Earth* these colors are used to characterize the natural landscapes of northern Shǎnxī, in *Black Cannon Incident* they are part of an aesthetic that excludes nature.

Cinematographers Wáng Xīnshēng and Féng Wěi have explained how they worked to establish the range of colors used in the film in an article entitled "Emphasizing the Expressive Function of Form," a title itself cognate with many of the slogans of Western modern art. Red, yellow, white, and black were taken as the main colors, and much work was done to exclude green and blue from most scenes by avoiding shots with sky in them and cutting down offensive vegetation.[71] Unlike *Yellow Earth,* in the context of *Black Cannon Incident* this amounts to the equation of modernization and industrialization with the exclusion of nature, and associates red, yellow, white, and black with the manmade (and dystopic) setting in which most of the film occurs. Yellow overalls, red plastic table tops, white walls, and black machinery are characteristic of the film.

These colors occur all across the film: even the furniture and the characters' clothes are usually confined to a palette that excludes blue and green. However, they also occur in forms that draw attention to themselves by being abstract rather than naturalized and integrated. Most obviously, there is the scene at the football field, where Zhào and the football coach talk as, behind them, a man paints an enormous billboard a bright primary red, like that of an abstract painting.[72] When Zhào and his girlfriend go to a rock concert, the singer appears against a background of black and white concentric rectangles, and when the manager speaks with a girl in red, they both appear against an abstract black-and-white pattern on the wall behind them.[73] Even the montage of shots of the sun that comes just before the closing scene of the film is highly abstract, with the sun rendered in yellow against a red ground, crossed by a few electricity wires, chimneys, cranes, or other elements of the industrial world.[74]

Not only is abstractionism invoked in this use of colors, but as indicated by the title of Wáng Xīnshēng and Féng Wěi's article "Emphasizing the Expressive Function of Form," so is their potential expressive function. As in *Yellow Earth,* it would be difficult to tie any single connotation to any of the four colors dominating the film, and indeed none of the essays by either the director or the two cinematographers tries to do so. Certainly, red does not simply mean communism (as it might have done in many socialist-realist films), or happiness (as in many traditional customs), nor does white mean death.

However, the colors are often primary and distinct, especially in the abstractionist uses mentioned above, making them powerfully attractive to the eye. They are used so extensively and exclusively within individual shots that it is almost impossible to avoid thinking about what their function might be in a particular scene. Overall, it can be noted that the use of red increases throughout the film as the situation grows more urgent and gets more out of hand. At first there is just a red umbrella Zhào trips over in the post office scene, but the film ends in a montage of red suns where, after the industrial accident, the entire screen is saturated with red. The director has mentioned to Berry on various occasions a fondness for the films of Antonioni, and so a reference to *Red Desert* (*Deserto Rosso*, 1964) seems plausible. In this sense, it may be that red connotes urgency in the film, although it may also be that the primary function of a highly controlled and stylized palette is simply to promote conscious thought on the part of the audience.

DISTANCIATION

In promoting conscious thought, colors, like the alienation effect, play a part in the final characteristic also associated with modern art to be discussed here: distanciation. This section will concentrate less on devices that share something in common with modern Western painting, however, than on modern drama and novels (and, as discussed in reference to empty shots in *Yellow Earth*, Chinese classical painting). This is because we will be detailing devices that promote narrative distension, functioning like the unresolved, often meandering plots of the modernist novel (*Ulysses*, for example), or the voids in the slowly unrolled Chinese scroll painting, both of which call upon and make space for the audience to engage in critical thought.[75]

Among the devices that promote this effect throughout *Black Cannon Incident* are empty shots like those found in *Yellow Earth*. Throughout Huáng Jiànxīn's film, there are montages of scenes from the worksite and sunsets which suspend development of the narrative in the film. In addition to the series of suns at the end of the film, scenes 24 and 5, for example, show various long shots of the worksite, and one shot of the sun, and there are also single shots of a yellow sun suspended in a red sky punctuating the film between other scenes.[76]

However, narrative distension in *Black Cannon Incident* bleeds beyond empty shots like those described above. Sometimes, there are whole scenes in which characters do appear and perform actions, but in which there is no dialogue and which appear to serve little narrative function other than to provide a space to think. For example, scenes 44 through 47 show Zhào doing some inspections in the plant at night while his girlfriend and her daughter prepare food at home.[77]

Even within scenes that serve very clear narrative functions, there is a tendency to append long tails in which the characters are often seen to be pondering the situation. For example, the scene at the football field where the wall is painted red ends with a long tail after the players have begun fighting, in which Zhào is seen wandering out of screen, his head presumably full of worries. At the end of the first Party meeting scene, after everyone except the manager of the plant has left, the manager is seen deep in thought as we cut to various remnants of the inconclusive meeting, such as cigarette butts in ashtrays. Then Zhào enters, and there is a silent shot/reverse-shot exchange between them, with no easily identifiable expression on either's face.

Another device that promotes distanciation besides emptiness is ambiguity, and there are whole scenes in the film which appear to be in some way part of the narrative (unlike, for example, the montages of the suns), but whose signification is very obscure. For example, there is the scene in the old Christian church. This scene is placed in the film after Zhào has found out why he has really been prevented from working with the German expert on the latter's second visit to help install the WD equipment, and we presume these scenes are consecutive. It draws attention to itself and suggests it must be important in some way by its clear difference from the industrial milieu that dominates the rest of the film, its exotic status in a Chinese context, and the presence of clear blues and greens in a film that otherwise works to exclude these colors. Zhào, who was brought up as a Christian, is shown on the threshold of the church observing worshipers, but does not go in. The signification of this scene is unclear, but it certainly calls upon the audience to consider the possible implications of the situation.[78] The same is true of the scene at the very end of the film, after the montage of suns, where Zhào watches a pair of little boys set up bricks like dominoes, knock them down, and then begin to set them up again. The green field is an unusual color in the film, and the epilogue-like position seems to suggest that the scene may be meant as a symbolic comment, but no precise signification is apparent.[79]

In addition to these delaying functions that distend the narrative and open up space in which the viewer is called upon to analyze ambiguous meanings, one final effect also found in many modern novels promotes distanciation.

This is a certain confusion over time. We know there are two visits by the German to the plant, and that the film begins from a point where the industrial accident has already occurred and the manager is recounting the "black cannon incident." Beyond that, however, things become difficult to figure out, as the film slips back and forth between different visits by the German and different intervening moments, without using any of the standard cinematic devices to signal flashback, such as a zoom-in to a close-up on a character's face accompanied by a dissolve, or even a voice-over explaining what is happening. This makes the film quite disorienting at times, and the viewer is again distanced and encouraged into conscious analysis.

TOWARD A POST-SOCIALIST AESTHETIC

Black Cannon Incident is probably less well known outside China than *Yellow Earth,* but inside China it is just as famous, having been one of the most successful Fifth Generation films at the box office.[80] Its look was also just as original, setting a trend for contemporary urban films, although most used it in a fairly superficial manner. For example, a Chángchūn Film Studio film about a group of single modern women all living together called *Strange Circle (Guài quán'r)* returned repeatedly to an image of a white taxi against a red shipping container. The camera is head-on, the red of the container takes up the whole frame, and then women in black enter, get in the taxi, and drive off. Huáng Jiànxīn further developed the aesthetic himself in his sequel to *Black Cannon Incident, Dislocation (Cuòwèi,* 1986).

In different ways, then, both *Black Cannon Incident* and *Yellow Earth* were highly influential films, and both worked to break the aesthetic stranglehold of socialist realism on the cinema and, in so doing, suggested many broader social criticisms. However, they also represent two extremes in a wide range of Fifth Generation and other films that appeared in the eighties and marked themselves out strongly from the socialist-realist tradition. As such, they did not constitute a new paradigm or formula so much as a nonformulaic formula. In the opening up of this postsocialist space, traditions within the fine arts, including painting, functioned not as set forms to be recreated in the cinema but as possibilities to be drawn upon. In turning to classical painting, *Yellow Earth* does not attempt to return to the past, but revives past traditions for very contemporary purposes. And in invoking Western modern art, *Black Cannon Incident* does not signify worshiping the West, but rather draws upon certain Western devices for very Chinese purposes.

1. Huáng Jiànxīn, "*Hēipào shìjiàn* chuàngzuò sīkǎo," in Chén Kǎiyán, ed., *Hēipào shìjiàn — cóng xiǎoshuō dào diànyǐng* (Beijing: Zhōngguó diànyǐng chūbǎnshè, 1988), p. 212.

2. For a full discussion of the institutional background to the Fifth Generation, see Tony Rayns, "Breakthroughs and Setbacks: The Origins and Struggles of the New Chinese Cinema," *Filmviews* 135 (1987); and Chris Berry, "Market Forces: China's Fifth Generation Faces the Bottom Line," *Continuum* 2, no. 1 (1988–1989), both reprinted in Chris Berry, ed., *Perspectives on Chinese Cinema* (2nd ed.), [London: British Film Institute, 1991]).

3. See, for example, Chén Kǎigē, Interview, *Playboy*, Chinese ed., May 1988; Huáng Jiànxīn, "*Hēipào shìjiàn* chuàngzuò sīkǎo," pp. 211–224; Tián Zhuàng-zhuàng, "Reflections," *Cinemaya* 5 (1989): pp. 14–19; Chris Berry, "Interview with Peng Xiaolian" and "Interview with Hu Mei," *Camera Obscura* 18 (1989); and Péi Kāiruì, "Zhang Yimou: Film Maker with the Golden Touch," *China Reconstructs* 37, no. 5 (May 1988), among others.

4. This model is also frequently referred to as the "classical mainland Chinese cinema." See, for example, Chris Berry, "Sexual Difference and the Viewing Subject in *Li Shuangshuang* and *The In-laws*," in Berry, *Perspectives on Chinese Cinema*. However, because we are also going to talk about classical Chinese painting in this article, we have avoided using the term "classical" in reference to film to avoid confusion.

5. One of the better-known examples of the construction of this sovereign-like subject position for the spectator/owner of post-Renaissance Western art is the nude, as discussed by John Berger in *Ways of Seeing* (London: Pelican Books, 1983). Here Berger points out that the female nude is physically positioned in such a way that she is displayed for the viewer, often looking in a direction that implies acknowledgment of (what is presumably) his gaze. In this way, the viewer is constructed by the painting as the owner of the nude woman. Foucault's famous discussion of the Velázquez painting *Las Meninas* (1656), at the opening of *The Order of Things* (New York: Vintage, 1973), makes a similar point about the function of perspective in Western realist painting in the construction of the sovereign subject.

6. See Berry, "Sexual Difference and the Viewing Subject," for an extended discussion of how the socialist-realist cinema draws upon the Hollywood model. Gina Marchetti also discusses the integration of Soviet and Hollywood styles with Chinese traditions in her article, "The Blooming of a Revolutionary Aesthetic: *Two Stage Sisters*," *Jump Cut* 34 (1989): pp. 95–106.

7. Paul Clark gives more details on the supposed indigenous qualities of this formula as opposed to the Soviet import, socialist realism, in his discussion of its introduction; *Chinese Cinema: Culture and Politics since 1949* (Cambridge: Cambridge University Press, 1987), pp. 63–64.

8. "Give prominence to positive characters among all the characters, to heroes

among the positive characters, to the principal hero among the heroes. Create special environment, character and personality and use all kinds of artistic media to make the proletarian heroes stand out. Reveal the heroes' inherent communist spirit" (quoted in David Laing, *The Marxist Theory of Art* [Sussex: Harvester Press, 1978], p. 79).

9. Discussed in Mary Ann Farquhar, "*Children's Literature in China*" (Ph.D. diss., Australian National University, 1983), p. 242.

10. Catherine Yi-Yu Cho Woo, "The Chinese Montage: From Poetry and Painting to the Silver Screen," in Berry, *Perspectives on Chinese Cinema*, pp. 21–29.

11. Paul Pickowicz, "Huang Jianxin and the Notion of Post-Socialism," (Paper given at the Cinema and Social Change in China, Hong Kong, and Taiwan Conference, UCLA [January 1990]), pp. 4–6.

12. "Nietzsche, Genealogy, History," in *Language, Counter-Memory, Practice* (Ithaca, N.Y.: Cornell University Press, 1977), pp. 139–164.

13. Esther C. M. Yau, "*Yellow Earth*: Western Analysis and a Non-Western Text," *Film Quarterly* 41, no. 2 (1987–1988): p. 24.

14. Ibid.

15. Chén Kǎigē and Tony Rayns, *King of the Children and the New Chinese Cinema* (London: Faber & Faber, 1989), p. 29.

16. Xiǎo Luó, "Huáizhe shēnzhì de chìzi zhī ài—Chén Kǎigē tán *Huáng tǔdì* dǎoyán tíhuì," in Chén Kǎiyán, ed., *Huà shuō* Huáng tǔdì, (Beijing: Zhōngguó diànyǐng chūbǎnshè, 1986), p. 277. Originally published in *Diànyǐng yìshù cānkǎo zīliào* 15 (1984).

17. Xiǎo Luó, "Wǒ pāi *Huáng tǔdì*—Zhāng Yìmóu tán *Huáng tǔdì* shìyǐng tíhuì," in Chén Kǎiyán, *Huà shuō* Huáng tǔdì, p. 285. Zhāng Yìmóu misquotes; this should read "*yì cún bǐ xiān*," not "*yì zài bǐ xiān*," although the meaning is the same. The parallel line is "when the work is finished, the idea remains" (*huà jìn yì zài*). In the Song period, Guō Ruòxū analyzed the notion of the highest form of painting, expressing an idea or *xiěyì*, and related this to the brushwork in "a one-stroke painting":

> When Zhāng Yànyuǎn said that only Wáng Xiànzhī and Lù Tànwēi were able to write and paint respectively in one brushstroke, this does not mean that an entire text or work was completed in one stroke but that, from start to finish, the brush moves under the aegis of the same influence, without any interruption in the inflow of vital energy (*qì*); thus, the idea precedes the brush and the brush circles within the sphere of this idea so that, once the painting is finished, the motivating idea is embodied in the work. (Translated from the French, Pierre Ryckmans, Les "*Propos sur la Peinture*" de Shitao [Brussels: Institut Belge des Hautes Études Chinoises, 1970]), pp. 16–17.

18. Xiǎo Luó, "Huáizhe shēnzhì de chìzi zhī ài," p. 277.

19. See Mary Ann Farquhar, "The 'Hidden' Gender in *Yellow Earth*," *Screen* 33, no. 2 (1992).

20. Chén Kǎigē, "Qiānlǐ zǒu Shǎnběi," *Diànyǐng yìshù* (Beijing), no. 153 (April 1985), p. 31.

21. Xiǎo Luó, "Wǒ pāi *Huáng tǔdì*," p. 286.

22. Ibid.

23. According to Farquhar's interview with the famous Chinese calligrapher and art historian Huáng Miáozǐ (in Brisbane, Australia, July 1991), there was traditionally no Cháng'ān school. After 1949 a painter called Zhào Wàngyún founded the School in Xī'ān; he was previously art correspondent for *Dàgōngbào* in Xī'ān and painted Northern (Héběi and Shāndōng) peasant scenes. After 1949 he became head of the Xī'ān Artists' Association. The Cháng'ān school centered on many artists who moved to Xī'ān from the Communist revolutionary base in Yán'ān. Zhào Zhènchuān was his son and a student of the Cháng'ān school's most famous painter, Shí Lǔ. Another painter from the region, whose work is discussed here, is Fāng Jìzhòng, presently vice-chairman of the Xī'ān branch of the Xī'ān Artists' Association.

For biographical notes, see Siu Fai Wing (Xiaō Huīróng) et al., eds., *The Hong Kong Gallery Centre Collection* (Hong Kong: Hong Kong Gallery Publishing, 1990). This work is in both Chinese and English. For a discussion of Shí Lǔ's work, see Féng Chuān, "Yi dào fāng chuān, Xīn yì wèi qù; Shí Lǔ xiǎozhuàn," *World of Collectors* (*Shōucáng tiāndì*) 4, no. 12 (1989), pp. 80–85.

24. Xiǎo Luó, "Huáizhe chēngzhì chìzi zhī ài," p. 265.

25. Chén Kǎigē, *Xīwàngpiān*, postproduction script of *Yellow Earth*, (1984), p. 2. For more detail, see Chén Kǎigē, "Qiānlǐ zǒu Shǎnběi," p. 31.

26. *Chinese Art 2* (Harmondsworth: Penguin, 1958), pp. 552–558.

27. Michael Sullivan, *A Short History of Chinese Art* (London: Faber and Faber, 1967), p. 111.

28. "*Huáng tǔdì*: Diànyǐng wánchéng táiběn," henceforth referred to as Film Script, Shànghǎi wényì chūbǎnshè, ed., *Tànsuǒ diànyǐngjí* (Shanghai: Shànghǎi wényì chūbǎnshè, 1987), p. 113.

29. Ibid.

30. Mary Ann Farquhar, "Huáng Bīnhóng, 1864–1955" (Master's thesis, Australian National University, Canberra, 1971), p. 21. Translated from Chén Fán, ed., *Huáng Bīnhóng huà yǔ lù* (Hong Kong, 1961). The most sought-after essays, according to Chén Fán (201), were those on brushwork and ink and, secondly, on composition.

31. Xiǎo Luó, "Wǒ pāi *Huáng tǔdì*," p. 286.

32. Farquhar, "Huáng Bīnhóng," pp. xiv, 25.

33. Xiǎo Luó, " Wǒ pāi *Huáng tǔdì*," p. 288.

34. Siu Fai Wing (Xiāo Huīróng) et al., p. 226.

35. Ibid., p. 289.

36. Ibid., pp. 289–290.

37. Farquhar, "Huáng Bīnhóng," pp. xiv, 25.

38. Xiǎo Luó, "Huáizhe chēngzhì de chìzi zhī ài," p. 276. Chén said, "Yellow

earth predominates in the composition of the shots" (*huàmiàn gòutú yǐ huáng tǔdì wéi zhǔ*). See also Xiǎo Luó, "Wǒ pāi *Huáng tǔdì*," p. 292.

39. Xiǎo Luó, "Wǒ pāi *Huáng tǔdì*," p. 291.

40. Ibid., pp. 291–292.

41. Film Script, p. 144.

42. Ibid., p. 143.

43. Xiǎo Luó, "Wǒ pāi *Huáng tǔdì*," pp. 291, 292.

44. Chén Kǎigē and Rayns, p. 1.

45. Yáng Píng, "A Director Who Is Trying to Change the Audience: A Chat with Young Director Tian Zhuangzhuang," trans. Chris Berry, *Continuum* 2, no. 1 (1988–1989): pp. 109–110. Reprinted in Berry, *Perspectives on Chinese Cinema*.

46. Ibid., p. 109.

47. Xiǎo Luó, "Wǒ pāi *Huáng tǔdì*," p. 295.

48. Simon Leys, *The Burning Forest* (New York: Holt, Rinehart and Winston, 1983), p. 28.

49. Ibid., p. 24.

50. See, for example, the discussion and translated excerpts of critiques of *Yellow Earth* in Geremie Barmé and John Minford, eds., *Seeds of Fire: Chinese Voices of Conscience* (Hong Kong: Far Eastern Economic Review, 1986).

From the point of view of painting, one of the most interesting articles is Meng Hongmei, "Yì zài bǐ xiān, huà jìn yì zài, *Huáng tǔdì* xiěyì de shī tán," *Diànyǐng xīnzuò*, no. 41 (September 5, 1985), p. 84. Meng analyzes the film in the filmmakers' own terms (i.e., *xiěyì*). From her analysis she concludes that there are two "faulty strokes" (*bàibǐ*; see note 17 for the meaning of this term in the context of "a one-stroke painting"). These are the Yán'ān Drum Dance and the Rain Prayer sequence.

51. See Sullivan, 111, and Ryckmans, p. 25.

52. Chén Fán, p. 61 (trans. in Farquhar, "*Huáng Bīnhóng*," p. 13). "To loosen his clothes and sit cross-legged" is a phrase describing the untrammeled mood of the true artist in Chuang Tzu (c. 369–c. 286 B.C.), perhaps the greatest of the early Taoist philosophers.

53. Huáng Miáozǐ, interview (Brisbane, Australia, July 1991).

54. Ní Zhèn, "*Huáng tǔdì* zhī hòu," Shànghǎi wényì chūbǎnshè, p. 196. Cited in Farquhar, "'Hidden' Gender in *Yellow Earth*."

55. Huáng Jiànxīn, "*Hēipào shìjiàn* chuàngzuò sīkǎo," p. 216.

56. See, for example, Lǐ Zhāo, "Fēnggéhuà de mólì—*Hēipào shìjiàn* yìshù fēnggé pōuxī," in Chén Kǎiyán, *Hēipào shìjiàn*, pp. 330–340. Kracauer's *Theory of Film: The Redemption of Physical Reality* (London and Oxford: Oxford University Press, 1960) was published in Chinese around this time under the title *Diànyǐng de běnxìng: Wùzhí xiànshì de fùyuán* (Beijing: Zhōngguó diànyǐng chūbǎnshè, 1981). In 1982 the famous translator, critic, and theorist Shào Mùjūn published his *Xīfāng diànyǐng-shǐ gàilùn* with the China Film Press, which also includes discussion of both theorists. A translation of a discussion of Bazin by Dudley Andrew appears in *Shìjiè diànyǐng*,

no. 6 (1981), a journal largely devoted to the publication of translations in which a number of Bazin's essays have appeared over the years.

57. For a contrast between the almost hyper-real naturalism of *Yamaha Fish Stall* and the stylization of *Black Cannon Incident,* see Chris Berry, "Chinese Urban Cinema: Hyper-Realism Versus Absurdism," *East-West Film Journal* 3, no. 1 (1988).

58. For a sampling of writings on this film, see Chén Kǎiyán, *Hēipào shìjiàn,* and Zhāng Zǐliáng and Zhú Zǐ, eds., *Huáng Jiànxīn xīn zuòpǐnjí* (Xi'an: Huàyuè wényì chūbǎnshè, 1989).

59. That such similar elements can be understood in reference to classical Chinese painting for one film and Western modern art for another should not come as any surprise; it is well known that many modern artists looked to a variety of nonrealist traditions for ways of differentiating themselves from the realist tradition, including the dramatist Bertolt Brecht, whose alienation effect was at least partly inspired by a performance of Beijing Opera.

60. It is clearly beyond the scope of this essay to consider the complete range of different paradigms for the "modern" that China has considered during the past 150 years; but it should be noted that even though it only became dominant in 1949, the socialist, and more specifically the Soviet model, held wide currency in China well before that: Jiāng Jièshí (Chiang Kai-shek) was trained in Moscow and built his Guómíndǎng (Kuomintang) Nationalist party on Bolshevik principles of democratic centralism.

61. Huáng Jiànxīn, "*Hēipào shìjiàn*—Fēnjìngtóu jùběn," scene 16, in Chén Kǎiyán, *Hēipào shìjiàn,* pp. 109–110.

62. For these and further details of the exposure of non-Chinese modern art in the People's Republic, see John Clark, "Recent Chinese Painting: Postmodernism and Expressionist Tendencies in Recent Chinese Oil Painting," *Asian Studies Review* (Australia) 15, no. 2 (November 1991): pp. 128–129.

63. Huáng Jiànxīn, "*Hēipào shìjiàn*—Fēnjìngtóu jùběn," scene 20, p. 114.

64. Ibid., scene 83, p. 177.

65. Ibid., scene 4, p. 102.

66. Huáng Jiànxīn, "*Hēipào shìjiàn* chuàngzuò sīkǎo," pp. 217–218.

67. Huáng Jiànxīn, "*Hēipào shìjiàn*—Fēnjìngtóu jùběn," scene 56, pp. 146–147.

68. Ibid., scenes 32, 34 and 67; pp. 124–129, 163–169. Huáng Jiànxīn specifies that this clock is four meters wide by three meters tall. This is the same width as the meeting room itself and only eighty centimeters short of the ceiling, which means that the clock takes up almost an entire wall in the room; "*Hēipào shìjiàn* chuàngzuò sīkǎo," p. 215.

69. Huáng Jiànxīn, "*Hēipào shìjiàn*—Fēnjìngtóu jùběn," scene 23, p. 117.

70. Ibid., scene 20, p. 114. Other examples of this construction include: the rock concert scene (scene 26, pp. 118–119), where the singer performs between a backdrop of concentric black and white, alternating rectangles and the camera; the scene between Hans and the incompetent alternative translator, Féng, after an argument

(scene 31, pp. 123–124), where they sit on part of the huge WD installation, one on each side of the screen, with the camera confronting machinery head-on; the scene during the "bullet incident" episode where the laborers climb a stairway outside a wall to ask for some bullets (scene 51, p. 141) and where the wall again forms a boundless plane confronted by the camera; and the scene in the hotel where the manager discovers that the woman in red on his staff speaks little German (scene 63, shot 259, p. 155) and where the two characters are squeezed between the camera and a wall with a black-and-white abstract pattern.

71. Wáng Xīnshēng and Féng Wěi, "Qiánghuà zàoxíng de biǎoxiàn gōngnéng," in Chén Kǎiyán, *Hēipào shìjiàn,* pp. 232–234.

72. Huáng Jiànxīn, "*Hēipào shìjiàn*—Fēnjìngtóu jùběn," scene 43, pp. 136–137.

73. Ibid., scenes 26 and 63, pp. 118–119, 155.

74. Ibid., scenes 88–95, pp. 182–183.

75. Although Huáng Jiànxīn has not discussed either of these possible antecedents, he is quite explicit that his efforts at "stylization" and the "absurd" are intended to promote distanciation and therefore thought on the part of the audience: see Huáng Jiànxīn, "*Hēipào shìjiàn* chuàngzuò sīkǎo."

76. Huáng Jiànxīn, "*Hēipào shìjiàn*—Fēnjìngtóu jùběn"; scenes 24 and 25 are on pp. 117–118, the series of suns at the end of the film appears in scenes 88–95, pp. 182–183, and examples of single suns include scene 35, p. 129, and shot 183, p. 138.

77. Ibid., pp. 137–138.

78. Ibid., scene 77, p. 173.

79. Ibid., scene 96, pp. 183–184.

80. In an interview on February 15, 1988, Wú Xiǎojīn, deputy director of planning and research for the China Film Corporation in Beijing, told Berry that *Yellow Earth* sold only thirty prints within China. Two hundred would be a more typical figure for a film. *Black Cannon Incident* sold ninety-nine prints, making it the most popular Fifth Generation film apart from *Secret Decree* at that date.

THE PAIN OF
A HALF TAOIST:
*Taoist Principles,
Chinese Landscape
Painting, and* King
of the Children

BY ĀN JǏNGFŪ

Taoism, a philosophy which was founded around the sixth century B.C. by Lao Tzu and later developed by Chuang Tzu, has greatly influenced the life and arts of Chinese people for thousands of years. It's not difficult to find Taoist influence in Chinese landscape painting, which has been the main traditional visual art form to present Taoist thought and ideas. As for Chinese film—a modern art form which has only existed in China for less than a hundred years—the Taoist influence is scarce. There are very few Chinese films that directly envision Taoist thought and ideals.

In 1988 one of the leading directors of new Chinese films, Chén Kǎigē, broke the silence with his *King of the Children* (*Háizi wáng*). This film successfully depicts the pain of "a half Taoist" during the Cultural Revolution (1966–1976) through powerful narration and visual expression (figure 5.1). Because the narration and visual expression are closely related to Taoism and the Taoist principles of Chinese landscape painting, the film has not been fully appreciated by either

I'd probably take a position half-way between worth and worthlessness. . . . though it might seem to be a good place, really [it] isn't — you'll never get away from trouble there. (CHUANG TZU)[1]

5.1 *King of the Children* (*Háizi wáng*, 1988) (courtesy of China Film Corporation).

Chinese or foreign audiences. This essay is an attempt to excavate the deeper meaning of *King of the Children* as it relates to Taoism and Chinese land-scape painting.

According to Lao Tzu, the Tao is the way of nature and of human life. Though born before heaven and earth, the Tao is nonbeing (*wú*) and gives birth to all beings (*yǒu*). The Tao is silent, empty, and hidden. It moves cyclically without becoming exhausted; it clothes and nourishes ten thousand beings but does not lord over them. If one wishes a harmonious life, he or she should live in Tao, practicing inaction, living a simple life, and reducing desires, in a state of genuine quietude (*jìng*). Other teachings derived from these principles include those that state: The softest in the world gallop the hardest in the world. Great fullness appears empty. The best way to govern a state is by no action.[2]

ĀN JǏNGFŪ

Following the teachings of Lao Tzu, Chuang Tzu emphasized that human beings can achieve freedom from the struggling, vulgar world. He suggested that people broaden their minds and make themselves identical with the Great Thoroughfare (*dàtōng*) by sitting and forgetting everything. In this way, they will wander with the ancestor of all beings (Tao) in the Broad-and-Borderless field (*kuànglàng zhī yě*), leaving no room for personal views and personal interests. "[J]oy, anger, grief, and happiness can never enter your breast. In this world, the ten thousand things come together in One . . . [L]ife and death, beginning and end will be mere day and night, and nothing whatever can confound you—certainly not the trifles of gain or loss, good or bad fortune!"[3]

Chuang Tzu also emphasized the inborn nature of human beings by stating that, just as it is unnatural to cut a crane's legs or to dress a monkey in a robe, many human activities go against the substance of the Tao.[4] By obeying their inborn nature, human beings can live freely and nothing will do them harm. Therefore, one must stop "carving and polishing" and return to plainness.[5]

Lao Tzu and Chuang Tzu lived in the Zhou dynasty, a time when the old political and economic systems were in a state of decline, and when production and consumption were increasing dramatically. Lao Tzu and Chuang Tzu wrote their teachings to persuade people to preserve their inborn nature by practicing inaction and by living in emptiness, silence, and purity. Their teachings acted as a note of resistance against the evils which were causing chaos among the people.

These teachings of Lao Tzu and Chuang Tzu greatly influenced ancient Chinese intellectuals who were frequently the victims of civil wars and shifts of power during the long history of the monarchic system. During those tumultuous times, glory and disgrace, failure and success, poverty and riches, loss and preservation, slander and fame, uselessness and usefulness all became twisted like changing clouds. It was easy for the intellectuals to adopt Taoism and to long to live in the Taoist way. To free themselves from the chaotic, vulgar world, many of them went to live or to travel in the forests and mountains. In the vast and tranquil natural world, they lived in simplicity and emptiness, and their spirits wandered with the ancestor of all beings. In this way, they sensed in quietude how everything is in order without human planning. These wandering intellectuals gained vigor from the Tao and became purified, thereby returning to their inborn nature.

When these ideas called for expression in painting, landscape painting was developed. Zōng Bǐng (A.D. 375–443), an intellectual of the Six Dynasties, said of the function of landscape painting: "Although I'm old and sick in bed, I can still wander in the mountains in paintings."[6] Chinese landscape paintings reflect these intellectuals' longings for nature and for the Taoist way of life. In these landscape paintings, the space depicted is vast because of the expansive sky (heaven) and the low stretch of land (earth). Chinese painters tend to express distance by the height and vastness of an object. In contrast to the Western system of perspective, huge mountains, lakes, and rivers occupy most of the space in a Chinese landscape painting.

Human beings appear as small figures, like dots, in this broad and borderless natural world. They seem to merge with nature (figure 5.2). On the other hand, the sense of vastness and emptiness is increased by these small figures. Some of these human figures are woodcutters, fishermen, farmers, cowherds—the sons of nature. Others are intellectuals—the friends of nature—visiting reclusive acquaintances in the mountains, playing chess, resting, or looking into the infinite heaven.

The tone of these landscape paintings is always silent and still. In many of them, the "blank" parts also play an important role, representing mist, vapor, or air through which the spirit of the Tao circulates. Both the figures in the painting and the spectator of the painting are absorbed into these mysterious, dark parts. They become identical with the Great Thoroughfare and wander with the ancestor of all beings, attaining a sense of fullness according to Lao Tzu's teaching that "great fullness appears empty."

Influences from Taoism and from Chinese landscape painting are clearly reflected in Chén Kǎigē's film *King of the Children*. The story takes place in a chaotic period: the middle of the Cultural Revolution. In the cities, all high schools were closed and older students were sent to the countryside. When the schools reopened later, only new students were allowed to enroll. By the time the story begins, the hero, Lǎogǎr, and his classmates have been sent to the southwestern border area of Měnglà[7] for seven years to work and to receive "reeducation" from the peasants and workers there. One would typically expect Lǎogǎr to become depressed during this period of labor; however, his characterization is that of a Taoist. He lives a carefree and idle life, wearing dirty clothes and keeping his hair uncut. He treats issues of promotion and demotion indifferently and looks upon his students as friends.

When Lǎogǎr was first ordered to teach in the commune high school, he felt surprised and hesitant. As a "full Taoist," he knew from his own experience that, during a period of social chaos, the act of acquiring knowledge is useless. Although he knew that the best way to live is to reduce one's store of knowledge and to pursue the Tao, he decided to take the job of a teacher because it was the first time he found his acquired knowledge useful to anyone. Due to his inner sense of Confucianism, he thought that there was some hope for the younger generation. This decision drew him back to the

5.2 Xiàng Shèngmó, landscape (dated 1649) (courtesy of C. C. Wang Family Collection). An intellectual stands under a tree, looking into the distance, trying to forget his sorrows.

vulgar world. From that time on, Lǎogǎr became "half Taoist" and "half Confucian."

In the commune high school, to his surprise, he sees that the students are learning only by rote. What is even more absurd is that useless and hypocritical political texts are used as the content for this rote learning. As a "half Taoist" and teacher, he feels responsible to free the students from "carving and polishing," and to help them return to their inborn nature. Instead of teaching them political texts, he begins to teach the students useful vocabulary words and ways of expressing themselves honestly.

At the same time, however, Lǎogǎr doubts that his teaching is really useful to the sons and daughters of the peasants and workers during this period of cultural desolation. As a "half Taoist," he is pessimistic. Whenever he sees or hears the cowherd of the village, he feels awkward and humiliated, and wishes he could become as free as the village boy. As Lǎogǎr helps the students gradually return to their inborn nature, he is fired from his position because of his Taoist teachings. By this act, he is freed from his painful position of being a "half Taoist" and returns to nature as more of a pure Taoist.

The Pain of a Half Taoist

Chén Kǎigē successfully expresses the content of this narrative in the visual form of the film. Following the principles of Taoist thought and of landscape painting, he sets the school in a mountain forest area on the border. This is a vast and tranquil world—an ideal place for a Taoist. The whole picture resembles a Chinese landscape painting, and the slow pace of the film reinforces this impression. In addition, there are more than one hundred landscape shots which directly express the vastness and "emptiness" of the film.[8] Like Chinese landscape paintings, most of these shots are still. The space is vast and empty because of the expansive sky and the low-lying land. The cowherd, Lǎogǎr, his schoolmates, and the children often appear as small figures in these shots, bathed in mist, while mountains and trees, though large, are often seen from a distance, hidden in mist. In only a few shots are there one or two trees in the foreground, but these are also hidden in mist, leaving a vast and deep space behind them. The vast and empty spaces substitute for the mysterious blank parts of the Chinese landscape painting where the spirit of the everlasting Tao circulates. In this vast space, the minds of the children are purified and all kinds of "polishing" and hypocrisy are abandoned.

A closer analysis will help us learn more about the function of these landscape shots. The cowherd, a son of nature, is exclusively in the landscape shots (except during one long shot of the school in which he is at a corner in the background, throwing mud and flowers at the blackboard as a way of mocking—and enlightening—Lǎogǎr). The cowherd seems to know that the best way to live in a period of cultural desolation is to practice inaction. His idle and free life is an act of rebellion against the absurdity of the schooling. He is identical with the spirit of the Tao around him and serves as an example of an ideal Taoist.

There is a similar story by Chuang Tzu in which Confucius (551–479 B.C.) meets an old fisherman. The old man who teaches him how to live in the Tao has the same effect on Confucius that the cowherd has on Lǎogǎr, making him feel awkward and humble.

In these landscape shots, Lǎogǎr always senses the power of the Tao (figure 5.3). Bathed in the spirit of the Tao, he receives the strength and inspiration to make progress in leading the students back to their inborn nature. At the same time, he receives inspiration about how to look in quietude at his awkward and distorted "half Taoist" position in life.

When Lǎogǎr goes to the school with his schoolmates, they are depicted in landscape shots. We note that Lǎogǎr feels a sense of awe from the tranquil and mysterious qualities of nature, as if his act of teaching is against the Tao. After he copies down the useless political texts for the students, he frees him-

5.3 Lǎogǎr (Xiè Yuán) looks into the distance, sensing the power of the Tao (courtesy of China Film Corporation).

self by returning to the landscape shots of the school playground. Bathed in the evening air, he plays with the stone roller, that symbol of the way tradition and politics "flatten" everything out, making everyone the same regardless of individual talents or interests. After searching for the cowherd and meeting the village singer, he sees his awkward position even more clearly. He mocks himself and spits at his own split image in the mirror. When he realizes how the students are distorted by this rote learning and by the absurd political texts, he is in a landscape shot in front of his house. He seems to breathe in the spirit of the Tao and, at the same time, plays with his sleeves in a self-mocking manner.

It seems that Lǎogǎr is now ready to lead the students back to a more natural kind of learning. In the classroom the next day, he begins to teach the students basic words. After the next landscape shot of Lǎogǎr in the evening light, he gives the students even more freedom: "You don't have to keep your hands behind your backs. You can talk if you want to. If it is really necessary, you can leave the class." The students feel free as birds flying to the blackboard to mark the words that they should have known. Their inborn natures are gradually restored. After the sequence in which Lǎogǎr walks through the woods alone, he begins to teach the students how to express themselves through a naive but natural style of writing.

Again, Lǎogǎr meets the cowherd in the landscape shots of the hillside outside of the school. When he offers to teach the cowherd and receives no answer, he feels awkward and humiliated. For the first time, the camera tilts up as if to press Lǎogǎr, the humble "half Taoist," into the earth. In subsequent landscape shots, Lǎogǎr and his students burn wood on the school ground. Lǎogǎr makes a bet with the student Wáng Fù, a completely Taoist action.[9] Closely following this, Lǎogǎr, Wáng Fù, and the other students appear in landscape shots in the woods by the river, where the teacher emphasizes his Taoist attitude again by advocating that they never write about an event before it happens. Back at the school again, he asks the students to write about the people with whom they are familiar, a natural but difficult assignment for the students because the subjects of such composition are not ancient heroes or political figures (as they have been instructed in the past), but real, living people.

In the last landscape shot before Lǎogǎr leaves the students, he teaches them a good-bye song, telling them to study and live according to their inborn nature. In the last group of landscape shots, Lǎogǎr steps over the stone roller with an air of self-mockery and walks into nature, facing a pale sun. As the students gradually return to their inborn nature, they appear more frequently in the landscape shots. For example, Wáng Fù first appears in a landscape shot after he and his classmates are freed by Lǎogǎr to mark unfamiliar words on the blackboard. In this shot, he walks down the hillside and disappears, as if it were the first time for him to be spontaneous with nature. In the landscape shots of woods and river sand, the students learn a further lesson about how to preserve their inborn nature. When Wáng Fù appears in the landscape shot again, he is at the stone roller, copying down the dictionary. He throws one or two stones, just for fun. Although he has lost his bet, it seems that he now knows a more natural way of learning.

When we examine the function of the landscape shots further, we find that Lǎogǎr's schoolmates, those friends of nature, approach and leave the school in these shots. They bring fresh air and vigor to the students who later join them in chanting a rebellious and mocking rhyme. Soon after chanting the rhyme, those young students step over the stone roller, for the first time, and walk down the slope into the mountain landscape shots.

Another function of the landscape shot is to stress the discordance between nature and the school. In the opening and ending of the film, the mist and clouds gradually clear to reveal the school buildings, which are later lost in the landscape, as they are swallowed up by the darkening mountains. These landscape shots both reveal and reabsorb the school. The classroom, with its heavy rooftop and claustrophobic sense of space, represents the artificial and hypocritical political pressure which has been placed on the children.

Although *King of the Children* was not well received by Chinese film audiences, its position in the history of Chinese art films is an important one. It expresses successfully the pain of a "half Taoist" who leads his students back to their inborn nature during a period of cultural desolation.

Notes

1. Burton Watson, *The Complete Works of Chuang Tzu*, in Records of Civilization: Sources and Studies, no. 80 (New York: Columbia University Press, 1968), p. 209.

2. Ellen M. Chen, *The Tao Teaching: A New Translation with Commentary* (New York: Paragon House, 1989).

3. Watson, p. 226.

4. Ibid., pp. 277, 160.

5. Ibid., p. 105.

6. Zōng Bǐng (courtesy name, Shǎowén) was a painter of the Minor Song dynasty (420–478). Known as an accomplished *ch'in* (zither) player and calligrapher as well, he is credited with the *Portrait of Jī Kāng, Portrait of Confucius and Disciples,* and *Lion Attacking an Elephant.* He refused numerous requests to serve as an official in the Eastern Jin (Tsin) and Song governments, choosing instead to join the White Lotus Sect of Huìyuǎn and Huìyǒng at Mt. Lú.

7. Měnglà is in Xīshuāng Bǎnnà, Yúnnán, the Dǎi semiautonomous region on the Burmese border.

8. The term "landscape shots" refers to those shots in which mountains and trees appear in the background, whether they are hidden or obvious. Most of these are long shots, although sometimes medium-long shots, medium shots, or even close-ups are inserted. In all cases, the function of the natural background remains constant.

9. By wagering anything the student might want, he shows a "Taoist" lack of concern for material goods. The subject of the wager is also a "Taoist" concept: the impossibility of writing about something before it happens—that is, being open to the changes of Tao and nature.

J U D O U :

An Experiment in Color
and Portraiture
in Chinese Cinema

BY JENNY KWOK

WAH LAU

CHAPTER 6

In his book *The Film Sense,* Sergei Eisenstein prophesied the coming of color in cinema. He speculated on how color, as another major element in the visual arts, could be used to heighten the artistic quality of films. His zeal for experimentation was strong enough to drive him to undertake the painstaking task of hand-painting some of his films, notably *Alexander Nevsky.* Today, when technology has made color the generally accepted form of film while black-and-white has become the exception, the element of color has not received as much attention as other aspects of film, such as editing and sound. This is partly due to the illusion that color is but a "natural" aspect of photography which, unless used in an abstract way, seems to need little analysis.[1]

However, if one agrees that the mise-en-scène of most films is a product of detailed design, one can easily recognize that the use of color is yet another means for an artist to manipulate a visual aesthetic which is basically culture-bound. Consequently, it is significant to map out possible relations between the visual orientation of a film and its cultural origin. The latter can shed light on the understanding and the evaluation of the former. In this essay I have selected *Judou (Júdòu,* 1990), a visually attractive film directed by the young Chinese director Zhāng Yìmóu, to discuss how the Chinese tradition in painting is creatively employed in filmmaking.[2] Before discussing the film, however, I will point out some of the significant aspects of Chinese painting which are pertinent to an appreciation of Zhāng's endeavour.

A Sketch of History: The Painter's Object

To many Western students of art, Chinese painting usually means monochromatic landscape paintings. The impression is only partly correct. In simplified form, the history of Chinese painting can be divided into the pre-Tang and post-Tang periods, with the Tang dynasty as the watershed. One of the major changes occurring during the Tang dynasty was the switch of artists' preoccupation from portraiture to landscape. In Chinese painting three classes stand out to be the major subjects of artists' depiction. They are portrait, or "figure painting," "birds and flowers,"[3] and landscape. While "birds and flowers" has been a constant sideline, portraiture dominated down to the Tang dynasty when it was gradually replaced by landscape painting.

The concept of narrative painting, which was found as early as the Qin and Han dynasties, emphasized the face as a major means of expressing the human being as a whole, and the relation between different figures portrayed within the same painting.[4] Gù Kǎizhī, one of the "Three Great Masters of the pre-Tang period," is admired for both his landscape paintings and his pictures of complicated groupings of human figures held together by strong psychological tension created through the use of space. This tradition of portraiture is different from that of the West in its basic orientation. While Western portraiture emphasizes the form of the human body, the Chinese concern is on human characterization as reflected through facial expression and relations between characters (figure 6.1).

During the Tang dynasty large compositions of landscape, figure painting, and single figure painting were popular.[5] Sensuous and richly colored figures as well as grand compositions of groups of mortals and immortals positioned in gardens and palaces are preserved in such museums as the Palace Museum in Taipei, and Hōryūji in Nara, Japan. These figures are usually painted dis-

6.1 Fāng Shìshù and Yè Fānglín, *The Literary Gathering at a Yángzhōu Garden,* China, 1743, Qing dynasty, handscroll (detail) (courtesy of the Cleveland Museum of Art, The Severance and Greta Millikin Purchase Fund, 79.72). The spatial arrangement of the three characters creates the tension of their relationship.

proportionately, and the buildings are projected in an isometric perspective (figure 6.2).

The lively optimistic spirit of the Tang dynasty is gradually worn down by the mid-Tang civil war. The attention of the artists shifted from the individual and small groups toward the larger world of nature, with the latter providing a source of refuge in the midst of social turmoil. Figure painting, which climaxed in the Tang, is slowly overcome by the tradition of poetic monochromatic landscape painting which carries a quiet contemplative mood initiated by Wáng Wéi, one of the great nature poets of the late Tang period (eighth century).

During the Song and Ming dynasties, painting schools were established which produced professional painters, or "academy painters," as distinguished from the scholar painters, or the so-called literati. The literati were a self-selecting group who were concerned with relating calligraphy and litera-

6.2 *Ladies of the Court,* China, Southern Song dynasty, handscroll (detail) (courtesy of the Cleveland Museum of Art, John L. Severance Fund, 76.1).

ture with painting and regarded professional painters as lesser artists. Their interest was in the use of ink (i.e., monochrome) and the depiction of nature, mostly landscape. Since the literati were usually associated with noted poets and writers, who therefore received special social status and who, in addition, could well articulate their theory on art, their preference for landscape painting became an important factor for the prolonged dominance of the genre in the rest of the history of Chinese painting.

THE USE OF COLOR

The idea of monochrome as the style of Chinese painting easily leads to a misconception that color primarily belongs to folk art. However, the long quote below from *Record of Famous Painters of All the Dynasties* (*Lìdài mínghuà jì,* A.D. 847), which is in turn taken from the note of Gù Kǎizhī (fourth century) on his painting of a Taoist pilgrim, will provide a glimpse of the Chinese artist's sensitivity to the role of color in painting.

JENNY KWOK WAH LAU

When the sun shines upon a mountain, its back should be shown in shadow. I will have a glorious cloud to the west, shining against the east. On a clear, bright day, the sky and water should be all blue, with bits of white above and below reflecting the sun. I must make clear the distances of the hills on the west, which start to rise from the east; half-way as it goes up, five to six purple rocks, shaped like frozen clouds, straddle the rounded mount in an upward direction, so that they seem to form the twisting movement of a dragon. A tall peak carries it straight up, while below spread the minor crests, so that the eye is led upwards. Then rises another peak of granite. It faces the sharp peak towards the east, and towards the west it leads into a reddish bluff standing by a sharp drop over a gully. In painting this reddish bluff overhanging the gully, I must show its terrifying grandeur. A Taoist master . . . sits there forming a group with the shadows of the rock on which he is sitting. Down in the gully some peach-trees on its banks will be appropriate. The master will be depicted as thin and bony, but with a distant look, his face towards the disciples, pointing to the peaches from his elevated position. Among the group, two disciples will be seen peering down over the cliff, perspiring with fright as shown on their faces. . . .

In painting human figures, make them seven-tenths of their height when they are seated. The dresses and colors will be faint; this is because the men are seen at a great distance in these high mountains. . . .

In the last section, there is a reddish-brown bluff. There should be a Buddha's head . . . like lightning. This bluff faces the cliff under the phoenix on the west of Yúntái to form another gully, with a clear stream coming out at the bottom. A white tiger, crouched on a rock, will be painted outside the cliff walls. Beyond, the picture drops abruptly. . . .[6]

Gù demonstrates here a maturity in the manipulation of color, not only its hue but also its luminosity, shape, distance, and contrast. Besides the obvious narrative scheme, the description of color bears much similarity to later Western realist art. Zhāng Sēngyóu, another major artist of the same period, offered a different approach. Zhāng is famous for his stylistic use of cobalt green in landscape painting, a technique which later was developed into the Cobalt Green landscape school. Under the influence of Hindu art, the use of such colors as gold, bright red, and bright yellow became popular especially during the late pre-Tang period. This can be seen from the famous wall paintings of grand paradise scenes in the caves of Dūnhuáng. The tradition of using brilliant colors for decorative and expressive purposes forms a genre called *nóng cǎi huà* (rich color painting).

During the cosmopolitan Tang dynasty, the dream of paradise reached its climax, while the Buddhist palette confined to red, black, and yellow is almost completely gone. The flamboyant color trend carried on for about two centuries until the contemplative landscape painting appeared in the late Tang period in which the use of color became subdued.

The final marriage of calligraphy with painting occurred in the late Song dynasty when poet Sū Dōngpō introduced the notion of literati painting as a genre. The characteristics of the genre are the refusal to imitate form and color[7] while pursuing the stylistic expression of rhythmic contours with brush and ink. But the "brush and ink" monochrome and the ideogrammatic approach transferred from calligraphy did not become dominant until the Yuan dynasty during which "idea writing" (xiěyì) became popular and thus paved the way for the calligraphic painting of the Qing "literary" style.

Despite the fact that, beginning from Song/Yuan, most literati regard the use of color as being unartistic and celebrate the notion that "if you have ink, you have the five colors," the use of color had not ceased. Color is used not only in "birds and flowers," the genre that flourished in the Song and Ming dynasties, but also in landscape painting in which such colors as white, yellow, and especially green remain active. But one must realize that, by this time, mainstream art's attention has shifted to the complementary use of color in relation to ink. The artist Qí Bǎishí is a good example of one who employs thick dark ink with brilliant colors (colorplate 5).

According to the contemporary Chinese art historian Zhu Zixian, in Chinese painting, color is used for both "realist" purposes[8] and for accentuating the "spirit" of what is being depicted. In Gǔhuà pínglù (A Survey of Ancient Painting, sixth century) artist Xiè Hè stated what has been called the "Six Canons of painting," the fourth canon being on the "suitability of type (by laying the suitable color)." Here, "suitability" does not mean pure representation of color, even if it is scientifically accurate. In this sense, the kind of realism alluded to by the Chinese is different from that of the West. Indeed, suitability is usually measured by the effect of color in creating the "spirit resonance" and "rhythmic vitality" of the painting, which is the quintessential criterion for judgment, including brushwork, stroke, and ink. This Chinese preference is related to the Taoist conception of nature. Given that qì is the vitality of the spirit, the essence of anything both human and nonhuman, the highest goal of art is to express it. The achievement of a painting is the presentation of the spirit rather than the representation of the physical form.

For this reason Chinese artists from all dynasties have been observant of the shape and color of a wide variety of objects and their relation to each other under different circumstances or at different times. Chinese artists are not hesitant to write about their visual experiences, such as the colors of the seasons and of the different times of the day, vegetation, water, sky, sun, moon, rock, mountain, buildings, temple, straw house, brick house, bridge, human skin, and so forth. Their aim is to present the inner spirituality of their object of depiction.

With the above understanding in mind, one can turn to the film *Judou* and observe to what degree it follows the aesthetics of Chinese painting. The investigation will show that the attraction of the film lies precisely in its untraditional cinematic adaptation of traditional painting which creates meanings that are new to traditional Chinese cinema.

Judou *and Its Visual Imagery*
THE IMAGE

The narrative of *Judou* takes place in remote rural China in the 1920s. Visually speaking, the film could have taken one of several possible approaches, such as following the so-called ruralism which negatively displays the poverty and backwardness of rural China[9] or the highly acclaimed (in the West) aesthetic approach of landscape art epitomized in Chén Kǎigē's film *Yellow Earth*. However, *Judou* does not follow any of these forms. It concerns itself neither with poverty nor with the landscapist penchant for pure nature. In fact, one is astounded by the grandiosity of shot composition and its use of both natural and artificial colors, especially of golden yellow.

If one compares *Judou* with *Yellow Earth,* it is not hard to realize that the power of both films lies not so much in their narrative as in their visual imagery. However, while *Yellow Earth* draws its discursive strength from traditional Chinese landscape painting,[10] the discourse of *Judou* works with a different tradition. The consistent use of flat frontal wide shots which reveals full-size characters positioned at relatively stationary spots reminds one of Chinese portraiture. This, in a sense, is not a coincidence, since the major theme of the film concerns itself with personality and human relationships which are also the basic theme of classical Chinese figure-painting.

The story begins with a young woman (Júdòu) married to an old man (Qīnshān) who is stingy, cruel, and sadistic. One can glimpse into his personality by observing his relation with his adopted son (Tiānqīng), whom he enslaves in his domestic dye factory. The first interaction in the film is a two-shot of Tiānqīng and Qīnshān.[11] Tiānqīng is back from his errand to collect debts for the old man. Following his entry into the house, the camera stops at a medium wide shot which shows Qīnshān eating at the table in front of the ancestral altar. Tiānqīng stands at the other end of the table and bends slightly toward him.

The men's gestures are in marked contrast. Qīnshān is sitting while Tiān-qīng is standing. The former raises his head arrogantly and the latter nods humbly. They have very different facial expressions. While the old man frowns with impatience, Tiānqīng always smiles apologetically. In terms of spacing, when Tiānqīng is handing money to the old man he prefers bending over, rather than moving even an inch closer. The dimly lit ancestral altar behind Qīnshān juxtaposed with his presumptuous domination over the youngster creates a sense of identification of the old man with the ancestral tradition.

Such a shot design makes use of the four elements in classical Chinese portraiture; that is, posture, facial expression, spacing, and environment to delineate not body forms but the spirit of, and the relation between, the characters. Since the shot is an uncut long take, it also functions like a scroll painting that obligates the audience to ponder its images and their relations. Like *Yellow Earth* which uses Chinese landscape painting as a new signifier to convey an idea inexpressible within the traditional socialist coding system, *Judou* also employs the tradition of figure painting to present what is previously unpresentable, namely the "spirit" of a person who has to live within and, at the same time, against her social environment.

Soon Júdòu and Tiānqīng fall in love, although under the feudalistic system they can only relate to each other in secret; and Júdòu becomes pregnant. As the film progresses, gerontocratic oppression, and a daring spirit of rebellion struggling within it, becomes more and more obvious. The ancestral altar inside Qīnshān's courtyard appears in many shots. But most of the time it is associated with torture—Júdòu's screaming or Qīnshān's being confined in a barrel that hangs in the air. One of the most dramatic moments of the narrative—the name-giving ritual for Júdòu's baby, a son (Tiānbái)—is also carried out in front of the altar. The scene begins with a frontal wide shot of the family elders sitting around the altar table. In the middle is the oldest grandparent, with his long white beard. The lighting is such that only the central portion of the frame is lit with a pale golden yellow sidelight. The rest of the composition is in a shadow out of which the audience can vaguely see the background altar with two big red lanterns hanging symmetrically on both sides, and a few other family members, including Tiānqīng, sitting or standing by.

The highly symmetrical frontal shot which again reduces the depth dimension resembles a Chinese painting which does not follow the rule of perspective. Then, as if to insist on the reading of a painting, the scene is further cut into a medium close-up frontal shot and a medium frontal shot. The first one is a two-shot of the white-bearded man and the man at his immediate left. The second one is the middle portion of the picture where four men are sitting at a table.[12]

The position occupied by each elder indicates his seniority. The eldest man is sitting in the middle while the "father" of the baby, Qīnshān, is standing at his back. Others stand around with their sides toward the camera. The eldest man is the most self-assured. With his shaking hand he writes down what the child should be called or in fact who the child belongs to. With the ancestral altar occupying the upper third of the frame, one cannot miss the point that this very act of building up and perpetuating the governing symbolic system is done with the ancestral blessing. But the solemn ritual is ironically portrayed. The elders choose the name Tiānbái for the newborn baby because together with his "brother" Tiānqīng their names form the idiom of qīngqīng and báibái, which literally means "innocent from any guilt." The irony lies in the fact that Tiānqīng is the adulterous father of the baby. By presenting a literal contradiction, which the film allows only its audience to know, the film challenges the governing symbolic system and the validity of the Confucian ideology behind it.

Interestingly enough, a similar shot of elders gathering is repeated in the latter half of the film after the death of Qīnshān. This time they are deciding on what Júdòu should do as a widow. Besides being a frontal shot with the white-bearded man in the middle, the lighting, color, and positioning of different characters also looks similar. But there is a slight difference in the use of space between the naming shot and this shot which is significant for the atmosphere that is generated. The latter exaggerates a large foreground and background area. Besides creating a spatial feeling of distance and a courtlike atmosphere, this large empty space is also a signifier of the absence of Júdòu to whom the decision is directed. In addition, unlike the naming scene in which there is some drama of character interactions which form different shots within the scene, this gathering is a one-shot straightforward declaration of the decision of the elders. Thus, like many shots in the film, the long take draws almost solely on the power of picture composition and invites the audience to feel the oppressive regime.

JÚDÒU I — QÌZHÌ

The drama of the film revolves around Júdòu's attempt to transform her life while in fact she is transformed by life itself. Jú dòu (and to some extent Tiānqīng) struggles for liberation from the Confucian Code of lǐjié, a system of moral rules that are based on filial piety and female sexual purity. Even if one does not know her story, one can almost sense it by reading her different images at different stages of the film.

Júdòu's first image appears early in the film. It is in the midst of the bluish clean morning air that one hears a few roosters crowing and sees a weak stream of yellow light coming from the morning sun. The high-angle shot reveals two big tile roofs surrounding a courtyard, which is the home and dye factory of Qīnshān. In the upper middle of the frame, where the courtyard is observed between the roofs, a tiny corridor can be seen at a distance. With the morning light hitting it, the corridor stands out a little clearer than its surroundings. A few seconds into the shot, the small figure of a woman comes out from a room and walks along the corridor. The shot lasts for a few seconds. Subsequent shots confirm that the woman is Júdòu. This frame composition of Júdòu in the courtyard is not unfamiliar to the Chinese eye. It resembles a classic isometric projection used in many of the grand garden paintings in which the figures are tiny but not unimportant. One learns to know such figures by relating them to their environment. Here, it is in the midst of a fresh and peaceful morning that the audience first comes to see Júdòu.

The scenes that follow show either the back of Júdòu or her vague image as seen from the point of view of the peeping Tiānqīng. The first time that she appears close up and clear is in her response to the nervous Tiānqīng, who falls a few steps on the stairway after shouting for her to come to work. A medium close-up shows Júdòu in brilliant yellow clothes smiling innocently. A few scenes later there are low-angle shots of Júdòu working high up in the scaffolding, lit by a very strong backlight from the sky which overexposes part of her image.

Tiānqīng's infatuation with Júdòu generates more medium and medium close-up shots of her. She is seen moving in and out of some beautifully backlit golden yellow fabrics which blend very nicely with her skin color, her yellow clothes, and the color of the morning sunlight (colorplate 6). Her two dark eyes create a sense of warmth and purity while the slight movements of her lips show a sense of tenderness. Watching Júdòu is like watching a figure-painting. Both her facial expression and the environment in which she is immersed suggest the same "spirit" of her personality. Júdòu is related to freshness, morning, sunshine, and golden yellow, the combination of which associates her with nature or even *tiān* (Heaven, the source of *qì*). Júdòu is not only beautiful; she is also a woman who possesses *qìzhì*, a fairylike aura that emanates from a person of character.

But the scene during the night is totally different. One is shocked to see the innocent woman being sexually abused. The next morning, a low-angle wide shot shows a stairway between two colossal panels crafted with traditional patterns. A shade of yellow light comes in from the left. Júdòu comes out from a room on the right. Tired and bruised, she trots down the stairs. Her tiny figure makes her look like she is being squeezed between the two high panels. The contrast of this sequence with the first causes an emotional revulsion against the old man who is the source of such cruelty.

In the next scene, Tiānqīng is peeping at the bathing Júdòu. She knows it and he knows that she knows it. What Tiānqīng sees, however, is not a Júdòu on the scaffolding, who is both reserved and vibrant. Suddenly one realizes that Júdòu has a high cheekbone, tired face, and a bruised body. Although the soft yellow light creates a sense of warmth, the haystack as well as the old wooden basin that makes up her "bathroom" give a sense of material limits and the limits of her position. Thus, as she turns around to show Tiānqīng her body, the feeling communicated is not one of sexual attractiveness but of the misery of the oppressed. Her turning toward Tiānqīng signifies not only her decision to be romantically involved with him but also a decisive step against the rule that operates against her.

TIĀNQĪNG

Before continuing with Júdòu, the film pays some attention to Tiānqīng, opening up yet another story that explains the doomed nature of her struggle. Contrary to Júdòu, who is a woman of *qìzhì*, Tiānqīng is a coward. In the opening shot one sees a blue sky that occupies almost half of the frame and a small figure walking under it in the midst of some farmland: it is Tiānqīng going home with a horse. The huge sky/tiny human figure composition reminds one of a Chinese landscape painting. The fact that Tiānqīng walks beside the horse instead of riding it gives an impression of a harmless rural boy. As described above, subsequent shots of his interaction with Qīnshān show his placidity and compliance.

Tiānqīng's innocent rural appearance is further highlighted in the first part of the film by a portraitlike shot which punctuates his first major encounter with Júdòu. In their conversation, Júdòu expresses her misery through telling the fable of the pig which is killed for the pleasure of men. She cannot control herself, and leaves in tears. Tiānqīng, who is caught by surprise, remains motionless and stares at Júdòu's back. The frontal full shot of a stationary bald head of barefoot Tiānqīng, standing with a cow by his side, resembles a still photo of a crude male which contrasts sharply with Júdòu's refined beauty.

Tiānqīng's cowardice never leaves him. Even the horse's neighing can scare him. In order to peep at the bathing Júdòu, he has to hide himself in the haystack beside his horse. At one point the uncooperative animal protests, and Tiānqīng is so frightened that he falls. Again, when Júdòu openly seduces him after the old man has left for an errand, he is very much afraid. The shot before they make love is a frontal one of both characters facing the camera with Júdòu embracing him from the back while he, out of fear, stands numb and motionless (figure 6.3). By comparing his timidity toward Júdòu with his eagerness to respond to the old man, the viewer indeed recognizes Tiānqīng's character through what he does for the old man and what he does not do for Júdòu.

The film's criticism of the Confucian ethic can be seen most clearly at this point. The person who most faithfully carries out such a tradition is portrayed as one with little strength of character. He passes on the tradition only out of placidity and cowardice. In the rest of the film one sees that Tiānqīng is unable to take a stand against Qīnshān and is never able to fully condemn the oppression suffered by Júdòu. The reason for his submissiveness is, as he states at one point, that "he [Qīnshān] is my uncle"—meaning that the rule of filial piety overrides any other concern.[13]

JÚDÒU II — FIERCE

While in the first half of the film the image of joy and love is vivid on the face of Júdòu, her image undergoes a change in the second half of the film after the old man learns about her affair. Because of his rage Qīnshān tries to kill the baby Tiānbái. Júdòu returns from her meeting with Tiānqīng just in time to rescue him. She fights with Qīnshān, curses him, and declares clearly to him that Tiānbái is not his. Her shrewdness contrasts sharply with her previous image of beauty and tenderness. Even the red dress that she is wearing turns into a kind of sinister mix of blue and red under the moonlight. In the other two murder attempts, Júdòu continues to be protective toward the baby but very hostile to the old man. Thus both her fresh fairylike and her helpless suffering image are gone. Júdòu has turned into a fierce woman who is struggling for survival.

The fierce Júdòu, however, is unable to fight a system which is beyond and above everybody. Although she gains the freedom to be with Tiānqīng after the old man has a stroke, this momentary liberation is soon reversed when Tiānbái grows older. One day Tiānbái is playing in the courtyard when Qīnshān tries to strike and kill him with a club. Accidentally, at the critical moment, the child turns around, faces up squarely to the approaching murderer, and innocently utters the word "Dad." The old man immediately seizes the

JENNY KWOK WAH LAU

6.3 Zhāng Yìmóu, *Judou* (courtesy of Miramax Films).

opportunity for revenge and reestablishes himself as the father, Júdòu as the mother, and Tiānqīng as the brother in the family. Once the former patriarchal order is recaptured, the system works by itself. Júdòu and Tiānqīng cannot keep an open relationship even after Qīnshān's death.

JÚDÒU III — EXHAUSTED

The last part of the film gives an image of an older, melancholy Júdòu. The smile and laugh have gone. After Qīnshān's death she has to dress in black as a sign of mourning. Every night she sits on the bed alone or stands in the midst of the big courtyard by herself. In order to avoid gossip, she has to stay away from Tiānqīng. Her meetings with him have to be carried out with great secrecy, since her son Tiānbái is resentful of the relationship.

Thus, the different portraits of Júdòu in succession tell a story. The change from a beautiful woman of *qìzhì* to a fierce, then tired, and then old and melancholy person forces one to reflect on her destruction. The image itself is the strongest evidence of the oppressive nature of a patriarchal order.

The visual impact of *Judou* lies not only in its composition but even more so in its unusual style of color. The use of color in *Judou* simulates the Chinese tradition of *nóng cǎi huà* (rich color painting).[14] One of the characteristics of *nóng cǎi* is that the gray tone of the colors tends to be heavier and stands out in an exaggerated way. The picture is meant to be explicit and expressive. This is in contrast to *dàncǎi huà* (light color painting), which uses a lighter gray tone and creates a more subdued mood. Another characteristic of the color used in *Judou* can be loosely described as "splashed ink" (*pōmò*, a name given to a genre of Chinese painting), which fills large patches of the frame with one kind of color in a highly idiosyncratic way. The emphasis is on the color rather than on the contour that delineates exact shapes. These techniques are not meant to be realistic but expressionistic.

In Chinese painting the effect of *nóng cǎi* is created by the use of different coloring chemicals. Similar results in the film are generated by both prop design and the effect of lighting. For example, in addition to the selection of some flamboyant colors for the hanging fabrics, the sensuality of their color is further accentuated by side- and backlighting. Thus the color red is either a strong vibrant red or a dark sinister red. In either case the color calls for a strong emotional response.

Furthermore, "splashed ink" style generates a spirit of freedom or rebelliousness in the film. One can see the free "splashes" of red, yellow, or green that occupy major parts of shot compositions. The notion of "freedom" refers to a technique of "splashed ink" which creates a flow of color on paper that results in variations of gray tone, luminosity, and intensity in different parts of a picture. In the film, similar results are achieved with lighting to create nuances of a color that fill part or all of the frame. The idea is to communicate a "powerful overall spirit," "a quality of having a life of its own"— the *qìzhì* of a motion picture.

Given that a major function of lighting in this film is the creation and manipulation of color following the tradition of Chinese painting, it is appropriate that the lighting seek a pictorial form that emphasizes the two-dimensional nature of a painting. The impression generated is quite different from the kind of lighting produced in Western cinema, which follows a more sculptural tradition of emphasizing perspective and dimensionality.

Throughout the film one can detect two major color schemes which follow the change of mood and narrative of the story. In terms of hue, bright red and golden yellow represent a positive mood in the story while blue and dark blue represent the opposite. Not only hue but luminosity and gray tones are employed to create the "spirit" of a picture as well.

The first portion of the film is dominated by the expressionistic use of bright red and golden yellow. This is accomplished by filling the frame with shots of fabrics or by the use of lighting such as that which occurs in the wide shot of the domestic factory in early morning, with slants of light shining through the interior of the courtyard (colorplate 7). The silhouettes of the machines and donkeys are positioned against the golden yellow mist inside the building. Side light is also used to accentuate reflection and the shininess of the color, such as the color of the liquid in the dye vat. When Júdòu and Tiānqīng make love beside a red-dye vat, the strong sidelight gives a shiny redness that adds strength and vitality.

This kind of brilliant red and yellow gradually disappear as the story progresses and the tragedy of Júdòu unfolds. A darker version of red and yellow is seen in such scenes as Tiānbái's birthday banquet or the name-giving ritual where the wooden building is brownish yellow rather than golden yellow. Even the former bright red and golden yellow color scheme of the sex scenes of Júdòu and Tiānqīng gives way to a darker yellow and grayish tone. Not only is the lighting less brilliant and gay, but the dark gray color of their clothing generates a sense of hardship until one realizes that, despite appearances, even sex with Tiānqīng inflicts pain on Júdòu.

In addition to the different meanings carried by the different hues, the contrast of bright and dark colors of the same hue also relays different messages. The most obvious example is in the use of red. (Traditionally red is an important positive color for the Chinese. The use of red in Chinese art has a long history, and red is the Chinese color for important rituals and ceremonies such as marriages, birthday celebrations, and so forth. But as the film is ideologically untraditional,[15] a rebellious use of color in defiance of the traditional code further accentuates its theme.) For example, in the first murder attempt on Tiānbái, Júdòu is wearing a red coat, which in the first portion of the film connotes a positive feeling. But here the red coat turns into a kind of dark or "dirty" (zhuó) red as a result of seeing it under the blue moonlight. The effect is unpleasant or even sinister. Other "dirty" red or yellow colors are seen in such scenes as the sex abuse scene, or when Qīnshān attempts to set a fire.

An extreme example of different kinds of red is found in the three major events of the film: the lovemaking scene beside a red-dye vat, the drowning of the old man, and the drowning of Tiānqīng, both of which occur in a red-dye vat. In all three sequences, the use of red is exaggerated by filling the whole frame with the color. However, in the first and last case, the red is quite similar. It is shiny and vibrant, while in the case of Qīnshān's drowning, the red is in fact mixed with black and hence is dark and "dirty." In fact, the last shot of Qīnshān's scene is taken from a high angle which shows the vat as dark rather than red. Sympathy is thus directed toward Tiānqīng but not Qīnshān.

While showing red in an unpleasant, sinister, or even monstrous manner carries strong critical overtones, the use of the colors blue, dark blue, and black is another scheme in the film which delivers a negative connotation. Examples are the night scenes of sexual torture in the beginning of the film, the murder attempt in the middle of the film, and the dark gray color of suicide at the end of the film.

The overall color of the film follows a line of development which starts with bright red and golden yellow. Then, as the tragedy grows the color becomes darker and darker until, in the end, after a long period of gray, gray green and gray blue, a shot of colorful fabrics reappears. Both Júdòu and Tiānqīng are getting old, but their passion for each other has not diminished. They are sitting on the scaffolding, and Júdòu serves a meal for both of them. Their silence expresses a strong affection for each other. Finally, they decide to "do it for the last time" in a dry well. The series of shots that leads to their entering into the well are filled with red and yellow, two colors which one otherwise finds only in the beginning of the film.

As the well lid is being closed, the scene fades to black. The following shot is a low-angle wide shot of the colorful fabrics hanging from the scaffolding, a shot that the audience is familiar with from the beginning of the film. But for the first time, the camera revolves more than ninety degrees. One realizes that something different or even unfortunate may take place. In the subsequent scenes, Tiānbái discovers the couple, "rescues" Júdòu, and kills Tiānqīng. If, as discussed above, bright red and golden yellow are positive colors that celebrate love and youthfulness, the return to the same color scheme in this last sequence of Júdòu and Tiānqīng indicates that the film does not condemn their relationship. Instead, it is the use of darker or even "dirty" colors in the middle section of the film which expresses criticism of the feudalistic system.

The last shot of the film is a low-angle shot that starts with the bright red and yellow fabrics hanging in the scaffolding. For the first time the fabrics are let loose and fly freely in the air. Then a very slow fade to white turns the fabrics into white while the background fades to black at the same time. The artificially dyed colorful fabrics turn into long pieces of white cloth which look like Chinese funeral couplets. Does it mean that the human effort of making artificial rules can only result in death? To end the absurdity of her own life, Júdòu sets fire to the factory. The frame is filled with yellow flames until the shot ends in a freeze-frame of an abstract mixture of splashes of golden yellow and bright red. Is this a positive ending which signifies the end of the oppressive machine, or is this a pessimistic gesture that indicates an inability to resolve the tension? The freeze-frame leaves the question open, and the color of the shot conveys an inexpressible feeling of awe.

In addition to conveying a narrative theme, the arrangement of color in the film *Judou* also follows a rhythmic pattern which adds to its liveliness. This is done by dividing the color system into a dominant and a subordinate scheme for different sequences. Bright red and yellow are the dominant colors in the first part of the film, while blue and gray blue are the subordinate colors. In the second part of the film the role of the two colors is reversed. The finale of the film contains an alternation between these colors which accelerates until it reaches the end where black is suddenly replaced by bright yellow and red.

Further, throughout the film there are intercuts of dominant colors and subordinate colors. For example, in the first part of the film where bright red and yellow are dominant, the scaffolding shots are intercut with the blue night scenes. In the final part of the film where black gray and blue gray are the dominant colors, the grayish courtyard is intercut with the yellow color of the building when seen under the golden evening sun. The intercut of the two color systems also happens within the same shot. For example, in the middle section of the film where blue is the dominant color, small portions of the frame are filled with red, such as in the bedroom shot. Or in one scene in the first part of the film, Júdòu's blue dress forms a "complementary" color in a sequence of red and yellow. Rhythm is thus created and carefully maintained by the interaction of two distinguishing color schemes, generating a visual tension in the film.

As director Zhāng Yìmóu once stated, his films celebrate life and must be both vibrant and thought provoking (figure 6.4).[16] *Judou* is definitely one of his major successes. The dramatic use of color creates a strong vibrancy while the somber tone of the film forces one to take the issues raised seriously. While *Yellow Earth* makes use of landscape painting as its mode of expression, the result yields, as in landscape painting, a contemplative effect. *Judou*, on the other hand, simulates the portraiture tradition and the style of *nóng cǎi huà*. The outcome is a highly idiosyncratic expression. Among the group

6.4 *Judou* (courtesy of Miramax Films).

of outstanding New Chinese Cinema films, these two works stand out for their progressive views and at the same time are visually complementary to each other.

Notes

1. Even the debate on colorization (of black-and-white classical films) raised in 1987 has not stimulated popular attention on the meaning of color in cinema.

2. The film *Judou* won the 1990 Golden Bear in the Berlin Film Festival and the 1990 Golden Hugo Award in the Chicago International Film Festival, and was the first Chinese film to be nominated for the category of Best Foreign Film in the Academy Awards.

3. "Birds and flowers" is a loose term for a class which in fact also includes other objects such as animals, vegetation, and so forth.

4. The famous Mǎwángduī tombs at Chángshā, dating to the mid–second century B.C., depict interesting interactions between the human world and the mythical

JENNY KWOK WAH LAU

world. The piece is an excellent example which reveals the level of sophistication that narrative painting had reached even at that early period of its history.

5. Excavation of tombs of the royal family in Cháng'ān, the capital of the Tang dynasty, has revealed richly painted walls with life-size figures of beautiful composition.

6. Translation by Lin Yutang, ed., in *The Chinese Theory of Art: Translations from the Masters of Chinese Art* (New York: Putnam's Sons, 1967), pp. 27–29.

7. Sū Dōngpō once said, "There are plenty of craftsmen who can copy all the details of form, but the inner nature of things, the whole is spoiled" (ibid., p. 92).

8. The notion of "real" here is different from that in realist art in the West. It means real according to the impression of the artist alone.

9. "Rural Film" has always been a genre in socialist Chinese cinema. But "ruralism" here refers to some of the "New Wave" films made after 1976 which, in contrast to the previous socialist policy of glorifying peasants' lives, portray the poverty and other problems common in rural China. For a time Chinese officials were not happy about the "negative" exposure of China to the world and called for a "restraint" on production of such films. *Yellow Earth* has not been favored by the Chinese officials for this very reason.

10. See the analysis by Esther Yau, "*Yellow Earth:* Western Analysis and a Non-Western Text," *Film Quarterly* 41, no. 2 (1987–1988): pp. 22–33.

11. "Two-shot" here is a production term referring to a shot that consists only of two characters.

12. These two shots are not the kind of medium and close-up shots employed in classical Hollywood films. The latter are usually taken from different angles in order to avoid a jump cut. The medium and close-up shots here are taken from the same frontal angle, thus functioning more like the cropping or enlargement of the original picture.

13. A detailed analysis on the ideology of *Judou*, especially of the notion of filial piety and sexual purity, can be found in my article "A Hermeneutical Reading of *Judou*," *Film Quarterly* 45, no. 2 (Winter 1992): pp. 2–10.

14. *Nóngcǎi huà* is also known as *zhòngcǎi huà* (heavy color painting). For a discussion of *nóngcǎi huà*, see *Goúhuà sècǎi yánjiū* (*A Study of Color in Chinese Painting*) by Zhu Zixian (Taiwan: Artist Publisher, 1984).

15. Ibid.

16. *Hóng gāoliáng: Zhāng Yìmóu xiězhēn* (*Red Sorghum: Snapshots of Zhang Yimou;* Beijing: Zhōngguó diànyǐng chūbǎnshè, 1988), pp. 38–44.

FILM AND THE VISUAL
ARTS IN JAPAN:
An Introduction

PART TWO

FILM AND THE VISUAL

ARTS IN JAPAN:

An Introduction

BY THOMAS RIMER

The essays that follow provide fresh and provocative means to look with new understanding at Japanese film.

The visual vocabulary aligned to the long traditions of the Japanese arts was highly articulated and understood, on all levels of society, long before the twentieth century placed the medium of film in the foreground of Japanese artistic accomplishment. It is not surprising therefore that this vocabulary, either explicitly or implicitly, has helped shape the kinds of images that directors, performers, and audiences alike found moving and meaningful during the course of development of the Japanese cinema. For those of us not born into this tradition, however, the rich variety of insight contained in the following pages can help to sharpen our own visual perceptions and make articulate, and so understandable, elements central to what has made the work of the great Japanese film directors so distinctive. To suggest Japanese "commonalities" between disparate films and directors, on the other hand, is not to suggest that their own individual accomplishments, unique to each, can or should be examined in any purely reductive way; rather, as these various authors indicate, the rich variety of responses that Japanese directors have drawn from their own traditions reveals their individual gifts to be all the more striking. In the same fashion, the wide-ranging insights provided in these essays cannot be reduced to any single theme.

Nevertheless, there are certain points in common.

First of all, using certain observations in Anne Hollander's book *Moving Pictures* as a starting point, the "Japanese case" does exhibit some crucial differences when compared to the uses made of the Western artistic traditions in European and American film. The most important difference, it seems to me, lies in the fact that, in the Japanese tradition, narrative does not play a central role. Of course, there are important examples of "emplotment" in classical Japanese art. The *emakimono,* or picture scrolls, were created to carry a narrative line, and the self-conscious, and successful, use of such techniques can be seen in such a film as Kinoshita Keisuke's 1960 *Fuefukigawa* (*The Fuefuki River*). In general, however, it has been rather the formal qualities of Japanese classical art that appear to represent what seemed most suitable for appropriation by Japanese film directors. Indeed, the challenge they faced was to find a way to allow these formal qualities to contribute to a dramatic, narrative film form. Some directors, as Satō Tadao points out in his essay, had a long-nourished appreciation for the Japanese classical arts and tested various ways to make use of such devices in their films. As these essays indicate, the Japanese visual heritage, in some fashion or other, informed virtually every directorial eye.

What are the most important of these visual qualities as seen in film? There would appear to be, on the basis of the propositions that follow, two general and related categories of possibilities.

The first is the primacy of the suggestive. Here, the intuitive is privileged over the literal statement. This is a principle long appreciated in traditional painting and poetry, where, to paraphrase the words of the great medieval poet Kamo no Chōmei (1153–1216), the colored leaves of autumn seen through a veil of mist are more beautiful than any clear view of the bright trees themselves, since their appearance through the mist permits the play of the viewer's own free imagination. In the case of film, as several authors suggest, the techniques of framing can be so arranged as to press the viewer on to seek suggestions of the greater world beyond the confines of the screen. In this regard, visual control can nurture a greater intuitive freedom on the part of the viewer.

The second, and related cluster of ideas, might be described as a strategy undertaken in the traditional Japanese arts (and thus by extension in film as well) to attempt to suggest the essence, rather than to imitate the outer appearance, of what is being portrayed, a point nicely articulated by Donald Richie in his essay. In the traditional arts, this idea perhaps finds its most evocative articulation in the words of Zeami (1363–1443), who, in describing the kinds of actions appropriate to the medieval *Nō* theatre, emphasizes that the performer must strive to exhibit on the stage the essence of a character, rather than merely creating any superficial outer resemblance. In such a view, the actor portraying an old man will not hobble about in some melodramatic way but will simply move more slowly than the musical rhythms would have him do; a woodcutter will suggest the difficulties of his lonely life but will not use coarse or broken speech. Again, this kind of technique asks a special engagement of the audience, which, while filling in what has been left out, becomes all the more highly involved in the work of art being presented.

In terms of film, how does this essence represent itself? There appear to be several means touched on in the pages that follow.

One of them, mentioned by Kathe Geist, is *emptiness* or "unknown space," the use of "nothingness" as a positive element in film composition. A look at medieval Zen ink paintings, with their large unpainted spaces, or a reminder of Zeami's insistence that the greatest moments of dramatic impact may well occur in the "empty spaces" in performance when the actor is doing nothing, shows a powerful pedigree for this principle. Another, noted both by Geist and Dudley Andrew, involves the conscious use of two-dimensional space as an organizing principle. Long a central strategy in the Japanese visual arts, this flattening procedure can produce a brilliant sense of pattern and design, film sequences that indeed can suggest "a woodblock print with dialogue supplied."

Both Cynthia Contreras and Satō mention a predilection for horizontal compositional techniques, suggesting both the *emakimono* picture scrolls which unroll horizontally from right to left and the sliding painted doors, or *fusuma,* that form such a central element in classical Japanese architectural space. Lastly, David Desser, D. William Davis, and others stress the importance for the viewer of Japanese film of what has been termed the primacy of perception; plot may represent the element that moves the film sequences along, but the observing eye dwells on, and learns from, the visual moment portrayed. The kind of concentration this act requires again suggests the need for a participatory audience, one that is prepared to enter actively into the process of response the film demands.

In addition, the Japanese film represents, for Andrew and virtually all the others, a collaborative and communal form of art, one in which director, technician, actor, and audience all make a necessary contribution that goes to make the film "understood," both visually and intellectually. This assumption too finds powerful roots in the Japanese arts, particularly in classical poetry, where contests and the writing of *renga,* or linked verse, demand just such collaborative skills, since individual poets functioned at once as creators, collaborators, and audience.

Such are the bare outlines of the visual grammar here explicated.

An examination of such aesthetic assumptions, sometimes assumed, sometimes articulated in the context of traditional Japanese culture, can help

Western viewers understand Japanese films from a perspective that brings a new kind of visual truth to the images presented in the films. Ironically, this kind of understanding based on explication may be necessary as well for a certain number of younger Japanese, whose own aesthetic assumptions have been slowly altered by the onslaught of many generations of imported Western attitudes. Indeed the concept of film itself as an artistic medium since its introduction into Japan has brought a whole new series of techniques and attitudes that have helped develop modern and contemporary Japanese visual understanding. These new possibilities were, of course, no more "alien" to Japan than they were to the United States or Europe, since they were those created by a largely new form of visual art. Nevertheless, as Satō and others point out, Western assumptions of space, time, and dramatic technique have come to play an increasingly important position in Japan's ever more international modern and contemporary culture.

The observations contained in the essays here, which do so much to explain the aesthetics of Japanese film, raise, as inevitably they should, another, further series of issues that might take another volume of this scope to examine. To me, the most crucial of these extended issues concerns the inevitable difference in attitudes and expectations between the traditional "viewer" and his or her modern counterpart, whether examined collectively in a group, as in a theatre, or in terms of how an individual contemplates a work of art. The kind of contextual aesthetics described above, in which the audience is expected to play a central role, is invariably altered when film audiences, who may bring little in the way of such traditional artistic preconceptions or proclivities to a film, are faced with certain of the kinds of formal aesthetic problems (and solutions) mentioned here. How can this particular aesthetic of the film involve the attention of an audience educated to ponder only its own contemporary concerns? After all, dramatic conflict and, increasingly, social commentary have become the focus of the form. How, then, are the concerns of "real life," doubtless the one common bond carried into the theatre by the audience, "reinjected" into film which embraces a formal pedigree?

A significant clue to this complex problem is suggested in Linda Ehrlich's essay. She defines a useful concept of "playfulness," in which traditional and modern elements are mixed in a sometimes self-conscious and fanciful fashion in order to achieve individual artistic effects. This kind of playfulness, of course, is possible because of the ability of certain Japanese directors to find a means to "distance" the audiences from their material, so that spectators can observe from without, as it were, even while remaining emotionally involved. Brecht and his concept of "alienation" (itself drawn from his understanding of the Asian theatre) need not be summoned in order to understand such techniques (although his observations are always piquant and helpfully unsettling). As Ehrlich points out, the techniques of a traditional Japanese art such as the *bunraku* puppet theatre—which, in the famous dictum of the greatest of the Tokugawa-period playwrights Chikamatsu Monzaemon (1653–1724), dwells in the "thin line between reality and unreality"—have long since become central to the Japanese understanding of the power of stylization in the dramatic arts.

Still, the traditional "code," that mixture of conscious and unconscious elements in the collective psyche of the audience that allows them to "read" a film or work of art, is inevitably breaking down, as one set of cultural baggage is exchanged for another. How deeply do these, can these heretofore accepted older Japanese "ways of seeing" continue on in the future?

There is, of course, another intriguing possibility, best explained by way of example. Kume Keiichirō (1866–1934), one of the most accomplished of the early Japanese painters in the Western style, lived in Paris for a number of years, where he worked closely with Kuroda Seiki (1866–1924), the doyen of Japanese painters in France. Kume's eye, as well as his technique, was therefore virtually formed in Europe. When he and Kuroda returned to Japan in 1893, they made a trip to Kyoto, the old capital, an experience that was to remain totally revelatory for Kume. The artist had never imagined what the visual and cultural nature of the artifacts of his own culture might be. Discovering them, or, in some sense, rediscovering them, he created a series of paintings that often show a striking mixture of Western techniques and Eastern aesthetic principles. Such works were utterly new; even now they still retain their freshness after the greater part of a century. If Kume's experience is at all typical, the future may show similar possibilities. Japanese directors and filmmakers with altogether contemporary (that is to say, largely Western) assumptions may continue to rediscover the same kind of excitement that Kume felt when he observed classical Japanese forms. Their excitement, like Kume's, can then produce something altogether new.

Certainly this kind of encounter must have been what fueled the inspiration of a director like Suzuki Seijun (born 1923), who, after making popular, commercial films for much of his career, began to use his own evocations of the Japanese past in a series of independently produced films he has created in the past decade or so. The newest and arguably most successful of these visual encounters with older Japanese traditions is his film *Yumeji*, first shown in 1990. In one sense, the film is a perfect example of the ideas suggested in Hollander's book: Suzuki took the elegant, winsome images of Takahashi Yumeji (1884–1934), the most popular and evocative painter of the Taishō period and mixed them with fanciful evocations of his life in a heady surrealist mix.

Suzuki's film is filled with all the excitement, and the occasional confusions, of a brilliant contemporary film artist discovering, as if for the first time, the powerful spell waiting to be cast by certain more traditional elements in his own culture. It seemed to me, on the day I saw the film, that the audience found itself altogether willing to be pulled along on Suzuki's path of self-discovery.

For such reasons, then, the classical assumptions that influence modern Japanese cinema pointed out in the essays that follow must not be seen in any way as attempts at some sort of visual archaeology. These great aesthetic classical principles thankfully seem merely latent, waiting for filmmakers, indeed artists of any kind, to reencounter them, so that they may find embodiment in new works that, however contemporary in spirit, may still pay homage to a traditional visual culture as resilient and satisfying as any in the world.

THOMAS RIMER

THE INFLUENCE OF
TRADITIONAL AESTHETICS
ON THE JAPANESE FILM

BY DONALD RICHIE

The parents of cinema are various: painting, photography, the novel, the drama. Their degree of influence, however, depends upon the culture being discussed. In the West one of the parents has been painting and its stepchild, photography. Even at its beginnings the film was seen as a new way of taking pictures ("painting with light") rather than a new kind of drama.

In the East, however, and particularly in Japan, the dominant parent was the drama. The infant cinema was regarded primarily as an extension of the stage. "There was thus ample reason to incorporate elements from the traditional theatre into early film performances, and into early productions as well. There was also reason, initially at any rate, to disregard any claims for realism, which in the West was considered essential in a photograph, be it still or moving." [1]

At the same time, to be sure, there was a continued painterly influence. In all film there is "the undying resonance . . . of the visual imagery of the past. . . . Much of this process is unconscious; and so it guarantees the same direct emotional response in eventual viewers, unhampered by any conscious recognition of consciously applied effects."[2]

The difference with the East lies in the nature of the influence. Western painterly influences on Western film have been defined as several: first, the specific source for the emotive power of film imagery, seen in "the distinctive rendering of light by the painters of the North European Renaissance"; and second, the painters' "ways of composing the space in pictures to suggest and invite psychological motion."[3]

In Asia, however, the rendering of light is not among major traditional aesthetic concerns. Shadows were seen as unavoidable in the dramas, and happily banished as soon as electric lighting became available. Though, once they were missing, shadows came to be valued by traditionally minded intellectuals,[4] the popular preference, in Japan at any rate, is indicated by the full, flat lighting of the *kabuki* stage and the full, flat lighting of the ordinary Japanese film.

The concept of light and shade as an aesthetic principle arrived in Japan very late—imported from the West. The nineteenth-century painter Shiba Kōkan wrote that Western painting was, consequently, superior to Japan's in that "it portrays light and shade, the shapes of solids, and their perspectives."[5] Perhaps the reason for these different systems of representing depth was that the concerns of traditional Japanese art lay elsewhere. Light and shade are of use only to an artist concerned with modeling, with rendering objects in space, with the verisimilitude of the rendering. If the artist has no need for depth, no way to handle perspective, and no desire for illusionism, he or she will then see small attraction in the possibilities of light and shadow.

Such an artist will be concerned with surface, with outline, with two-dimensionality. He or she would not be interested in the literal kind of art we know as mimetic. In fact, "the principle of mimesis is an exotic and alien import into late nineteenth-century Japan."[6]

This did not mean that something like mimesis was missing. It meant merely that the Western concept of this quality was not in evidence. There are various kinds of imitation (which is what mimesis consists of) and what is realistic to one culture need not to be to another.

The reasons are obvious. In terms of film they have been defined thus:

> Imagine we are interested in the basic "language" elements through which a film communicates. . . . To facilitate our analysis we make certain assumptions about the characteristic response to any particular configuration of "terms" in this language. . . . This in turn depends upon a set of psychological assumptions

about the ways in which we emotionally respond to particular perceptual situations and such assumptions are themselves grounded in a body of psychological theory and knowledge. . . . [In] our society people respond to certain perceptual situations in the expected way. But in another society different patterns . . . alter the particular psychological response.[7]

The assumptions underlying Japanese art are different from those underlying Western art. This includes definitions of the nature of reality and consequently any artistic depiction of it. Japanese mimesis, for example, has been defined as "a tendency to value symbolic representation more highly than realistic delineation." Thus "mimesis meant not an imitation of outward appearance but a suggestion of inner essence, for true reality lay under the physical surface."[8]

A number of results arose from this assumption. Not only did "Western-type realism" develop slowly, but art as well became "a means by which a glimpse of higher reality" was made visible "to the ordinary eye." There was another result as well. This "mimesis assumed a selective presentation of the beautiful, and discouraged the artist from dealing with the humble and vulgar aspects of human experience. Consequently the artist tended to choose nature for his subject, avoiding the depiction of everyday occurrences," and predictably, "elegance was·one of the main types of beauty favored."[9]

These conventions disposed Japanese art—and, later, cinema—toward an aestheticism which is still a salient aspect. The patterned surfaces of painting or print, the considered composition of film directors Mizoguchi Kenji and Ozu Yasujirō, Kurosawa Akira and Ichikawa Kon—whether the subject requires this degree of aestheticism or not—are alike in this concern.

It has been said that traditional Japanese culture was indeed structured "with its aesthetic values at the center," and that "aesthetic concerns often prevailed even over religious beliefs, ethical duties and material comforts."[10] This being so, they certainly prevailed over the claims of an illusionistic realism.

To this end, various assumptions were codified. There was, however, little formal aesthetic theory. It was not until the late seventeenth century that a Japanese theoretical work finally appeared. This was the *Hanchō Gahō Taiden* (*The Authoritative Summary of the Rules of Japanese Painting*), and the author was himself a painter, Tosa Mitsuaki.

From this work a few principles may be deduced. One of its most famous entries states: "If there is a painting which is lifelike and which is good for that reason, that work has followed the laws of life. If there is a painting which is not lifelike and which is good for that reason, that work has followed the laws of painting."[11]

Of interest here is that an alternative is being proposed to what the West would consider a primary mimesis, the following of the laws of life. Apparently equal to the lifelike is what the West could only call artifice.

Mitsuaki goes on to imply that though all good works are perhaps "life-like," this quality is not to be encompassed by copying outside appearances. Rather, it is the inward laws of nature that one is after. To find these one must "go beyond the laws of life and enter a sphere governed by the laws of art." [12]

Thus the two kinds of painting are not equal after all. One follows the "laws of life" only to go beyond them and enter that presumably higher sphere governed by the "laws of art."

Almost any traditional Japanese artist follows the latter, though to do so he must sacrifice the former. For example, when painting bamboo, says Mitsuaki, "do not let branches grow at every joint, nor let leaves grow on every branch." [13] So much for the claims of lifelike realism.

So much, too, for any need for realistic modeling, for shade and light. These have no place in traditional Japanese concepts. And, perhaps consequently, in the cinematic extension, there is also little concern for depth, for modeling, for illusionary space.

The two-dimensional aspect of Japanese cinema is well known. Scenes from Mizoguchi's films are compared to those in handscrolls, Ichikawa's, to woodblock prints and modern graphics, Kurosawa's—in the later films—to classic *byōbu* (standing screens).

At the same time, of course, film is "realistic" to a much greater degree than is the painting or the print. Still, this "realism" is created through means so selective that one must suspect that the laws of art are being consulted at least as often as are the laws of nature. To the Western eye, nature never looked as it does in a Mizoguchi scene, or domestic architecture as it does in an Ozu film.

One of the reasons for this impression is that a number of compositional premises, quite different from those of the West, are accepted by both the artist and the filmmaker. Perhaps neither considered these premises, but they are there—a part of a specific culture, the Japanese.

To begin with, there is the premise concerning space. In the West, we feel that emptiness has no independent function. Only what is full is interesting, and we are not encouraged to contemplate what we would find vacant. Eastern aesthetics, however, suggest that the "empty" carries its own weight.

This emptiness must first be defined, however, and both Chinese and Japanese painting manuals insist that emptiness does not appear until the first mark is put on the paper. Only then does the surface become, by contrast, empty.

This is an important aesthetic precept, one which extends throughout

DONALD RICHIE

much of Japanese culture. In the Japanese garden, for example, the "natural" is not achieved until the rock is moved and the bamboo shifted. Before then, nature was not present, just as on a blank page emptiness was not present. Space is not reticulated until it is contrasted. This creates an area where the full and the unfilled are balanced in a manner of which the West knows little. There is, to be sure, a Western theory of negative space, but its definition and its use are far different.

This empty/full dichotomy informs much traditional Japanese art. In *ikebana* flower arrangement, for example, the spaces between the stems and branches define the space just as much as do the stems and branches themselves. Or, in the scroll landscape, the bottom is full, the top empty. The same is true of the ordinary hanging scroll, or the page of Japanese type.

This empty/full dichotomy also appears in the noticeable balance of firmly anchored empty spaces in the compositions of Mizoguchi, in the empty sides of Naruse Mikio's scenes, in the often horizontal divisions of Ichikawa, and in the famous "empty shots" of Ozu.

Another premise different from ours involves the direction in which the eye is led, the way "through" the balanced masses of the filled and the unfilled. One "reads" a Western composition by beginning at the left and continuing to the right. This is the theory—one reads a picture as one reads a sentence.

Japan has a similar convention, the difference being that the Japanese sentence is read from top to bottom and from right to left, just as often as it is nowadays read from left to right in the Western fashion. This, transferred to space, results in compositions which the West finds piquant or singular or unexpected—all qualities which Westerners have ascribed to Japanese film compositions.

Indicative is the way in which a single line—the diagonal—is interpreted in the two cultures. The West assumes that a line which begins in the lower left-hand corner and rises across to the upper right is expressing accepted qualities: endeavor, difficult but successful progress, and so on. This is because "movements running from lower left to upper right are commonly sensed as ascending."[14]

In Japan, however, the same line, read from right to left, has almost opposite connotations. The descending diagonal is seen as a graceful line leading to repose, to rest, to an accord with nature, with the way things are.

Thus, in film, the same line, the striving, triumphant diagonal—workers pulling a cannon in Eisenstein's *October;* the graceful resigned descent of the flowering grasses as seen in Mizoguchi's *Sansho the Bailiff* (*Sanshō Dayū,* 1953)—is "read" in completely opposite manners.

7.1 Mizoguchi Kenji, *The Loyal Rōnin of the Genroku Era* (*Genroku chūshingura*, 1941–1942) (courtesy of the Japan Film Library Council).

Another visual difference is the way in which the completed composition is framed. All views are partial; all need to be framed or else they would not be views. Thus the position of the frame—what is shown and what is not—had long been considered important in the cultures of both East and West.

Here, too, there is a dramatic difference in assumptions. Westerners often seem to believe that space is already so filled that all we need to do is cut out a portion, as it were, by placing the frame over it. Japanese, on the other hand, often seem to feel that space itself is so empty that we first place the frame and then, as it were, select the things to put into it.

It is as though an empty area has been originally envisioned and then filled according to the laws of art rather than the laws of life. In film, though there are many directors (Ōshima Nagisa, Imamura Shōhei, Hani Susumu) who are "Western" in the assumption that reality is outside the frame as well, and that the director chooses his portion of an already filled area, there are more—a number including Mizoguchi, Ozu, Naruse, Kurosawa, and Ichikawa—who create compositions within the studio and transmit a view of reality which is closed and composed.

Here the laws of art are most important. Kurosawa, like Ozu, never de-

DONALD RICHIE

7.2 *Midori* section of *The Tale of Genji scroll* (*Genji monogatari emaki*) (courtesy of the Gotō Museum, Tokyo).

parts from his script once it is completed. It is a blueprint through which to realize the envisioned (laws of art) film. Naruse refused when possible to work outside the environment of the studio, where his carefully selected compositions could be controlled, and the aesthetic effect judged. And many are the stories of Ozu switching about objects on a table between scenes, about Kurosawa shaping the snow or arranging the grass.

In such films (such scrolls, prints, screens), we are being shown a self-contained world, one animated not by natural forces but by the human mind. This view is anthropomorphic, and is indeed what one might expect from a culture which finds that emptiness has no quality until a person has made his or her mark, and that nature is not natural until a person has intervened to make it so.

It is also not surprising that Japanese painting and printmaking should have so affected the look of Japanese film in such a direct manner. Not only are the aesthetics of the traditional Japanese film based upon the aesthetics of Japanese art, but also the scene itself may refer to such original impetus in a manner directly imitative.

In Mizoguchi's *The Loyal Rōnin of the Genroku Era* (*Genroku chūshin-gura,* 1941–1942), there are scenes known to have painterly originals. The conference scene (figure 7.1) is based on one of the scenes in the famous handscrolls illustrating *The Tale of Genji* (*Genji monogatari*). This scene is taken from such an angle that one is reminded of the unroofed chambers in the scrolls (figure 7.2). At the same time the composition, in film as in scroll, becomes an "acknowledgement of the pictorial surface." [15]

Influence of Traditional Aesthetics on Japanese Film

There are many more examples, but perhaps more important to this discussion is this acknowledgment of similarity of purpose between artist and filmmaker. This has remained strong. For example, "even at the risk of going against professional theory, Ozu was always more concerned with making each shot a beautiful composition than with continuity."[16]

These concerns remain noticeable well into this century. "The flattening of the image in the work of, say, Ozu after 1933 may legitimately be regarded as a deliberate 'throwback' . . . and the persistence of 'primitive flatness' in so many Japanese films during the 1920s" may be seen as "accidental." Yet "insofar as it was determined by the general 'surface orientation' of the arts of Japan . . . it was, of course, no accident at all."[17]

This flatness, this concern for aestheticism, and this willingness to accept the appearances of traditional Japanese art are seen even in directors as supposedly Westernized as Shinoda Masahiro and Kurosawa.

Two small examples: in the former's *Under the Cherry Blossoms* (*Sakura no mori no mankai no shita,* 1975), the many scenes of the blossoms are rendered as friezes in the manner of the Kanō school, a Momoyama period–like framed profusion; in the second episode of Kurosawa's *Dreams* (*Yume,* 1990), peach blossoms are likewise rendered as friezes, blossoms alone, one framed scene after another like panels in a classical screen.

Though the influences of the traditional aesthetics of Japan are not now often seen in the works of younger, contemporary directors, or at least not seen so directly, these influences remain. Usually, however, they are of a more complicated lineage. The two-dimensionality of the Japanese print became the two-dimensionality of the *manga* "cartoon" strip, and it is this later two-dimensionality which informs the flatness of Itami Jūzō's *Tampopo* (1986). The steady stare of, let us say, the Zen scroll is transmuted into the steady gaze of the long, distant scene of Mizoguchi, but these are further influenced by the patient regard of Antonioni and the idiot goggle of TV watching to create the long, distant dance-party scene in Somai Shinji's *Typhoon Club* (*Taifū kurabu,* 1986).

Japan's rejection of the representational, a trend still continuing, goes then beyond a mimetic theory to reach a cognitive theory, and it is this which becomes visible in Japanese art, be it classical *waka* poetry, landscape gardening, painting, the haiku, flower arranging, or filmmaking. Though the direct influence of traditional Japanese art upon Japanese film may be seen as minor if the view is restricted to simple resemblance, it is vast indeed if the view is enlarged to consider the implications of a complete theory of aesthetics.

DONALD RICHIE

Notes

1. Donald Richie, *Japanese Cinema: An Introduction* (Oxford: Oxford University Press, 1990), p. 2.
2. Anne Hollander, *Moving Pictures* (New York: Alfred A. Knopf, 1989), p. 5.
3. Ibid., p. 6.
4. Tanizaki Jun'ichirō, *In Praise of Shadows,* trans. Edward G. Seidensticker and Thomas J. Harper (New Haven: Leete's Island Books, 1977).
5. G. B. Sansom, *The Western World and Japan* (New York: Alfred A. Knopf, 1950), p. 233.
6. Earl Miner, ed., *Principles of Classical Japanese Literature* (Princeton: Princeton University Press, 1985), p. ix.
7. Andrew Tudor, *Theories of Film* (New York: Viking Press, 1973), pp. 60–61.
8. *Kōdansha Encyclopedia of Japan,* s.v. "aesthetics."
9. Ibid.
10. Katō Shūichi, *Form, Style, Tradition: Reflections on Japanese Art and Society* (Berkeley: University of California Press, 1979), p. 4.
11. Ueda Makoto, *Literary and Art Theories in Japan* (Cleveland: Western Reserve University Press, 1967), p. 4.
12. Ibid., p. 131.
13. Ibid., p. 141.
14. Edward Lanners, ed., *Illusions* (London: Thomas and Hudson, 1977), p. 104.
15. Noël Burch, *To the Distant Observer: Form and Meaning in the Japanese Cinema* (Berkeley: University of California Press, 1979), p. 117.
16. Satō Tadao, *Currents in Japanese Cinema,* trans. Gregory Barrett (Tokyo: Kodansha, 1982), p. 189.
17. Burch, p. 118.

JAPANESE CINEMA AND
THE TRADITIONAL ARTS:
Imagery, Technique, and
Cultural Context

BY SATŌ TADAO
Translated by Ann Sherif

C
H
A
P
T
E
R

8

The imagery and techniques employed in modern Japanese cinema bear a relationship to traditional culture and the arts. In this article, I will discuss the ways certain traditional concepts of imagery and techniques in the visual arts carry over in Japanese film, and also look at the influence of traditional Japanese music and theatre on Japanese cinema.

Mountains and Rivers

Landscapes were a favorite subject of traditional Japanese and Chinese painters. With mountainous landscapes, painters sought to evoke the mystical realms of Taoism, where immortals dwell. Images of rivers and lakes in these paintings suggest the Buddhist concept of flux and impermanence. This predilection for natural subjects, therefore, does not simply reflect a love of nature, but must be understood in relation to its cultural context.

There are countless popular Japanese films that include Mount Fuji as a symbol of no-

8.1 Kinoshita Keisuke, *Ballad of Narayama* (*Narayama bushikō*, 1958) (courtesy of the Japan Film Library Council).

bility and stability, but mountain imagery does not typically otherwise figure prominently in Japanese cinema. Notable exceptions are the two excellent films based on Fukazawa Shichirō's novel *The Ballad of Narayama* (*Narayama bushikō*). The earlier film version was directed by Kinoshita Keisuke in 1958, and the later by Imamura Shōhei in 1983. The story takes as its setting a small village located near Narayama, or Mount Nara (a fictional mountain). In this village, it is the practice to take people who have reached the age of seventy to the mountain and abandon them there (figure 8.1). The scarcity of food and the poverty of the village render this custom a practical necessity, and the villagers view it as desirable because they believe that they will encounter the *kami* (Shinto deity or god) of the mountain there. Although Fukazawa based the story of abandoning the elderly on legend rather than on historical fact, he did not make up the belief in the divinity of certain mountains. Such beliefs still exist in contemporary Japan. These indigenous beliefs concerning mountains bear no direct relationship to the Taoist or Buddhist traditions that inspired landscape painting.

In the film versions of *The Ballad of Narayama*, the climax comes when a man and his elderly mother reach the peak of Narayama and stumble upon

SATŌ TADAO

8.2 Imamura Shōhei, *Ballad of Narayama* (*Narayama bushikō*, 1983) (courtesy of the Japan Film Library Council).

piles of human skeletons. The audience does not feel revulsion at this shocking scene, but instead a sense of surprise at this evidence of a very basic, primitive human regard for nature as sacred.

After the man has set his mother down among the skeletons and turns to make his way back to the village, it begins to snow (figure 8.2). Both parent and child rejoice at the snow, which they believe to be a blessing from the *kami*, because it will hasten the mother's death and thus reduce her suffering. This snow episode was not part of the original legends or folk tales about Narayama, but was added by Fukazawa. Significantly, in landscape painting, snow often represents purity, purification of the heart and mind, and the will to survive.

River imagery is incorporated in Japanese films far more frequently and with greater effect than in Western cinema. A prime example of this can be found in the wildly popular "Tora-san" comedies *It's Hard to Be a Man* (*Otoko wa tsurai yo*), of which over forty appeared between 1969 and 1993. Each film begins with Tora-san, an itinerant peddler, traveling back to his native Tokyo. Inevitably, he appears on the banks of the Edo River, which flows through Tokyo. Many of the scenes that involve Tora-san confessing his feelings to someone else also are set along the banks of a river. *Tora-san Goes to Vienna* (*Otoko wa tsurai yo: Torajiro kokoro no tabiji*, 1990), the forty-first of the series, finds Tora-san in Vienna. Here again, we find Tora-san having an intimate talk with the female protagonist, this time on the banks of the Danube.

Over the long history of Japanese painting, it became the practice to portray rivers and their banks as places conducive to expressing and confronting one's emotions. In landscape painting, this probably sprung from the use of river imagery to symbolize the Buddhist negation of human desire and attachment (figure 8.3).

Ozu Yasujirō's *A Hen in the Wind* (*Kaze no naka no mendori*, 1948) concerns a man who returns from the Pacific War only to discover that his wife resorted to prostitution once during his absence in order to pay their son's hospital bills. The man visits the inn where his wife worked for one night as a prostitute. Later, he encounters a prostitute who is eating her lunch down by the riverside. Their conversation reveals that she too is an essentially good-hearted woman who was forced into prostitution by financial necessity. She tells him that she comes down to the river in order to escape from the filthy inn. The riverside is the perfect place for these two—a prostitute and a repatriated soldier wishing to cleanse himself of the spiritual defilement of his wife's prostitution—to speak frankly to one another.

In Ozu's *Early Spring* (*Sōshun*, 1956) as well, a riverside becomes the

8.3 Kenko Shōkei, (fl. ca. 1478–1506), *Landscape,* Japan, Muromachi period, mid fifteenth–early sixteenth century, hanging scroll, ink on paper (courtesy of the Museum of Fine Arts, Boston, Fenellosa-Weld Collection, 11.4127).

SATŌ TADAO

8.4 Mizoguchi Kenji, *A Story from Chikamatsu* (*Chikamatsu monogatari*, 1954) (courtesy of the Japan Film Library Council).

scene of the protagonist's confession of his private difficulties. The man's marriage has floundered because of his extramarital affair, and his company has transferred him out of the Tokyo office. Down by the river, he speaks with his friend about these concerns.

Mizoguchi Kenji also made effective use of river imagery. His *The Story of the Last Chrysanthemum* (*Zangiku monogatari*, 1939) contains a touching love scene, set on the banks of a canal, in which a man and woman, separated by class and social status, confess their love for the first time. A similar couple in *A Story from Chikamatsu* (*Chikamatsu monogatari*, 1954) are in a small boat on a lake when they make known their feelings (figure 8.4). In *Sansho the Bailiff* (*Sanshō Dayū*, 1954), the slave girl, Anju, helps her brother Zushio escape from a slave camp, but then decides to kill herself rather than be tortured into giving away her brother's whereabouts. She drowns herself in a pond. Mizoguchi's cinematographer, Miyagawa Kazuo, filmed this pond scene beautifully, giving the dark surface of the water an almost mystical quality. Many other of Mizoguchi's films feature such use of water imagery. In most instances, the scenes involve people who are attempting to confront their own feelings or those who wish to wash away some disgrace or impurity.

In the films of such directors as Kurosawa Akira, Imamura Shōhei, and Ōshima Nagisa, all of a younger generation than Mizoguchi and Ozu, effective use of river and lake imagery is relatively rare. Perhaps this relates to these directors' distance from traditional Japanese culture.

Aside from landscape painting, Japanese scroll painting (*emaki*) also had an impact on Japanese cinema. When viewing a handscroll, one unrolls the painting gradually in order to see a story unfold. Unlike contemporary comic strips, the pictures on the scroll are not each enclosed in a frame, and the scroll appears to be one continuous illustration. However, the appearance of a central figure or figures throughout the painting indicates that the scenes are, in fact, discrete and the action sequential. In cinematic terms, this is akin to a moving shot of the camera that follows the actions of a single character. In the *emaki*, the action moves from right to left, and is usually seen from above. Often when actions take place indoors, the artist removes the roof of the structure to reveal the events within. Frequently, stylized mist or clouds conceal objects on the periphery of the scenes. Human figures are fairly uniform throughout the scroll and are always viewed as part of a long shot, never in a close-up (colorplate 1).

Certain aspects of the *emaki* bring to mind the cinema, but only in a very limited sense. In *emaki*, close-ups, montages, and a variety of points of view do not exist, nor is there any division between scenes.

The Case of Mizoguchi

One Japanese director familiar with the *emaki* tradition was Mizoguchi. From the mid-1930s, Mizoguchi tried employing extreme long moving shots, with no close-ups. He particularly favored mounting the camera on a crane and shooting from above. These techniques find their most complete realization in his two-part *The Loyal Rōnin of the Genroku Era* (*Genroku chūshingura,* 1941–1942). This three-hour and thirty-five-minute epic contains 160 shots in all. The average shot in this film lasts one minute and twenty seconds. Although a five-minute shot is not unusual in film now, at that time, a one-minute and twenty-second shot was considered radically long. The film contains predominantly long shots, with no close-ups at all. In addition, the director made considerable use of bird's-eye views. Although many contemporary critics praised this movie, others expressed their astonishment and displeasure at Mizoguchi's rebellion against cinematic techniques such as montage, and his return to the simplicity of the *emaki*.

Mizoguchi also took full advantage of certain structural features of Japanese houses that allow for continuous, uninterrupted shots. Traditional Japanese homes have removable sliding doors (*fusuma* and *shōji*) rather than walls and doors that are fixed in place. In the summer, these dividers are often removed, resulting in a continuous, unpartitioned space. Therefore, it is relatively easy to move the camera around and to film continuously people's movement from room to room, room to hallway, hallway to entryway. Mizoguchi would sometimes shoot as one scene what had been two or three scenes in the script, even if the setting changed and extensive camera movement was required.

This brings to mind the *emaki* tradition of painting houses without roofs in order to show the entire interior and the actions of the people inside. The painters regarded the portrayal of people's surroundings and social interaction as more important than the faithful and detailed representation of the figures themselves. In a like manner, Mizoguchi would do his utmost to include two figures in a shot rather than an isolated figure. He was thus able to emphasize the dynamic relationship between his characters. Naturally, this resulted in an increase in his use of long shots and bird's-eye views.

Such characteristics of Mizoguchi's art derive from his firm belief in the importance of performance. In his later years, Mizoguchi himself was aware of the influence of traditional painting on his work and even told cinematographer Miyagawa Kazuo that he wanted to shoot "without breaks, like the *emaki.*" Mizoguchi's distinctive style, which he began to create around 1935, came partly from his pursuit of realism. From the time of such films as *The Loyal Rōnin* and *The Life of Oharu* (*Saikaku ichidai onna*, 1952), the camerawork in Mizoguchi's films has an elegance also akin to the leisurely movements of classical Japanese dance.

"Bird and Flower" Imagery

In the *emaki*, the abundance of seasonal references such as grasses and flowers contributes to the atmosphere of elegance. This focus on the seasons in *emaki* derives from the painting style called *Yamato-e*, popular from around the tenth century. The *Yamato-e* had its roots in native, rather than Chinese, styles. Paintings rich in seasonal subjects, the *Yamato-e* adorned the folding screens of aristocratic residences (figure 8.5). Classical Japanese poetry (*waka*) was also included on this type of painting. Nature and the four seasons are a major focus of *waka*, and the *Yamato-e* served as illustrations for the verse.

Of all seasonal imagery, the cherry blossom is the most popular, to the point of becoming a cliché. When in full bloom, the cherry evokes the joy of springtime. The short season of the cherry blossoms suggests Buddhist notions of transience and evanescence, as well as the sorrow of parting.

This short-lived flower also symbolizes the samurai notion that the warrior should not cling to life, but instead die honorably and beautifully. The numerous film versions of Chūshingura all feature a scene in which Lord Asano commits ritual suicide, or *seppuku*. Cherry blossoms flutter down over him as he carries through on this fatal act. These symbol-laden flowers elevate his suicide to the level of an elegant ceremony, celebrating the honorable suffering of a proud warrior.

One director who employed the cherry blossom in a particularly fresh and successful manner was Ichikawa Kon. His *Makioka Sisters* (*Sasameyuki*, 1983) features a stunning final scene, which involves a man who has finally married off his sister-in-law. He sits drinking sake beneath the cherry trees, as the blossoms scatter around him. This scene reveals with great delicacy his conflicting feelings of happiness about her marriage and the sadness of parting. Thus, Ichikawa utilizes two symbolic aspects of cherry blossoms in a single scene.

Such painting styles as the *Yamato-e* and the *sansuiga* (landscape painting), popular from the fifteenth century, show the predilection of Japanese

8.5 Hanabusa Itchō (1652–1724), *Celebrations of the Twelve Months*, Japan, Edo period, eighteenth century, six-fold screen; ink, color, and gold on paper (courtesy of the Museum of Fine Arts, Boston, Fenellosa-Weld Collection, 11.4219-20).

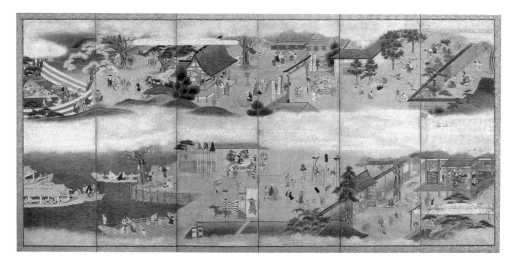

SATŌ TADAO

painters to focus on landscapes. The "bird and flower" paintings [1] prominent among artists of the Kano school (sixteenth to eighteenth centuries) exhibit an even greater tendency to the decorative and elegant (figure 8.6). These "bird and flower" painters often focused on subjects of symbolic importance, such as the crane and the pine tree, images associated with longevity and good fortune. The rising sun was another auspicious subject. The moon represented the companion of lonely souls.

Painters under the patronage of feudal lords (*daimyō*) produced these gorgeous paintings as decoration for ceremonies and for the residences of their patrons. Even with the popularization of art and a mass, rather than exclusively elite, audience, this preference for "bird and flower" motifs continues in modern Japan. In the early modern period, such decorative styles predominated and did not give way to the custom of family portraiture, popular among the Western aristocracy and bourgeoisie. It was not until photography became widespread that many Japanese people hung pictures of human subjects, such as the emperor or family members, in their homes.

Another example of the use of such images can be found in Horikawa Hiromichi's *Naked General* (*Hadaka no taishō*, 1958). The story takes place during and immediately after the Second World War. The central character is based on an actual person, Yamashita Kiyoshi, who was a brilliant painter and who suffered from mental illness. Yamashita avoided military service during the war by wandering from place to place. Horikawa carefully in-

8.6 Kanō Shoei, *Birds, Flowers, and Pines,* Japan, Muromachi period, sixteenth century, six-fold screen, ink and color on paper (courtesy of the Museum of Fine Arts, Boston, Fenellosa-Weld Collection, 11.4347).

cludes different types of flowers in the scenery of each area that Yamashita visits, despite the desolate wartime conditions.

Shibuya Minoru's *Doctor's Day Off* (*Honjitsu kyūden*, 1952) includes bird imagery. This heartwarming comedy depicts a poor urban community in the early postwar era and the dedicated physician who serves the local people. In the final scene, a shell-shocked former commissioned officer orders some people from the neighborhood to fall into line, like soldiers, and to salute a flock of geese flying by in the evening sky. The neighbors feel pity for the harmless, gentle young man and do as he says. The doctor then remarks that the geese are young pilots, who were injured in the war and are flying home to their mother. The image of a flock of geese represents powerless people who gather together for comfort and assistance. This symbolism is found in Japanese verse and "bird and flower" paintings.

Kurosawa Akira's *Rashomon* (*Rashōmon*, 1950) also exhibits a link with the symbolism of "bird and flower" painting. This film, made during the desperate years after the war, contains shots of the sun seen from a dense forest floor. Kurosawa conceived of using a shot of the sun as background for the scene in which the robber (Mifune Toshirō) rapes the wife of a samurai (Kyō Machiko). Because it was technically impossible to shoot the sun straight on, cinematographer Miyagawa Kazuo decided instead to film the rays of the sun through the filter of the leaves and branches of the forest.

In "bird and flower" paintings, the sun is often shown rising above the ocean. It is either a very auspicious image, or else it symbolizes a deity that watches over good and evil in the human realm. In *Rashomon*, the sun is not auspicious. Rather, it appears as a watchful deity. Specifically, the sun represents a supernatural being that exerts a powerful moral sway over people in a desperate situation. Although this reverence for the sun exists in Japan, no filmmaker before Kurosawa thought of shooting the sun straight on, because of the technical difficulties.

The moon, in contrast, is easily captured on film, and thus one finds it often in Japanese cinema. In prewar films, directors often set love scenes under the cover of night, because romantic love was not considered a proper topic for daytime scenes. The moon constituted an important element of nighttime scenes, acting as a witness who affirms the lovers' emotions. The moon also appears frequently in films as the companion of wanderers and travelers. One example of the use of the moon can be found in Imai Tadashi's *Muddy Waters* (*Nigorie*, 1953). The film, based on three short stories by Higuchi Ichiyō (1872–1896), focuses on the difficult lives of women during Japan's early modern period (late nineteenth century). One of the stories concerns the daughter of an impoverished former samurai family who is married to an elite bureaucrat. Dismayed at the emptiness of her marriage, the woman tries to find refuge in her parents' house, but they force her to return to her husband. When she leaves her parents' house, a bright moon shines high in the night sky. The woman hires a ricksha, only to discover that the driver is her old lover (figure 8.7). The two reminisce about the feelings they once had for one another and the happy days that they shared. The waxing moon is a most suitable background for these companions in misfortune, because even a sliver of moon eventually becomes a full moon.

Portraiture

While many Japanese painters dealt in natural subjects, there were also those who depicted human figures. When one compares the human figures in these portraits, like the one of Fujiwara Kamatari (figure 8.8) and those in the *emaki,* the latter frequently look rather sad, perhaps because of the bird's-eye perspective common in the genre. The figures in the portraits, in contrast, are viewed from the front and slightly below, conveying a sense of grandeur.

Several aspects of these portraits—the attitude and posture of the subjects, the orderly, almost geometrical sense of form, and the fact that the view is from below—bring to mind the films of Ozu Yasujirō. Although several of his earliest films have been lost, all of Ozu's extant works are consistently shot from a low vantage point. The placement of the lens is lower than that of someone sitting down, and often is from the perspective of someone who is lying down. Rarely does one find a person shot from above, as if Ozu regarded such a camera angle as insulting.

In a traditional Japanese house, one sits directly on tatami (straw mat) floors, rather than in chairs, and sleeps on a futon on the floor, rather than in a bed. This fact presents particular problems to Japanese directors. When a group of people are carrying on a conversation in a tatami room, they usually do not move from a seated position. In a room with tables and chairs, people may stand up or move around the room during a conversation. One person may be seated and another standing while they talk. This allows the director to present the cast in a variety of positions in relationship to one another, and thus to heighten the dramatic effect easily. In a tatami room, however, it would seem rude for one partner in a conversation to stand while the other sits, because it would appear as if the person standing were looking down on the seated person. Conversations set in tatami rooms tend to lack motion and movement. As a result, it is extremely difficult to create visual variations in such scenes, and they easily become slow paced and dull.

8.7 Imai Tadashi, *Muddy Waters* (*Nigorie*) (courtesy of the Japan Film Library Council).

As I explained in connection with the *emaki,* Mizoguchi Kenji took advantage of the openness of Japanese residential architecture and favored long, fluid shots that move seamlessly from room to room. This results in a heightened dramatic atmosphere, in which the actors could hardly remain in one seated position for long. In Ozu's films, one rarely finds scenes in which the actors are standing and moving within a room. This approach could easily become monotonous and flat, but Ozu gives beauty and interest to his movies by filming all actors from a set position. In the portrait, Fujiwara Kamatari sits in a tall, rigid position that expresses dignity, while Ozu's actors usually are relaxed and leaning forward. Both visual compositions have in common a calmness akin to that of geometric design. Ozu would carefully pose his actors, down to the angles of their heads and torsos, in order that everyone in the scene would assume the same posture. There is, however, no evidence that Ozu researched Japanese portraiture. Rather, the two artists likely came upon this common technique in their effort to display the human figure at its most beautiful.

8.8 Portrait of Fujiwara Kamatari, Japan, Kamakura period, fifteenth century (courtesy of the Cleveland Museum of Art, Leonard C. Hanna, Jr. Fund, 83.5).

Japanese Cinema and the Traditional Arts   177

Japanese filmmakers have also been inspired by the techniques of the Edo-period *ukiyo-e* (woodblock print). In contrast to artists of earlier centuries, the Edo printmakers portrayed a wide variety of subjects. In response to the varied tastes and interests of the mass audience of merchants, samurai, and so on, the *ukiyo-e* printmakers did portraits of courtesans of the pleasure quarters, actors of the *kabuki* theatre, as well as landscapes. Ordinary workers and erotic scenes were also popular subjects. These printmakers did not cater to the aristocracy or the moneyed classes. Rather, they aimed at a broad audience, by having publishers produce the prints in large quantities and sell them in shops. While earlier artists were obliged to adhere to certain orthodox styles and subjects, the *ukiyo-e* artists had to invent new techniques constantly in order to maintain their following. Even in their landscapes, the printmakers devised surprising and unique designs and perspectives. For example, Hokusai, in his *One Hundred Views of Mount Fuji* series, made the famous print that shows Mount Fuji rising up from between ocean waves. Another of the series has the mountain coming up from behind some woodcutters hard at work. Perhaps because this became such a familiar technique in *ukiyo-e,* Japanese filmmakers often expend energy creating similar visual compositions, which involve placing an object in the foreground of the scene. In the slang of Japanese movie sets, this is known as *"mido poji."* This term derives from the name of cinematographer Midorikawa Michio (abbreviated as Mido), who was active in the 1920s. He excelled at innovative camera positions (*poji*).

Mizoguchi's *The Life of Oharu* contains a good example of this type of deep focus shot. The heroine, Oharu, is found guilty of romantic involvement with a man from a lower class. As a result, she and her parents are banished from the capital. Mizoguchi shot the three retreating figures as they walk along the riverbank from beneath a bridge. This beautiful shot composition, with the bridge in the foreground and the three small figures in the distance, serves well in evoking the pathos of exile. The *ukiyo-e* prints of Hiroshige and others contain many examples of this type of view from beneath a bridge.

Yamanaka Sadao, a brilliant director of the thirties (most of whose films have, unfortunately, been lost), had a great fondness for *ukiyo-e* prints and often drew on them for inspiration. Notable is his skillful manipulation of contrasting foreground and background in deep focus shots. For example, he would shoot the roof of a large building in the foreground and have the tiny figures of actors fighting in the distance.

Ukiyo-e artists took great pains in their composition and the poses of their subjects. Some prints show a woman from behind, with her head turned just slightly so that the viewer can see a bit of her profile. With only the woman's attractive body and part of her head visible, the viewer is encouraged to imagine the beauty of the woman's face. The *ukiyo-e* printmakers also refined their portrayal of subtle details of the female figure, such as the nape of the neck (considered especially erotic in Japan), slightly mussed locks of hair on an otherwise perfect coif (a suggestion of sexuality), and the eroticism of certain facial expressions. These *ukiyo-e* aesthetics have influenced women since the Edo period. In the twentieth century, many actresses have emulated the poses of the women in *ukiyo-e*, and cinematographers have chosen camera angles reminiscent of *ukiyo-e* perspectives.

Another connection between *ukiyo-e* prints and Japanese cinema can be found in the portrayal of men and sexuality. In the world of *ukiyo-e*, artists did not show samurai in romantic situations. Confucianism did not regard romantic love in a positive light, and therefore brave, strong, and moral men were not supposed to be interested in sex and romance. The Edo-period audience for *ukiyo-e* prints, as well as the theatre, naturally clamored for romance and eroticism, but the heroes of such romantic prints and plays were beautiful but physically and emotionally weak men, who were often effeminate. Such characters were called *nimaime,* or second person, as opposed to a premier or main character, who would be manly and heroic. The men portrayed in *shunga* (erotic prints) belong to this *nimaime* group. Although they may be paying their partners, the *nimaime*'s approach to sex is not businesslike or cold. Their female partners therefore could also abandon themselves to erotic pleasure. Beauty in this type of print derives from the negation of the strength, authority, and masculinity of the samurai.

This distinction between heroic, masculine men and weak, beautiful ones persists in some Japanese films. Kurosawa, for example, always used masculine samurai types for his main characters. In contrast, Mizoguchi predominantly employed *nimaime* types, as in *Utamaro and His Five Women* (*Utamaro o meguru gonin no onna,* 1947), which portrays the famous *ukiyo-e* artist Kitagawa Utamaro. Mizoguchi focuses on Utamaro's arrest and persecution by authorities because of his *shunga* prints. Together, the films of Mizoguchi and Kurosawa represent the two extremes of male roles in Japan.

In a number of Mizoguchi's films, the director uses *ukiyo-e* prints to suggest sexual activity. Censorship laws strictly prohibited eroticism in film during Mizoguchi's career, and he could only refer to the explicit imagery of *shunga*. The influence of *shunga* can be seen in many movies of the 1970s and later, as with Ōshima Nagisa's *The Realm of the Senses* (*Ai no koriida*, 1976). From the 1970s through the 1980s, the Nikkatsu Studios produced many soft-core "Roman porn" movies. The films of popular director Kumashiro Tatsumi share with the *ukiyo-e* a stylized, romantic approach. Examples of this are his *Sayuri Ichijo — Moist Desire* (*Ichijō sayuri — nureta yokujō*, 1972), *The Four-and-a-Half-Mat Room in Back — Soft, Secret Skin* (*Yojohan fusuma no urabari — shinobi hada*, 1974), *Street of Joy* (*Akasen Tamanoi — nukeraremasu*, 1974), and *The Red-Haired Girl* (*Akai kami no onna*, 1979). All of these films center on men and women to whom only the pursuit of erotic love has meaning. The films delicately portray the psychology of sexual partners and the ways they seek to stimulate one another emotionally. This quality imparts a certain sentiment and artistry to the films, in contrast to much of American and European erotic cinema, which shows mechanical, emotionless sex in an exaggerated manner.

Tradition and the West

What explains the presence of traditional elements in some Japanese films and their absence in others? This can be traced to differences in generations of directors, their education, and exposure to art. Many non-Japanese people think of traditional Japanese arts as central to the cultural milieux of contemporary Japan, while this is not, in fact, the case. Schools and universities have taught only Western music for the past century.[2] In art classes as well, teachers instruct the students in methods of Western painting and sculpture, not in ink brush painting or *Nihonga* (Japanese-style painting). In Japanese high schools, the drama clubs perform Western-style drama, rather than *kabuki*. Rarely do students read *kabuki* plays in class. Japanese playwrights adopted Western-style theatrical methods about eighty years ago, and now they are the mainstream.

In the late nineteenth century, government officials introduced Western art and music into school curricula. They thought that, in order to resist the Western powers and to make Japan a strong nation, it was necessary not only to learn Western science and government, but also to abandon "worthless and barbaric" Japanese arts and replace them with Western ones. Even during the Second World War, when Japanese nationalism reached its height, this policy did not change fundamentally. This is because the leaders themselves had learned Scottish and Irish folk melodies with Japanese lyrics in elementary school and felt nostalgia for such songs. The militarists chose war songs with Western melodies. In the visual arts as well, the militarists found Western techniques more useful for propaganda posters and publications. The Japanese visual arts tend to be elegant, stylized, meditative, and sometimes unabashedly erotic, and therefore unsuitable for rousing enthusiasm for battle. Traditional painters were commissioned to do illustrations for wartime publications and posters, but they failed to create effective works. Painters who worked in oil and who used the techniques of realism found much greater success.

From the late nineteenth century, Japanese artists, musicians, and actors looked to the West for inspiration. As a result, contemporary Japanese are more familiar with Western painting, music, and theatre than with Japanese art. For example, in Kurosawa's *Dreams* (*Yume*, 1990), the episode starring Martin Scorsese centers on Van Gogh. To a Japanese audience, the inclusion of Van Gogh does not seem exotic or unfamiliar, because Van Gogh is better known to many Japanese than most Japanese painters.

The fact that art education in Japanese public schools has become thoroughly Westernized does not mean that Japanese peoplc have become Westernized psychologically or emotionally. Traditional Japanese arts have not, moreover, disappeared from the scene. Although the traditional arts have been excluded from the formal classroom, a wide variety thrive in contemporary Japan. Parents teach their children to play the bamboo flute (*fue*) and drums (*taiko*) that are an integral part of festivals. Older geisha teach younger ones the *shamisen, koto,* and ballad singing used to accompany dance. Many people take private lessons in traditional music. In addition, *kabuki* is performed regularly, and traditional painters command respect and prices comparable to that of artists who work in oil.

In the final analysis, however, it is Western music that provides the Japanese the basis for their understanding of music. Exposure to traditional music tends to be sporadic. Scholars have, however, pointed out the fact that much of the music composed in Japan now contains elements of traditional Japanese music, although this may be unconscious on the Japanese composers' part. Every Japanese artist is unconsciously influenced by the traditional aesthetics and outlooks that are an integral part of Japanese culture. Traditional-style rooms contain an alcove, or *tokonoma,* in which a hanging scroll of Japanese painting or calligraphy is displayed. Designs and patterns derived from *Nihonga* adorn women's kimonos. The kites that children fly at New Year's are decorated with pictures of warriors in the style of prints popular from the seventeenth century. Yet even these vestiges of traditional aesthetics are becoming increasingly rare.

In the 1920s, some Japanese elementary school art teachers possessed liberal ideas about teaching. Rather than having their students simply copy orthodox models, as was prescribed by the Ministry of Education, they encouraged their students to draw or paint whatever they wanted. This ran counter to the practice of traditional arts, and was considered a progressive, Western method. Kurosawa himself was heavily influenced by one such teacher in elementary school. Kurosawa was a painter for a time, and even after becoming a film director, he would do paintings of certain scenes and show them to his crew. His style, influenced by Fauvism, features strong, angular forms that seem to jut out from the confines of the canvas. Kurosawa's paintings have much in common with his films. Kurosawa dislikes confining the actor to the limits of the frame; his actors move with great vigor and dynamism, threatening to burst out from the edges of the screen, as *Ikiru* (1952) and *Seven Samurai* (*Shichinin no samurai,* 1954) illustrate.

In 1933, at age seventeen, Ichikawa Kon started working at an animated film studio. He studied Walt Disney and the Fleischer Brothers' movies[3] and made his own animated shorts. Eventually, he became an assistant director of dramatic films and, in 1947, began making his own movies. Ichikawa's exposure in his youth to Disney characters and Popeye clearly influenced his approach to filmmaking. This is evident in his simplification and exaggeration of forms and of actions. Ichikawa's *A Crowded Streetcar* (*Man'in densha,* 1957) concerns modern society's emphasis on uniformity and denial of individualism. In this film, Ichikawa deliberately directed his cast to move in a machinelike manner and to keep blank, frozen expressions on their faces. He had them perform like puppets, a technique learned from animated film.

The older generation of Japanese film directors came in closer contact with the traditional arts than do younger directors. Mizoguchi as a youth briefly apprenticed to a painter of kimono designs. Subsequently, he studied oil paintings for a year and worked on the sets for the first comic opera performed by Italian performers in Japan. At the same time, he was a fan of traditional Japanese theatre.

Ozu came from a family that had deep ties with the traditional arts. Although Ozu did not have formal training in Japanese painting, he was quite proficient. He was also a devotee of the *kabuki* actor Kikugoro VI and even made a documentary about him. As a young man, however, Ozu had been a fan of American film. At home, Ozu lived in thoroughly traditional Japanese-style surroundings, while in public he wore fashionable Western clothes.

Kurosawa studied oil painting as a youth and was still in his teens when he gained recognition as a professional painter. He could not make a living from painting alone, so when he was twenty-six years old, he applied for a job as an assistant director at a movie studio. Film director Yamamoto Kajirō, who interviewed Kurosawa for the position, later commented that he was impressed with Kurosawa's knowledge of Japanese art. Kurosawa also had an interest in traditional theatre, especially *nō*. Mizoguchi and Ozu, in contrast, were fond of *kabuki*.

Although *nō* and *kabuki* are both types of theatrical performance, they bear a deep connection to the visual arts. This is not simply because the costumes and props are traditional in style, but also because the highly stylized poses of the actors find their basis in traditional aesthetics. In *kabuki*, these important exaggerated poses are called *kimaru*. The *ukiyo-e* artists were especially fond of capturing these moments.

Various aspects of the *nō* theatre have influenced film directors. When Kurosawa was making *Throne of Blood* (*Kumonosujō*, 1957), he instructed the actors to imitate the expressions of *nō* masks suitable to each of their roles (figure 8.9). Similarly, Mizoguchi employed different aspects of the *nō* theatre in his 1953 *Ugetsu* (*Ugetsu monogatari*), especially in the scene where the beautiful ghost (played by Kyō Machiko) appears in the abandoned, rotting mansion. First, the open room that faces onto an exterior, wall-less corridor and garden coincides in style with the *nō* stage. The corridor, in both the *nō* theatre and in Mizoguchi's film, represents a passageway that links this world and the realm of the spirits. The gorgeous kimono worn by Kyō Machiko is actually a *nō* costume belonging to the head of a *nō* school. The music that emanates from the next room when Kyō Machiko begins dancing is that of the *nō* theatre. Mizoguchi asked composer Hayasaka Fumio to use the flute and drum of the *nō* theatre in his composition of this music. Because Japanese learned Western music in school, almost all film scores were Western in style, from the time of the talkies on. However, since Mizoguchi's successful use of this mysterious, beautiful sound in *Ugetsu,* various directors have included traditional Japanese music in their scores.

Mizoguchi was a greater devotee of *kabuki* and the *bunraku* puppet theatre than he was of *nō*. The inspiration of *kabuki* and *bunraku* is evident in many of his films. Two of these—*Woman of Osaka* (*Naniwa onna,* 1940), the story of a *bunraku* puppeteer, and *The Life of an Actor* (*Geidō ichidai otoko,* 1941), which concerns a *kabuki* actor—have unfortunately been lost. One can see Mizoguchi's use of the traditional theatre in a number of his other movies, such as *The Story of the Last Chrysanthemum, The Life of Oharu,* and *A Story from Chikamatsu.* The beautiful, stylized *kimaru* poses of *kabuki* actors are in evidence in these films.

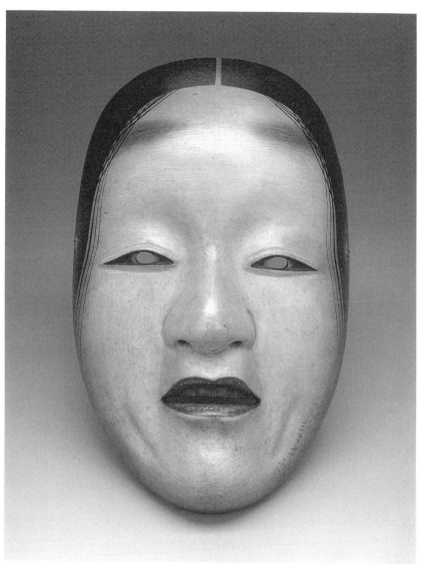

8.9 Deme Mitsunori (d. 1723), *Nō Mask of the Shakumi Type*, Japan, Edo period, eighteenth century, wood with polychrome (courtesy of the Museum of Fine Arts, Boston, William Sturgis Bigelow Collection, 11.5955).

While Mizoguchi's films are examples of the imaginative use of *kabuki* theatre, the influence of *kabuki* can also be seen in the ubiquitous period films (*jidaigeki*, or historical dramas). They feature stereotypical, exaggerated acting, flashy sets, and gaudy makeup and costumes. In his *Rashomon* and *Seven Samurai*, Kurosawa consciously broke away from the stale *jidai-*

geki. Not only did he present realistic sets and costumes; he also directed his actors not to assume the beautiful, stylized poses typical of *jidaigeki.*

Two differing approaches to tradition may be instructive. Kinugasa Teinosuke, the director of *Gate of Hell* (*Jigokumon,* 1953) and numerous other *jidaigeki,* had his actors look through the camera finder in order to figure out ways to attain the best *kimaru* pose within the frame of the camera lens. In contrast, Kurosawa, since *Seven Samurai,* shot scenes with several cameras at once. The cast did not know which take would actually be used and therefore became less conscious of the camera and moved more freely, which resulted in powerful performances. If Kinugasa's method is a traditional one that places emphasis on the beauty of forms, then Kurosawa's approach finds its conceptual basis in modern Western oil painting, which goes against decorative and stylized approaches and attempts to give expression to that which comes from within. However, it would be a gross oversimplification to call Kinugasa a traditional director and Kurosawa a Western-style director. Kinugasa was the first director in Japan to create a Western-style avant-garde film, as his *A Crazy Page* (also called *A Page of Madness; Kurutta ippeiji,* 1926) demonstrates (figure 8.10). Kurosawa was heavily influenced by Japa-

8.10 Kinugasa Teinosuke, *A Crazy Page* (also called *A Page of Madness; Kurutta ippeiji,* 1926) (courtesy of the Japan Film Library Council).

nese tradition, as can be seen in his affirmative treatment of the samurai spirit and his emulation of many aspects of the *nō* theatre.

It is misleading to label Japanese directors simply "traditional" or "Western." This is because their films reflect not only the riches of many cultures of the world, but also elements of a wide variety of Japanese traditions from different ages.

Notes

1. "Bird and flower" painting denotes a kind of Chinese painting first established during the Tang period, and which grew in importance during the Song, Yuan, and Ming dynasties. This term is used loosely to include "paintings wholly devoted to flowers, flowering branches, insects, butterflies and similar subjects" (Hugo Munsterberg, *Dictionary of Chinese and Japanese Art* [New York: Hacker Art Books, 1981], p. 15).

2. Only Tōkyō Geijutsu Daigaku has departments of Japanese painting and music.

3. Max and Dave Fleischer were the creators of such animated characters as Popeye and Betty Boop.

GENROKU CHŪSHINGURA
AND THE PRIMACY OF
PERCEPTION

BY D. WILLIAM DAVIS

C
H
A
P
T
E
R
9

Donald Keene, writing about Mayama Seika's monumental search for the historical forty-seven *rōnin*, or masterless samurai, was obviously not aware of Mizoguchi Kenji's 1941 film adaptation of Mayama's stage play. Professor Keene is quick to distinguish the scholarly historical intent of Mayama from the Chūshingura vulgarizations that were a staple of the Japanese screen from its birth.[2] This is similar to a literary critic defending the historical respectability of, say, Gore Vidal, opposing his work to the romanticized whitewash of Ford's *Young Mr. Lincoln*.

Mizoguchi's film, however, is different. In its own way, it is just as austere and uncompromising in its visual style as Mayama's is in its literary style. Moreover, this issue of historical discrimination—the need to sort out the authentic from the meretricious, the need to see clearly—is one which is explicitly taken up in Mizoguchi's adaptation of Mayama's play. It is taken up in the leading character of Ōishi, who deliberately vacillates in his plans for revenge to lend an appearance of

The excessive attention to historical detail which is sometimes obtrusive in Genroku chūshingura *is certainly not true of the films on the subject, which follow oft-tried patterns of good and bad guys fighting and eliminate the shadings that Mayama was so careful to establish.*

(DONALD KEENE)[1]

weakness and dissolution. There is also a strong element of visual discrimination in Mizoguchi's version, a tendency to use film techniques that inscribe a Japanese way of seeing. Specifically, Mizoguchi employs visual cues that appropriate the perceptual experience of *kare sansui* dry landscape gardens, the perspective system of *Yamato-e* painting, and other classical Japanese design features.[3] *Genroku chūshingura* is an "episode film," in that its primary interest lies not in an epic chain of cause and effect, but in an episodic attendance to the primacy of perception, to borrow a famous title from Maurice Merleau-Ponty.

Genroku chūshingura, made on the eve of Japan's entry into the Pacific War, is a model of both virtuosity and restraint. The virtuosity of its cinematography, setting, and acting restrains the headlong trajectory of its narrative and the stock character of its heroes. By the time Mizoguchi made his version of the legendary story of the forty-seven *rōnin*, there were already scores of filmed Chūshingura renditions.[4] Before that, the story had been commemorated countless times in *rōkyoku* and *naniwa bushi* songs, in *kōdan* ballads, and in the *kabuki* and *bunraku* puppet theatre.[5] Because of this overwhelming intertextuality, Mizoguchi could assume in his audience a bewildering array of preconceptions and connotations about the myth of the loyal forty-seven, and so re-present the tale as an exercise in perceptual renewal.

To presume to deliver all the offspring of pregnant connotations in *Genroku chūshingura* is pure arrogance, similar to attempting an exhaustive analysis of the Easter passion of Christ or the story of Passover. But these analogies are useful to bring out the manner in which *Genroku chūshingura* sacramentalizes Japanese tradition and Japanese perception. Mizoguchi could take for granted a familiarity with so many elements of plot, character, allusion, and allegory, thus freeing him to concentrate his energies, and his camera, on the problem of "defamiliarizing" the Chūshingura tale. This takes place on two registers or aspects: a thematic aspect which is related to the film's characterization of Ōishi as the ideal samurai, and a perceptual aspect which directly guides or trains the spectator's attention to specifically Japanese forms of contemplation. Here Mizoguchi's style invokes the sacred by means of interlocking techniques, like framing, camera movement, and long takes. This sacramental style encourages spatial and tactile explorations of the Genroku world (a period of intensely creative urban culture which flowered between 1688 and 1704). By abandoning oneself to these imaginary explorations, the spectator learns to perceive in a way consonant with traditional Japanese aesthetics and religion.

These "training exercises" in Genroku perception encourage familiarity

D . W I L L I A M   D A V I S

and facility with formal design and behavior from a remarkable period of Japanese artistic renaissance. They build from the bottom up an awareness of the modularity of space as it is organized by Japanese interior design and an experience of how collective spectatorship can afford clues to deciphering a social situation. The perceptual provides a foundation for thematic lessons in discerning real from apparent motivations in specific situations. Style in *Genroku chūshingura* functions to plunge us deep into a perceptual experience of the Genroku world in the hope that spectators may become comfortable with its ways of seeing and perhaps take with them the desire to practice this way of seeing when the film is over. This is the intended effect of the film, as a *kokusaku* ("national policy") project: a nationalistic promotion of the classical Japanese heritage to fire up the war effort. Mizoguchi was not alone in the effort to render classical Japanese arts and ethics as a monument to Japanese identity.[6] The function of the film's style, however, as a training exercise in indigenous perception is revealing in its own right.

Chūshingura is a vendetta story whose culmination is complicated by the legal repercussions of the act of vengeance by the *rōnin*. Due to his ceremonial inexperience, the Lord of Akō loses his temper and wounds Kira, the master of ceremonies, in the palace of the *shōgun*. This is a capital offense, and Akō is sentenced to commit ritual suicide. His estate is confiscated, and his now masterless samurai vow revenge against Kira. The *rōnin* are led by Akō's erstwhile treasurer, Ōishi Kuranosuke, who must deal with the dilemma of taking the law into his own hands and the obligation he is under as a samurai to avenge his dead master. Where is his primary loyalty—with the *shōgun* or with his master? Is he bound by the laws of the land or by his personal relationship to his lord?

Ōishi's dilemma is made more difficult by public speculation over whether, and how, the Akō vendetta will be carried out. The land has been at peace for one hundred years, and there is an awareness that martial discipline in the samurai classes is at a low ebb. Ōishi and his faithful *rōnin* must go underground for two years, pretending to lose themselves in drink and dissolution, before they vindicate both themselves and the *bushidō* code that binds them with a brilliant strike against Kira on the anniversary of the Lord of Akō's death. The story structure and characterization pose questions about the codes that govern samurai ethics in a time when those ethics seem most anachronistic. Chūshingura asks the key question of what it means to be a true samurai when the very necessity of the samurai institution is in doubt.

Mizoguchi's insistence on the most expensive and authentic period detail in materials, artifacts, and acting style is legendary. But what sets this film apart from other period epics is the camerawork and editing used by Mizo-guchi to explore the space that he so painstakingly constructed. It is a percep-tual experience, not merely a recording of historical authenticity, that Mizo-guchi sought to convey. The images are constructed in a way that prioritizes, and sometimes makes problematic, the process of perceiving. Moreover, these images go by in an almost seamless flow, arising "naturally" from the serenity of setting and design.

Genroku chūshingura is a masterpiece because it transcends drama, or rather because it brings drama into a perceptual realm that seems to have little to do with its overt subject matter. Although *Genroku chūshingura* is a deadly serious historical tract, Mizoguchi plays games with our perceptual apprehension of space and objects at a local level. He asks that we focus our attention on things that are not directly relevant to the story, which attenu-ates the narrative but concentrates the style. In so doing, we involuntarily come to regard the film as a whole, as well as the legend of Chūshingura, with an intensive aestheticism that merges with the sacramental.

Garden of Stone

One can think of *Genroku chūshingura* as a story of perceptual discovery, because the issues with which the characters struggle are clearly exemplified in the style of the film, which in turn is determined by spatial articulations in architecture and landscape. To illustrate, consider the opening sequence of the film, which concentrates on various points of observation on Asano's at-tack. The opening sequence offers a good example of how spatial articula-tions can conceal or reveal social realities. A motif of circularity governs the staging and shooting of the opening act of violence, ironically the only physi-cal conflict to appear in Part 1 of the film. Asano's attack on Kira initiates a disruption of a harmonious state whose tremors shake the entire country and reverberate for centuries. Techniques which encourage perceptual contem-plation are correlative to the social discriminations necessary for honorable judgments in a time of ethical uncertainty.

Mizoguchi presents Asano's attack on Kira so as to favor Asano, but not so much as to allow the spectator to identify with Asano by sharing either his optical or emotional point of view. By using a combination of eccentric character blocking and misleading eyelines, Mizoguchi is able to firmly an-chor our conviction that Kira provoked Asano, but is also able to avoid a corresponding approval of Asano's outburst. Furthermore, the circular motif that develops out of the subsequent pandemonium lends a sense of calculation and containment that is consistent with Ōishi's (and the film's) deliberate style.

In a medium shot, we see Kira bitterly denouncing the "ignorance and rudeness" of his colleague to another member of the court, Lord Kajikawa. Kira is talking about Lord Asano, of course, and his agitation becomes more intense as he spits out his belief that Asano is a committee member "in name only, unable to carry out the various functions" according to the appropriate forms and rituals. In the absence of opportunities for valor on the battlefield, a high-ranking samurai could only show his cultivation through mastery of courtly niceties. To be accused of barbarity in this regard was cruel gossip indeed.

The surprise is that this is not gossip at all, but open slander. As Kira's barrage of ridicule mounts, he looks to the left, away from the camera and Lord Kajikawa, with unbounded contempt. Then the two men move out of frame left to reveal a small figure crouching in the shadows no more than twenty feet away. We suddenly realize that Asano has heard Kira's entire tirade against him, and moreover that Kira must have been looking toward Asano because of the direction of his glance. Kira's invective to Lord Kajikawa is retroactively revealed as not aristocratic gossip, but a direct slap in the face, a deliberate insult to one whose stature and livelihood depends on his ceremonial relationships with *shōgun* and emperor (figure 9.1).

Rather than heightening Asano's emotional humiliation, Mizoguchi maintains his camera distance on the outraged figure and even veils his face in shadow. We cannot identify with Asano's emotional response due to the delay in the revelation of the deliberate, personal quality of Kira's remarks, the medium-long distance on Asano's figure, and the insufficient lighting of his face. These barriers to identification lend an impersonal significance to the episode: an act whose importance lies less in its psychological causes than in its social consequences. The narrative problem of motivating Asano's assault and subsequent vendetta is established, but at the same time it is depersonalized, drained of psychological imperatives, so as to encourage reflection not only on the commission of a personal injustice but also on the nature of inninjustice in a particular social formation.[7]

That just two shots can be invested with such dramatic possibilities is testament to the care (and duration) of Mizoguchi's decoupage. How does the rest of the introductory scene encourage perceptual concentration at the expense of narrative legibility? The style of the opening scene accentuates the explosive violation of the contemplative peace that ordinarily obtains in an imperial house. Working against this, however, is a motif of circularity—in camera movements around the periphery of the courtyard and in editing pat-

9.1 Mizoguchi Kenji, *The Loyal Rōnin of the Genroku Era* (*Genroku chūshingura*, 1941–1942) (courtesy of Shōchiku Co., Ltd.).

terns—that evokes a sense of quiescence and resignation. This implacable stasis persists throughout the film, adding to the quiet calculation, claustrophobia, and even paranoia that stands in for overt onscreen action. The perceptual qualities of the opening sequence evoke a duality of plenitude and potential excess—a duality graphically figured in the depiction of the *kare sansui* dry landscape occupying the center of the space.

This dual function is contained in the opening shot of the rock garden (3.a; see page 194), framed by two posts of the palace veranda. With painstaking slowness, the camera tracks rightward past two or three of the posts before swiveling right to show the Kira-Asano interchange. This is the canonical way of experiencing (i.e., walking around) a *kare sansui* garden, like the famous Ryōanji in Kyoto, which synthesizes the contemplative practice of Zen Buddhism with the design principles of *shoin* (aristocratic) architecture. The garden itself consists simply of pure white gravel raked into straight rows, a textured plenum punctuated intermittently by the black posts on its surface.

This setup clearly shows a concern to reproduce the *kanshō*, or *zakan*, a central compositional view of the garden "suggestive of a picture and suitable for long and studied viewing."[8] The *kanshō* evokes the Zen practice of pro-

9.2 Mizoguchi Kenji, *The Loyal Rōnin of the Genroku Era* (courtesy of Shōchiku Co., Ltd.).

longed, intensified perception as a means to heightened consciousness, and the posts which intermittently frame our view call attention to the intervals/relationships between objects, called *ma*. The measurement of *ma* is the central principle of traditional domestic architecture in the Muromachi period. Specifically, the intervals between the posts are called *ken* (written with the same character as *ma*), whose distance of around six feet eventually was standardized at 1.8 meters, the standard length of tatami mats and of all other measurements (columns, beams, *shōji* screens, etc.) necessary for building a Japanese house.[9] The fact that the majority of shots taken around the palace use oblique angles that separate the action planes with the garden between them shows a solicitation of our discernment of intervals, of the relationships *between* things as well as of things in themselves (figure 9.2).

The moving camera also privileges the proprioceptive, or bodily, aspect of perception. A static "view" is established and held, then everything moves in vertiginous flux, only to resolve itself again into a new tableau open for perceptual scrutiny. There is a demand for the viewer's perceptual participation in order to get involved in *Genroku chūshingura*'s intrigues and second-guessing. When we accept this, we find our perceptual arsenal and our endurance strengthened. This is consistent with the film's ideological project:

Genroku chūshingura *and the Primacy of Perception*   *193* the training of a certain perceptual facility with traditional Japanese forms and designs.

As a sequence of shots, the opening attack forms a relatively self-contained cell, a circular structure in time as well as space:

1. (Credits)
2. Stasis: oblique shot of ceremonies
3. Long take: shattering of perceptual plenitude
    a. Rock garden: tracking right
    b. Kira insult
    c. Revelation and attack of Asano: tracking left
4. Match-on-action: Kira circles left
5. Straight cut: Kira's flight, circles left
                        (Cut on Tsunatoyo's glance)
6. Long take, crane in: Asano's struggle in foreground; Kira goes out in background
7. "Scroll-shot": tracking left
8. Stasis: high angle shot of interrogation room

The sequence clearly shows a balance between moments of stasis at the beginning and end, punctuated by the rising action of the attack itself (3.c), the chase, and the denouement. This temporal structure, however, is determined by the spatial orchestration of the action around the periphery of the garden.

Consider the way in which the camera moves around the palace (see figure 9.3): First, the camera is positioned obliquely to the corners of the structure so that two planes of action are simultaneously visible. With one exception (shot 4), the action is staged in two places at once, a foreground and a background veranda. The action is intensified by the "empty" space of the garden between them. Next, the tracking and cutting of the first three shots are motivated by Kira's hasty retreat from Asano. Although the first tracking movement around corner #2 follows Asano in his headlong assault on Kira, Asano is actually chasing Kira, who motivates Asano's and the camera's movement. When Asano catches up, drawing his sword with a blood-curdling yell, the shot breaks into a match-on-action to shot 2, elaborating the view of the attack from Kira's side. In this second shot, as in the first, the camera is placed obliquely to corner #2 in the same place as its initial position looking across corner #1.

Again, Kira quickly moves offscreen left, but this time a straight cut to shot 3 anticipates Kira's arrival into the space (rather than tracking with

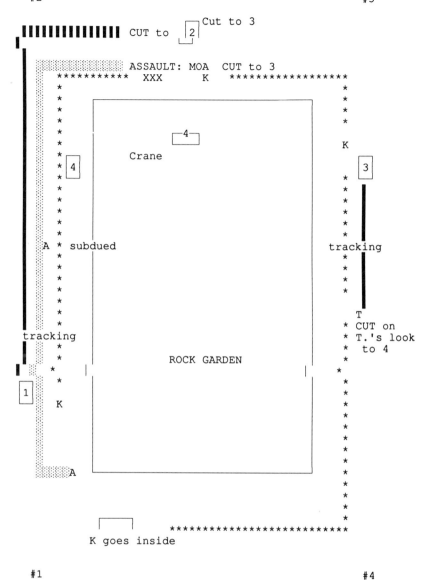

9.3 *The Loyal Rōnin of the Genroku Era*: opening attack.

Kira's movement). The angle of shot 3 corresponds to corner #3 as shots 1 and 2 correspond to corners #1 and #2 (i.e., showing two planes of action taking place at oblique angles to one another and separated by the space of the rock garden). In shot 3, the camera briefly tracks along the corridor with Kira, but is interrupted by the presence of a new character, Tsunatoyo, who steps into the frame and momentarily controls the angle of view. Rather than following Kira, a cut to shot 4 puts us inside the garden looking in at Asano's hysterical struggle. This is in clear violation of the circular tracking and cutting pattern initiated by Kira's flight around the courtyard.

With a complicated crane movement, the camera follows Asano as he moves, kicking and screaming, around corner #2 in a counterclockwise direction, opposite that of Kira. The struggling Asano moves left, while the camera swivels around with him until it is positioned looking straight down the corridor toward corner #1, where the entire incident began. Since in almost every shot Kira is shown scurrying out of frame left, and since he has already gone around three corners, it is no surprise to see him in shot 4 shuffled into the background and out of sight through *fusuma* sliding doors. Meanwhile, the sputtering Asano lies on his face in the foreground while an official reprimands him and asks for his ceremonial robe.

The pattern of circular camera movements and shot changes established from the outset is therefore fulfilled, in an unexpected way. What was apparently a violation of the circular pattern in the cut on Tsunatoyo's look turns out to be just a shortcut to the original place where everything began. Kira's insult takes place in corner #1, where he eventually disappears after running around the entire periphery of the courtyard. This gives the episode spatial as well as narrative closure—but with some differences. First, there is no oblique angle that segregates two planes of action by means of the empty garden space. Asano's arrest and Kira's disappearance are separate planes of action, but they are spatially continuous. Second, the frantic movement of characters and camera have subsided by the end of shot 4, as if the initial camera position inside the garden has a cauterizing effect on the rapid lateral tracking movements of earlier setups. The circularity and closure of this sequence is hardly reassuring, however; the style evokes finality, but also futility. There is the sense that this was a disaster waiting to happen, an inevitable paroxysm borne of long, steady, implacable repression.

If we must specify the precise moment of explosion, we would have to choose the match-on-action device which heightens the intensity of the assault (shot 3). This is important in light of Noël Burch's contention that Mizoguchi's tendency to use "centripetal" camera movements is a sustained challenge to the proscenium-like frontality of Western codes of camera/figure placement.[10] The match-on-action is a privileged *departure* from the norms of Mizoguchi's style, which accounts for its accentuating function here.

In Western editing codes, the match-on-action is a nearly infallible way of smoothing over a potential disruption in the spatial flow; in *Genroku chūshingura,* it intensifies the disruption initiated by Asano's attack. While viewers assimilate the revelation of Asano's presence and infer the deliberateness of Kira's insult, they are confronted with a sudden shattering of the stately serenity of the opening moments. The assault itself, the match-on-action, the sudden flooding of multiple planes with shouting, milling samurai—all add up to a perceptual barrage whose motivation is not psychological, but social. What kind of society is it where a breach of etiquette causes the disintegration of the social fabric?

Because the perceptual plenitude of the opening moments is so fragile, we expect further violent disruptions. But they are not forthcoming, and this conveys an edginess, a heightened perceptual vigilance in the expectation of other paroxysms of repressed passion.

A change of location completes the sequence in a sort of coda to the actual attack and shows the respective places where Kira and Asano are taken. A characteristic tracking shot of Kira being hurried through the back rooms of the palace is a good example of what Burch calls a "scroll shot," a successive interpenetration of spatial modules intermittently blocked by latticework, *shōji* screens, and pillars.[11] This shot recalls the credit sequence, a traveling series of landscape images, as well as the delicate rightward tracking movement in the garden inside the palace. The modularity-in-motion of the scroll shot underscores the importance of the emptiness at the center of intervals, relations, and measurements. Staging the action on separate planes requires a double vision, as in Asano's attack on Kira, and the scroll shot similarly splits our attention from the primary narrative event by intermittently blocking it from view.

Finally, a high-angle shot on the place of Asano's interrogation completes the sequence. Structurally, the shot brackets the very first shot of the film, a static oblique angle on some imperial ceremonies. The interrogation room is composed using parallel perspective; that is, two vanishing points define the perspective of the large room in the style of medieval Japanese paintings of the *Tale of Genji* and other classical works (note figure 7.2). The structural and spatial symmetricality of the sequence gives it a closed, hieratic quality consistent with its dual function of initiating the narrative trajectory and providing a pretext for an indigenous perceptual inscription.[12]

In summary, the opening sequence of *Genroku chūshingura* is anomalous in its spectacular burst of passion and violent action, but its circular structure telegraphs the subsequent containment of chaos through perceptual concentration. Hollywood films domesticate the irrational through the proposal and eventual solution of a narrative enigma; *Genroku chūshingura* does it through the displacement of narrative by perceptual, aesthetic, and religious contemplation. Style serves narrative in Hollywood, but in *Genroku chūshingura* style renders narrative peripheral, partly because the narrative is already so familiar to Japanese audiences. The primacy of perception is fully established in the opening sequence and invites the perceptual experience of the Genroku world. By exploring spatial arrangements more than character psychology, our perception is both constrained and opened up, and we begin to realize that in the realm of Genroku ethics, as in aesthetics, less is more.

What kind of perceptual experience, then, does the film invite us to have in Mizoguchi's Genroku world? More than anything else, our perceptions are solicited by the slowness and gravity of monumental evocations. The imagination is not sufficiently quickened by the task of puzzling together the cause and effect of the overall narrative chain, and Japanese audiences know the story by heart anyway. We are left then, with a critical appreciation of ritual exchanges, objets d'art, interior design, architecture, and the very space of the Genroku era.

Not surprisingly, the reversal of the priority of narrative over style has a political significance. As David Bordwell writes of the narrational strategies of revolutionary Soviet cinema: "The conventionality of the large-scale narrative articulations promotes a moment-by-moment 'microattention' to the unfolding *syuzhet* [or plot]. . . . The task is to make these givens vivid, or as the Soviet directors were fond of saying, *perceptible*."[13] A similar process is at work in *Genroku chūshingura*, except that the "microattention" demanded of us by Mizoguchi is perceptual rather than narrational. That is to say, in this film the perceptual *is* the narrational, and this is the film's nationalistic mission. The "default" back to perceptual style from narrative comprehension presumes a normative status for narrative characterization and causal relations that *Genroku chūshingura* aims to challenge. Even so, the slowness of the film arising from its narrative attenuation is, to say the least, difficult.

Ultimately, the perceptual invitation offered by *Genroku chūshingura* calls the pertinence of "drama" into question. The demands and pleasures of this film are mostly extradramatic. There are stories in such forms, but usually they are pretexts for other kinds of artistic or spiritual activities (e.g., ritual as community consolidation). The traditional Japanese forms and designs beckon like forgotten ancestors, and the gate through which we enter is perceptual.

D . W I L L I A M   D A V I S

By what techniques and to what ends does Mizoguchi open up our perception? One side of this is the "poverty" of narrative, action, and drama. More positively, Mizoguchi uses interlocking techniques of framing, camera movement, and the long take to encourage spatial and tactile exploration of the Genroku world. In abandoning oneself to these explorations, the spectator learns a mode of perception that is consonant with traditional Japanese aesthetics and religion.

Take for instance Mizoguchi's "flying" crane shots. These shots propel us straight up into the air as much as thirty or forty feet, affording a bird's-eye view on the action below. Given the preponderance of interior setups and modular spaces, these crane shots have quite a liberating quality. Another reason for this quality is the way in which these shots transcend boundaries—fences, curtains, and walls—that modularize the space below (figure 9.4). Finally, these shots are reminiscent of the high parallel perspective found in classical screen paintings.

According to Margaret Hagen, a perceptual psychologist, the perspective system used by *Yamato-e* classical painting is marked by aerial views that combine a station point distance of infinity (there is no vanishing point in these pictures) with perspective lines that are parallel (figure 9.5).[14] This contrasts with European "natural" perspective which uses a middle-distance station point with converging lines of perspective. The very great height of the station point lends a "God's-eye" view that is impartial and detached. It also necessitates the depiction of roofless and wall-less buildings in order to show any human activity, as in the anonymous Edo-period paintings of *rakuchū-rakugai* (figure 9.6). Unlike the scientific reproduction of optical perspective in the Renaissance,

> the Japanese artist is not placed by perspective in the composition of the picture, nor is the observer. The work of art created is a separate entity unto itself, an object of contemplation, not an extension of the self. A Japanese composition does not depict a personal, momentary view through a window, subject to change from the slightest of observer movements.[15]

Yamato-e paintings connect historically to garden aesthetics: in the Heian period a monk named En'en used *Yamato-e* scroll paintings as source material for his garden designs; Sesshū, the most innovative ink painter of the Muromachi period, also designed stone gardens which "put to practice the precepts of a style that discovers five distinct colors in the gradations

9.4 *The Loyal Rōnin of the Genroku Era* (courtesy of Shōchiku Co., Ltd.).

of monochrome black ink . . . a strongly Japanized version of a Chinese tradition." [16]

We can reasonably assume that Mizoguchi wished to pay homage to the technical hallmarks of classical Japanese painting because of his considerable training as a painter, and because his crane shots simply look a lot like these paintings. But these flying crane shots may have a more important role to play than mere citation. If Hagen is correct in assigning to this perspective system a removal of both painter and observer from the depicted scene, these shots may function as perceptual anomalies with respect to Mizoguchi's other techniques that so strenuously solicit the observer's activity. If these shots express or embody a "theological" self-sufficiency, they are consistent with the overall ideological project of the film but inconsistent with the ongoing engagement of Mizoguchi's techniques with the spectator's perceptual faculties.

As with other kinds of camera movement, the flying crane shot always moves with deliberate slowness, directing our attention to the unfolding transformation of vision rather than to the sensation of movement as such. One of the best examples is a shot of a grief-stricken vassal who meets Lord Asano at his place of suicide (scene 7). A high-angle crane shot along a wall shows Asano approaching, then descends and stops as Asano greets his loyal

D. WILLIAM DAVIS

9.5 *Horse Race at the Kamo Shrine,* Japan, Edo period, six-fold screen (courtesy of the Cleveland Museum of Art, Purchase from the J. H. Wade Fund, 76.96).

vassal. He gets ready to step through a gate in the wall, leaving his vassal behind. As he goes through, the camera moves straight up, allowing a view of two actions separated by a barrier: Asano walking bravely across the courtyard to the curtained area where he will disembowel himself, and his retainer kneeling at the gate, stunned with grief and shock.

This shot shows that Japanese organization of space and action into separate modules is not limited to interior design; the outdoor layout of yards and gardens follows much the same principle. Space is geometrically partitioned both outdoors and indoors. High-angle shots in particular are very similar to the "roofless" parallel perspective of the *Tale of Genji* and *rakuchū-rakugai* paintings. Establishing and closing shots of the Palm Room, where Asano is interrogated, use a very high camera height and angle. They come early enough in the film that they also function as norm-establishing shots, because they underscore the boundaries that divide space. An outer boundary is constituted by elaborately painted *shōji* and *fusuma,* and is accentuated by the bodies of outward-facing guards stationed at intervals along the periphery. Within this space, an inner boundary is fashioned by high paper screens set up to form a makeshift interrogation space for Asano. Its smallness is belied by the opulence of the Sesshū splashed-ink paintings on its inside walls. These splashed-ink paintings represent landscape and journey motifs that convey pilgrimages and other devotional regimens even as they exemplify a technique of quickness, spontaneity, and improvisation (figure 9.7). After the interrogation, the makeshift modularity of Genroku interiors is signaled by

Genroku chūshingura *and the Primacy of Perception* 201

9.6 *Sights in and around Kyoto* (courtesy of the Tokyo National Museum and Sho-gakukan Inc.). An example of *rakuchū-rakugai*, also known as *funaki-byōbu*.

D . W I L L I A M   D A V I S

9.7 Shūgetsu, *Haboku Landscape,* Japan, Muromachi period, hanging scroll (courtesy of the Cleveland Museum of Art, Purchase from the J. H. Wade Fund, 76.59).

Genroku chūshingura *and the Primacy of Perception*   *203*

the same high angle on Asano's departure, with the accompanying disassembly and removal of the Sesshū screens (scene 6).

Our first introduction to Ōishi (scene 10) is by way of a spectacular crane shot which starts high over the Akō castle walls and gradually descends to follow Ōishi as he moves inside among the stewards, taking inventory. The offscreen sound of the counting and sorting is associated with Ōishi before we even see the source of the noise. But it is important that Ōishi is not initially introduced precisely within this space, but as a tiny lone figure contemplatively standing outside the castle walls. This invests him with an authority carried along as the shot follows him through the more mundane surroundings of the castle inventory. Ōishi's stature is magnified by the perceptual concentration lavished on him as a lone figure in such a large visual field.

A similar effect is achieved in the scene where Ōishi refuses entrance to his old friend Tokubei, who wants to help defend the Akō castle (scene 15). Tokubei is a peasant who used to serve the Asano clan and, together with his young son Monzaemon, is ready to sacrifice himself in honor of his former clan. But under no circumstances will Ōishi allow them to help in such a capacity: "I won't ask jobless samurai to help us hold the castle; it would be a disgrace." Tokubei is scandalized that Ōishi may be willing to give up the castle, but Ōishi retorts that he will not take orders from Tokubei. At this moment the camera cranes up on Tokubei and his son as Ōishi walks away, giving the exchange a broader thematic significance and the composition a more "elevated" scale. There is something that makes the flying crane shot feel "exalted" (if only through conventional linguistic associations); perhaps it is through subliminal awareness of the physical impossibility of such views that the monumental connotations are conveyed. In addition to this, there may be a class consolidation suggested in that the bravery of Tokubei and Monzaemon is fitting allegiance to the Asano clan given Ōishi's commitment to help the Akō farmers and shopkeepers weather the coming hardships. The flying crane shot on these two peasants may be a visual prefiguration of their apotheosis through suicide.[17]

There is also a virtuosic, swooping crane movement down onto the nō performance that opens Part 2. A typically oblique aerial shot of the roofs and buildings opens the sequence; a gliding motion downward briefly shows the performance onstage, then the camera pans to reveal the gallery audience along the periphery of the courtyard. Finally it reaches the place of honor, then cranes in before coming to rest and cutting to a medium shot of Tsunatoyo. What is striking about this shot is the concentration on the audience more than on the performance itself. One would imagine that Mizoguchi

D. WILLIAM DAVIS

would linger on the play a little longer, because this sequence is the first in Part 2 and would present few motivational problems for the narrative. This is forthcoming later, however, in Tsunatoyo's spear dance; for now, it is the layout and scale of the audience's gallery that takes center stage. Not the performance itself, but the whole spectacle—performance, audience, physical arrangement, atmosphere—alerts us to a characteristically Genroku scene.

Having introduced the perceptual address of one of the film's more complicated techniques, it is time to fill in the functions of *Genroku chūshingura*'s more basic means of affecting the viewer. In terms of shot scale and framing, there are two principal kinds of setups in *Genroku chūshingura*. One is a medium shot capable of accommodating two to three seated figures, and like these figures, the shot is placed about three or four feet above the floor. After the French term for American medium shots, I call these *plan Japonaise* (*p.J.*), which also happen to be an ideal position for viewing Japanese objets d'art. The other main setup is an extreme long shot, with or without camera movement, that usually emphasizes a configuration of congregated figures, as in shots of the assembled *rōnin*. There is no negative space in either shot. This implies that empty space is as important as the figures and objects that fill it. When the spatial disposition of objects and people contributes as much to the significance of the scene as does the dialogue or action, it is fair to conclude that the camera's organization of the spatial field is a visual parameter which does not differentiate between object and background, positive and negative space.

Of course, *Genroku chūshingura* is not an abstract film, and there are areas of greater and lesser visual interest. But the most interesting elements in the shot will be configurations, not just figures; that is, combinatory *patterns* of space, people, and objects rather than clearly delineated things sitting or moving in neutral surroundings. There is an egalitarianism in the shot composition of *Genroku chūshingura* that is at odds with the hierarchical compositional legibility of Western shot scale and framing.

Consider Noël Burch's description of the articulation of space in the Japanese film image:

> In the projected image . . . , depth cues, such as axial character movement and receding, converging lines are, in the most common instances, *overridden* by the effect of surface, due primarily to the predominance of the quadrilateral. Thus, the film image becomes, *predominantly,* the planar projection of the three-dimensional cells, static in each of their successive arrangements, which constitute the pro-filmic dwelling-space.[18]

Burch's italics reveal his preference for attributing flatness and surface orientation to Japanese cinema's articulation of space. This is simply substituting one hegemony for another, in which Japanese cinema allegedly promotes a two-dimensional field, in opposition to Western cinema, whose codes encourage a three-dimensional diegesis. In *Genroku chūshingura*, the *plan Japonaise* and the collective compositions in the long shots do not suppress three-dimensionality; rather, they play with it as one element among others.[19]

Mizoguchi often evokes "invisible" forces generated by onscreen perceptual activity. He composes the image around the perceptual forces (eyelines, figure arrangement, costume, and movement) that articulate the mise-en-scène. In scenes of ritual configurations, where a group of people engage in some ceremony or collective activity (like worship or aesthetic contemplation), these invisible perceptual forces are clearly motivated. For instance, consider the reaction of the Akō vassals when they are officially informed of Lord Asano's enforced suicide. An extreme long shot from the back of the hall shows a large number of samurai kneeling and waiting for the news from Edo. When the messenger is formally introduced to Ōishi at the front, the samurai all inch forward on their knees to hear and see better. The overall appearance of the scene is one of unsettled organic movement, as first one part of the congregation shifts and fidgets, then another. Since the samurai are all dressed and coiffed alike, their fragmentary movement resembles a swarm of tiny creatures whose repose has been disturbed.

A sequence of *p.J.* medium shots follow which lend more intimacy to Ōishi's bewilderment at the sudden death of his lord. Then a 180-degree reverse angle shows a deep focus view of Ōishi grieving in the foreground, with the mass of samurai in the background, huddled like a hundred copies of Ōishi with his dark costume, bald pate, and erect topknot. As he reads Lord Asano's farewell poem ("More frail than petals scattered by the wind / I bid a last farewell and leave spring behind"), the mass of shiny heads and pointy topknots drop out of sight as the samurai begin to weep and lower their heads to the floor.

It is a very odd scene for its graphic qualities and might even be comic were the grief not so intense. Such collective orchestration of gesture and feeling seems improbable. In *Genroku chūshingura*, however, it is the most emotionally wrenching scenes that employ these configurations of "objectified spectatorship." Perhaps we are approaching something culturally specific in such representations, in that expressions of great feeling are magnified by objective echoes of its impact on other people, and on the physical configuration of the ritual.

Framing and shot scale of the cinematography in *Genroku chūshingura* give space a more active role in the composition than simply providing neutral background. In the long take and in Mizoguchi's camera movement, the role of duration similarly comes forward as a dimension that is radically slowed down, if not quite arrested. The moving camera and the long take "stretch" time in a similar way that framing of the mise-en-scène "magnifies" space.

Consider first some perceptual functions of the static long take. Generally, when a stationary setup is held for an inordinate length of time, for example for more than 30 seconds (0:30), there is a dual intensification that takes place. First, the long take encourages something like a mental close-up in which the spectator begins to see that a denotative function is being "overtaken" by some other purpose. The spectator will begin to look for connotative meaning in the shot, especially as an indication of expressive intensification. Some clear instances of this are the scenes in which Tamon bravely appeals the hasty judgment on Lord Asano in Part 1 (scene 5) and Lady Asano reads about the attack on Kira in Part 2 (scene 5). These are both extremely long takes (almost 5:00 and 2:30, respectively), and both are scenes in which the emotional pitch of the dramaturgy rises as the shot is held. These shots show a correlation between dramatic intensity and duration.

In addition to dramatic intensification encouraged by the static long take, a perceptual intensification takes place as well. The static shot of long duration is not without the movement of the spectator's focus of attention. The longer a shot is held, the more time there is to "decompose" the composition into its parts. There is plenty of time for this, as *Genroku chūshingura* has an average shot length of about 1:30.[20] We begin to analyze facial expressions, background objects, spatial relationships, shadings of light and dark, shapes, lines, and textures. With Mizoguchi's images, the sustained perceptual concentration encouraged by the long take always pays off in a way consistent with stylistic and ideological goals of the film, as a particular shot early in Part 2 can illustrate:

Lord Tsunatoyo is interrogating Sukeimon about his real intentions concerning the vendetta. Because his sister attends Tsunatoyo, Sukeimon arrives at the Tsunatoyo mansion apparently to watch a *nō* play. But his real reason is to discover the movements of Kira. The long take showing the interview with Suke lasts more than 3 minutes, although it breaks down into three static shots linked by crane movements. For 0:45, a *p.J.* shows Tsunatoyo insouciantly drinking sake, flanked by two beautiful courtesans who replicate the direction of his gaze. The camera cranes and pans around the shoulder of the nearer courtesan until it comes to rest exactly behind her, with Tsunatoyo on the extreme left side of the frame and Sukeimon at the extreme right. This deep focus composition, dominated by the back of Tsunatoyo's courtesan, lasts 1:30 before the camera cranes along with Tsunatoyo when he gets up. Sukeimon appears to be three times smaller than Tsunatoyo and his courtesan because he is so far away. In the background, over the shoulders of Tsunatoyo and his courtesan, is a line of more attendants, including the sister, looking across at Sukeimon.

The perceptual force of this composition is clearly with Tsunatoyo; the effect of the eyelines and perspectives is to practically push the hapless Suke right off the screen. Compositionally, the body of the courtesan forms a massive barrier between Tsunatoyo and the remote Sukeimon, lending a sense of disproportion and futility to the exchange. The shot is composed using an angular-isomorphic perspective, typical of Edo-period courtesan woodcuts, in which an angular, corner illusion organizes the space while maintaining a picture plane isomorphic with the plane of the screen.[21] In Edo woodcuts the lines stretching deep into the picture do not converge, but remain parallel (figure 9.8).

In addition, there is a concealed geometry to the shot whose central axis is covered up by the body of the courtesan in the foreground. A vertical line extending from floor to ceiling would be visible, because of the support beam in the center that forms the corner of the room. This corner is blocked by her body however; thus the picture looks skewed, as if all the characters were facing each other on the same axis with the room running downhill to the right. If the camera were high enough, one could see the rectangular shape by following the edges of the tatami mats at the periphery of the room, but the camera is placed at the same level or lower than that of the characters. The shot actually shows the inside corner of a rectangular room, flanked on one side by a line of courtesans and on the other by Sukeimon. This is hard to see, however, because the huge figure of the courtesan blocks the view.

This is the way Mizoguchi seems to approximate the isomorphic perspective used by woodcut artists. He compels us to *infer* the geometry of the room for it to make visual sense. At the same time, the perspective, composition, and speaking role lend perceptual priority to Tsunatoyo's side of the frame. The only thing to catch our interest on Sukeimon's side is a small puff of smoke from his pipe. This very unbalanced composition eventually cranes over to a smaller-scale *p.J.* again, this time with Tsunatoyo and Sukeimon in medium shot (0:50). Consistent with the previous two setups replete with attending courtesans, this part of the shot has Suke's sister worriedly watching her brother's exchange from the background.

9.8 Hasegawa Yasumasa, *Playing the "Hand Game,"* Japan, Edo period, hanging scroll (courtesy of the Cleveland Museum of Art, the Kelvin Smith Collection, given by Mrs. Kelvin Smith, 85.260).

Such an elaborately composed serial shot underscores the organizational work of perception. I agree with Burch that such visual fields, whose design may be indebted to the *emakimono*, the *kare sansui*, or the *kabuki* stage, demand a "reading."[22] But this does not involve a Brechtian distanciation effect; on the contrary, the spectator's attention is *solicited*, not alienated, in order to work out the spatial configuration of the scene. In these compositions, a constant encouragement of perceptual involvement is the presence of perceptual forces inside the picture, such as eyelines and body positions, that visually complement, or confound, the empirical spectator's activity. The perceptual cues with which spectators work are the same as those used by the characters in the image; they are an invitation to put ourselves into the scene, assuming, of course, a suspension of one's awareness of the planar properties of the images (pace Burch). Often there are spectator-surrogates in the image whose sole purpose is to contribute their bodies and attention to the overall perceptual design, extending an implicit invitation to the spectator to do likewise. Robert Cohen and Dudley Andrew, among others, have noticed the "detached observer" convention in Mizoguchi's work and have speculated about its status as spectator and authorial stand-in.[23]

Because the film is so fixated on Japanese forms and traditions, Burch insists that its techniques "offer an absolutely unique *ceremonial commentary* on the representational system of the Western film."[24] Mizoguchi is hardly offering a ceremonial commentary on Hollywood; he is interested in forging a uniquely Japanese film style that operates on its own terms, as an inherited legacy from Japan's indigenous artistic heritage. Everything about *Genroku chūshingura* indefatigably emphasizes the artistry in Japanese architecture and design, costume and manners, paintings and gardens. More than this, the systematic patterns of decoupage invite a mode of perception that reflects the serenity, decorum, and tenacity of the depicted historical world. I say "tenacity" to indicate that *Genroku chūshingura* is not a mere indulgence in nostalgia, but a serious ethical and political exhortation. Its aesthetic devices, especially its framing, camera movement, and the long take, are "training exercises" in Genroku perception: awareness of the modularity of space, especially as organized by Japanese interior design; the experience of collective spectatorship and how it offers clues to deciphering a situation; the austere pleasure of duration and its concomitant virtues of patience and discernment. The film offers a mode of perceiving along with its represented world that affords those who wish a new way of seeing an opportunity to indulge in a Genroku "feast" for the senses.

But if *Genroku chūshingura* is such a feast, it is one that requires some fasting from the satiation of narrative appetite. It works on the spectator incrementally, encouraging a small-scale intensive scrutiny of things that do not necessarily further the plot. *Genroku chūshingura* promotes the primacy of perception over narrative comprehension due to the solicitation of close perceptual scrutiny. Its gravity, restraint, and uncompromising stylistic rigor pull distinctly toward a way of seeing that is ineffably Japanese.

Genroku chūshingura *Segmentation*

PART I

1. Credits
2. *Edo:* Asano attacks Kira in the Pine Corridor for his insulting remarks on Asano's ignorance of court etiquette.
3. In the Palm Room, Chamberlain Tamon interrogates Asano, then the cowardly Kira.

D. WILLIAM DAVIS

4. Lady Asano is told of the attack.

5. Tamon pleads for leniency, but the counselors of the *shōgun* have condemned Asano to commit suicide.

6. Asano is held in Tamura's castle, while the dissenting counselor Kofu praises Tamon for his courage and support.

7. Asano's vassal Gengoemon gets permission to see his master for the last time. Gengo and Asano exchange farewells outside the place of ritual suicide.

8. Lady Asano's maids cut her hair.

9. Asano's men receive word that his Edo castle is to be confiscated.

10. *Akō:* At the Asano castle, Ōishi Kuranosuke, Asano's chamberlain, is criticized for calculating the fief's assets, but he explains that he must think of the people in Asano's domain.

11. Messengers arrive with word of the verdict of the *shōgun*. Ōishi reads Asano's last words and a poem to the bereaved samurai.

12. Ōishi broods and keeps his wife and family ignorant of his intentions.

13. Onodera arrives from Kyoto to tell Ōishi that other lords support him and possibly even the Emperor. Ōishi is overcome with relief.

14. Edo retainers complain that Ōishi is delaying the revenge out of cowardice.

15. Ōishi's wife Riku and children are apprehensive. Her cousin summarizes the situation. An old friend, Tokubei, and his son arrive and ask to help with any plans, but Ōishi refuses.

16. Edo retainers demand to know Ōishi's plans, and refuse their support in blood.

17. Tokubei and his son wait outside the castle, chagrined at their exclusion.

18. Meeting of loyal retainers. Ōishi's proposal: surrender the castle and disband, but bide their time to kill Kira and avenge Asano.

19. Tokubei has killed his son and stabbed himself outside the castle. On finding them, Ōishi confides his plan to the dying man.

20. At Ōishi's home, retainers Yasubei and Kazuemon are angry that he is not there. Ōishi's son Matsunojo leads them to Kyoto while Riku declares her intention to stand by her man.

21. *Kyōto:* Yasubei and Kazuemon find Ōishi drunk in a geisha teahouse. They witness his offensive behavior to a highly placed lord who wishes to retain him. They leave in disgust. Ōishi throws off his feigned drunkenness and recalls his son, telling him that they must patiently wait.

22. At Ōishi's home, loyal retainers arrive to tell Ōishi that since the Asano house has no hope of being restored, they must proceed with vengeance. He agrees.

23. Riku asks Ōishi for a divorce on account of the community's disapproval, and he consents. She and the younger children leave Ōishi.

Genroku chūshingura
PART 2

1. Credits
2. *Edo:* During a *nō* performance, Lord Tsunatoyo wonders whether to ask the *shōgun* to restore the Asano house. Sukeimon, an Asano retainer, sneaks into the performance because he knows Kira will be there. He is recognized and brought before Tsunatoyo, who questions him about the vendetta. Suke only criticizes him for allowing the *shōgun* to pass such harsh judgment on Asano. Kira arrives and Suke rushes impetuously to kill him. His sister restrains him and promises to help him kill Kira at that night's *nō* performance.
3. That night, Suke attacks a *nō* actor he believes to be Kira, but after a scuffle discovers it is Lord Tsunatoyo himself. He upbraids Sukeimon for his impetuosity, and the young man accepts the criticism. Tsunatoyo then goes to perform before an audience which includes Kira.
4. At Lady Asano's home, Ōishi arrives to pay his respects to the memory of Asano on the anniversary of his death. Ōishi meets with some resistance from the old servant Godayu, but he is admitted by Lady Toda. Lady Asano sees Ōishi, but she criticizes him for not avenging her husband and refuses to let him burn incense to his memory. Before he leaves, Ōishi gives a packet of poems to Lady Toda for Lady Asano.
5. That night, Lady Asano talks with Lady Toda. They discover Ōishi has left not poems but an account book. A message is thrown over the wall: the forty-seven *rōnin* have attacked Kira's mansion and killed him.
6. Lord Asano's grave: the *rōnin* arrive and offer thanks for their victory, placing Kira's head on the grave. Ōishi declares they must surrender instead of committing suicide on the spot.
7. *Kumamoto:* At Lord Hosokawa's mansion, flowers arrive from Lady Asano. They are taken to the imprisoned *rōnin*. The elder group of *rōnin* express their gratitude, and the younger group offer to entertain the messenger, Horiuchi. After the flowers have been arranged on the altar, all bow in thanks to Lady Asano.
8. Crosscutting: Laughing, the younger group asks Hara to dance. Ōishi and his group sit somberly. Hara finishes his dance, and Jūrōza plays the flute. This sends old Horiuchi out weeping.

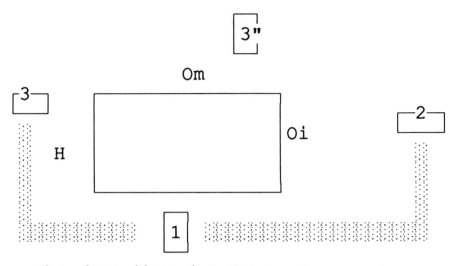

9.9 *The Loyal Rōnin of the Genroku Era:* Omino's ruse (scene 9, part 2).

9. Omino's ruse: Horiuchi tries to pass off Omino as a page boy, but Ōishi is not taken in. She says she must see Jūrōza (figure 9.9).
10. Jūrōza and Sukeimon discuss Omino, who was used as a spy on Kira. Suke tells him to soften his heart.
11. Horiuchi and Omino explain to Ōishi that she has been disowned by her family because Jūrōza failed to marry her. Ōishi finally agrees to let her see Jūrōza. He arrives and pretends not to know her. Then he calls himself her father's son-in-law.
12. The sentence arrives from the *shōgun:* the *rōnin* must commit suicide. Hosokawa provides a farewell meal, for which they express their thanks.
13. The execution procession is interrupted by Ōishi's discovery that Omino has killed herself.
14. Horiuchi prays over Omino's body as the *rōnin* commit suicide one by one. Jūrōza offers to let Ōishi go first, but Ōishi must go last, smiling as he meets his fate.

Notes

Thanks to Paul Clark for reading and providing helpful commentary on earlier drafts of this essay. Special thanks to T. R. White, whose speculations on the formal importance of *kare sansui* and *manga* started some provocative trains of thought.

1. Donald Keene, "Variations on a Theme: *Chūshingura*," in *Chūshingura: Studies in Kabuki and the Puppet Theater,* ed. James Brandon (Honolulu: University of Hawaii Press, 1982), p. 20.

2. See Brian Powell, *Kabuki in Modern Japan: Mayama Seika and His Plays* (London: Macmillan, in association with St. Anthony's College, Oxford, 1990), for a full discussion of Mayama's historical reconstruction of the events on which the *kabuki* and puppet plays were based.

3. *Yamato-e,* a "characteristically Japanese" school of painting, grew in importance during the Heian period. The subjects for *Yamato-e* were often taken from Japanese historical or literary sources.

4. Gregory Barrett estimates it was filmed more than eighty times between 1907 and 1962 (*Archetypes in Japanese Film: The Sociopolitical and Religious Significance of the Principal Heroes and Heroines* [Selinsgrove, Pa.: Susquehanna University Press, 1989], p. 23). In *The Japanese Film: Art and Industry,* expanded ed. (Princeton: Princeton University Press, 1982), Joseph Anderson says he stopped counting at 220 features dealing with the Chūshingura story (p. 446).

5. See Barrett (*Archetypes*) for a good discussion of this genealogy of Chūshingura evolution across different media (pp. 26ff).

Naniwa bushi (also known as *rōkyoku*) are a popular solo stage entertainment featuring narrative ballads about popular stories or historical events, accompanied by the *shamisen* (a fretless, three-stringed plucked lute).

6. Note D. William Davis, "Back to Japan: Militarism and Monumentalism in Prewar Japanese Cinema," *Wide Angle* 11, no. 3 (July 1989): pp. 16–25.

7. Contrast this depsychologizing gesture with the characterization of women in the film, who are given the opposite function of magnifying the personal and psychological consequences of the samurai ethos.

A caveat: *Genroku chūshingura*'s opening scene, with its paroxysm of violence and hysteria, is highly atypical of the rest of the film. There is too much action here for our stylistic analysis to hold good for subsequent parts of the film. But this is consistent with the narrative and stylistic concentration on the disjunction of expectations and reality. This has a historical aspect too, given the traditional status of Chūshingura as a vehicle of swashbuckling action. The unsuspecting spectator, flushed with the news of Japan's first strike on Pearl Harbor, would look forward to an action-packed evening of samurai exploits. But he or she has another thing coming. The opening scene of *Genroku chūshingura* is transtextually motivated, in violation of its literary source (not only is there no opening attack in Mayama's play, but Kira does not appear even once [Keene, p. 13]). It is a norm from which Mizoguchi decisively departs in the rest of the film.

8. *Kōdansha Encyclopedia of Japan,* s.v. "gardens."

9. Ibid., *Japan,* s.v. "architecture, traditional domestic."

10. Noël Burch, *To the Distant Observer: Form and Meaning in the Japanese Cinema* (Berkeley: University of California Press, 1979), p. 240.

11. "[In the 'scroll shot'] the pro-filmic organization of architectural space is such

that the passing lens produces successive tableaux which appear as both discrete and inter-penetrating. This is a major effect of the *emakimono*. In these shots Mizoguchi achieves a corresponding fusion of the two fundamental and opposite aspects of lateral camera-movement as such: successive stages versus steady flow" (ibid., p. 229).

12. Burch writes that symmetry in Japanese architecture is reserved for temple structures, but gives no citation (p. 238). If true, this is consistent with my argument that the sequence invites semireligious perceptual concentration and vigilance, despite its spectacular action.

13. David Bordwell, *Narration in the Fiction Film* (Madison, WI: University of Wisconsin Press, 1982), p. 242 (italics in original).

14. Margaret Hagen, *Varieties of Realism: Geometries of Representational Art* (Cambridge University Press, 1986), 114. See also Hagen and Rebecca K. Jones, "Cultural Effects on Pictorial Perception: How Many Words Is One Picture Really Worth?" in *Perception and Experience,* ed. R. D. Walk and H. L. Pick (New York: Plenum, 1978).

15. Hagen, p. 145.

16. Itoh Teiji, *The Gardens of Japan* (Tokyo: Kodansha, 1984), p. 178.

17. The *kare sansui* dry landscape garden itself was a product of the upward mobility of the *kawaramono*, or outcasts. Outcast gardeners, denied access to the written traditions of stone-setting priests, were compelled to design "withered mountains and water" (*kare sansui*) gardens of astounding creativity, thus gradually earning the right to become Jishū temple gardeners by examination (Itoh, 80). (Jishū is a Zen Buddhist sect that took in outcast gardeners to teach them the intricacies of *kare sansui* design.) In this way, Zen priests cooperated with these people, acting as mentors and patrons, to help bring the *kare sansui* style to birth (p. 176).

18. Burch, p. 200 (italics in original).

19. To be fair to Burch, he singles out Mizoguchi as a director who likes to use character movement in "contradiction" to the predominant two-dimensionality of the image space. But what Burch sees as a contradiction, I see as an essential element of Mizoguchi's stylistics, and perhaps of the monumental style.

20. Donald Kirihara, *Patterns of Time: Mizoguchi and the 1930s* (Madison: University of Wisconsin Press, 1992). Compare this with an average shot length in Mizoguchi's *Story of the Last Chrysanthemum* (*Zangiku monogatari,* 1939), about 1:00; *Sisters of the Gion* (*Gion no shimai,* 1936), 0:33; and *Osaka Elegy* (*Naniwa hika,* 1936), 0:23.

21. Donald Weismann, *The Visual Arts as Human Experience* (Englewood Cliffs, N.J.: Prentice Hall (1970), pp. 186–187.

22. Burch, p. 70; p. 108, esp. n. 18; pp. 116, 118.

23. Robert Cohen, "Mizoguchi and Modernism: Structure, Culture, Point of View," *Sight and Sound* 47, no. 2 (Spring 1978); Dudley Andrew and Paul Andrew, *Kenji Mizoguchi: A Guide to References and Resources* (Boston: G. K. Hall, 1981).

24. Burch, p. 240 (italics in original).

WAYS OF SEEING

JAPANESE PRINTS

AND FILMS:

Mizoguchi's Utamaro

BY DUDLEY ANDREW

C
H
A
P
T
E
R

10

I

In a delicately suggestive book entitled, *Dire l'éphémère,* the author meditates on the uncanny resemblance between the art of cinema and that of Japanese woodblock prints (*ukiyo-e*).

> Once alerted to the possibility of a correspondence between woodblock prints and film, between *ukiyo-e* and the art of movement, evidence of such correspondence begins to accumulate as when a shore is enriched, wave after wave, with shells, algae, and starfish.[1]

While this correspondence adds to our sense of a distinctively Japanese aesthetic that emanates from these beloved popular arts, the evidence of that correspondence comes from the cultural sphere within which these art forms, separated by over a century, took hold. To take these arts together is to take an interest in the social situations that permitted them to thrive and to look for the surprisingly similar cultural functions they so patently aimed to fill. Many critics might lead an inquiry into the social role and consequence of art. I choose John Berger because his immensely popular *Ways of Seeing* directly announces its mission to reach beyond and through art to the culture that produces and consumes it.[2] In fact, Berger has never addressed Japan at all; his historical materialism ties him to the Occidental culture he so effectively analyzes. Yet his book can spur our inquest because it so boldly lays out the issues these arts cannot help but raise: first, the problem for modern art, dear to Walter Benjamin, of the technological reproduction of copies; second, the issue, linked to this, of the role of the artist, particularly the status of genius and originality; third (and this is where Berger has struck the nerve of our age), the scandal of the female body within the economy of artistic production and consumption.[3]

Berger's views are popular and controversial enough to deserve this transportation to the Orient.[4] A cultural examination of Japanese print- and filmmaking, tied to Berger's agenda, may come back to criticize the theory that launches it. How Western, in fact, and how modern, are these linked problems in art: mechanical reproduction, the male genius, and the female body?

At first glance *ukiyo-e* centrally involves all three issues, and involves them in such a way as to "alert us" to its rapport with cinema. To begin, both media require collective, artisanal labor of production and a literal machinery of reproduction. Both forms were initially and primarily commercial and secular, responding to middle-class values and interests. Both were looked at suspiciously by a political and religious hierarchy that occasionally invoked its power of direct censorship. Unauthorized, both forms felt their way along the floor of everyday life, learning to fill certain needs of an inarticulate public. Moreover, both were obsessed with the erotic representation of women by men, a few of whom were taken as, or took themselves as, mavericks and geniuses.

Ukiyo-e may mark the earliest clear step in the increasing "democratization" of aesthetics. Its appearance in multiple copies automatically began to devalue the notion of the "signed original," the art object precious in its singularity. Although this did not completely eliminate the worth and pride of artistic ownership, it certainly brought about gains in exhibition possibilities, amounting to a fundamental change in the social use of art, a change Walter Benjamin believed that photography and the cinema were on the point of fulfilling in our century.[5]

Compared to a patronage system whereby a wealthy noble supports an artist for the novelty and distinction of his work, *ukiyo-e* depends on gradual variation within controlled proliferation. As would be the case in film studios, the ratio between distinctiveness and predictability must favor the latter. Few artists could risk major changes in subject or style. For *ukiyo-e* depended on the Japanese penchant for "repetition and variations on a theme," a penchant evident after the Second World War when the "public remained faithful to the films of Tōei, Shōchiku, Nikkatsu because these studios provided them with specific products that were variations in tone on the same themes."[6]

Two genres dominated *ukiyo-e,* that of *kabuki* actors and that of beautiful women, accounting for 80 percent of all prints produced in the eighteenth century. Moreover, prints were often published as books or linked in series as different poses of a famous actor or well-known beauty. Publishers must have negotiated with their artists like the heads of studios who in the 1950s decided each year how many samurai films, home dramas (*shomingeki*), and historical epics (*jidaigeki*) to venture, as well as which actors and actresses to feature. In both cases producers listen to their distributors who claim to be in close contact with the masses hungering for entertainment. Distributors in both media claim to possess the ability to recognize or anticipate popular fads and needs. And so an informal feedback loop links the populace to the source of the images they pay to look at.

Such a democratic, as opposed to aristocratic, system depends on the urbanity of the populace, on its literal urbanity. Because of the governmental edict that noble families reside, at least part-time, in the capital, unprecedented construction took place in the seventeenth century, bringing to Edo the most skilled, intelligent, and crafty workers and artisans in the land, all without their families. The money and ambition that quickly gravitated to Edo was strictly regulated so as to keep the social structure in place (samurai on top) even if the middle classes were becoming dominant economically. Excess money, much of which could not be passed down, spilled over into the well-known industries of pleasure that *ukiyo-e* chronicled and to which it contributed. By advertising personalities and places, these prints widened the popularity of pleasure and increased its connoisseurship even among samurai who languished in a period of enforced leisure. Actors, hungry for fame or notoriety, modeled apparel and poses, in what became at this time the largest city in the world, a city by all accounts overstuffed with bachelors. *Ukiyo-e* thus developed in productive rapport with the *kabuki* theatre, teahouses, and brothels of the Yoshiwara district (figure 10.1).

It was common for publishers of prints to book seats for their artists at the first performance of a new production so that depictions of scenes from it, and portraits of actors in the new costumes, could be sold to audiences during most of the play's run. . . . the prints even influenced the designers of sets, who often created their flats and backdrops with the styles of certain print makers in mind. And some of the actors developed certain poses, knowing that they would appeal to the print artists.[7]

As for courtesans and teahouse beauties, one can imagine the importance to them of what amounted to metropolitan and even national publicity in the dissemination of prints showing them off in fetching apparel and attitudes.

In fact the informal industry of pleasure, centered in the Yoshiwara district, was horizontally coordinated. Even before Yoshiwara, *kabuki* had been directly linked to prostitution. After 1680 the printing industry was involved as well. It should not surprise us that many of the earliest examples of *ukiyo-e* (Moronobu's) depicted explicitly sexual acts.[8] Even when such subjects came under severe censorship (in 1720 and again in 1790), the image industry was geared to take advantage of, and augment, the largely erotic obsessions of Edo.

Just as social historians describe the flowering of the Yoshiwara district of leisure as a displacement of repressed political and economic ambitions, so can we account for the eighteenth-century "refinements" of theatre and graphic art as sublimations of this hypereroticism. Curiously and symptomatically, the merchant and artisanal classes, blocked in their social ambitions by a repressive hierarchical society, reproduced a hierarchical structure in the Yoshiwara. Courtesans, teahouses, and entertainers of all sorts were classified by a fine-meshed semiotic system that translated into product differentiation and a strictly, if informally, regulated scale of costs.

Nowhere was this more evident than in the printmaking sector, where prices of prints depended on a network of factors, all of which obscure or thwart the democratic revolution this art form seemed to promise. When mechanical reproduction sapped from pictorial art the aura of its uniqueness, its rarity, putting pale copies of art in everyone's hands, the prestige associated with ownership or even with familiarity should have ended. Once the actual worth of the artistic material (the gold leaf of illustrated manuscripts) or the literal rarity of originals (the uniqueness of each oil painting) had been deflated by the press and then by the photograph, one might have expected preciosity to fade from the cultural discourse about art. But discrimination seems endemic to aesthetics even in the age of democracy or socialism, for its method, like that of capitalism, is competition and its result is elimination of the weak.

As would be the case in the era of studio filmmaking, while most products slipped into the well-worn tracks of genres, a certain percentage reached for particular "distinction." Connoisseurs became the acolytes of art, helping to

DUDLEY ANDREW

10.1 Okumura Masanobu, theatre interior, *ukiyo-e* (courtesy of the Cleveland Museum of Art, Gift of Mr. and Mrs. J. H. Wade, 16.1154).

set the scale of value for prints that were equivalent in material worth.[9] An early version of the auteur theory developed whereby the primary criterion of distinction among the thousands of available prints was the name of the designer.

Thus Kitagawa Utamaro's name, like Mizoguchi Kenji's a century and a half later, stands out from the nameless artisans he worked with, and from the less renowned artists he competed against. Similarly a star system developed rapidly in Tokugawa Japan where courtesans, teahouse girls, and actors vied for recognition in their representations just as much as in their vocations. Stars and artists (those artists who achieved stardom) quickly became bankable signifiers of value in the democratic world of *ukiyo-e*, as they surely would in the cinema. Walter Benjamin was the first to recognize this economy where the aura that evaporated from the work of art condensed onto the person of the star associated with the work.[10] He had in mind the cinema, but as we have seen, he might have been speaking of *ukiyo-e*.

And so, just as in the eighteenth century when the city of Edo went wild for prints, gobbling them up by the thousands through shops, at theatres, and from street hawkers, so from 1925 to 1960 more than five hundred Japanese films a year tried to satisfy the millions who weekly bought tickets. Limited by jealous authorities in the topics they were allowed to treat, *ukiyo-e* artists and connoisseurs devoted their lives to pursuing the delicate and literally sublime expressions one could create with line and color on paper. Such exorbitant concern with technique and style, found in the more famous prints by Utamaro, Haronobu, and Sharaku, conjures up Japanese cinema once again, for out of the hundreds of filmmakers laboring in that industry, the names of only a handful are known to us: the supreme stylists like Mizoguchi, Ozu, Kurosawa.[11] The situation of the popular arts in Japan, then, comes down to this: under the pressure of social restrictions, but within a general atmosphere of plenty, the proliferation of its products permits a commercial art industry to support style and abstraction, resulting in the adulation, the fetishization, of certain artists and their (specifically erotic) concerns.

II

A startlingly transparent allegory of this whole process lies before us in a 1946 film about *ukiyo-e*, Mizoguchi's *Utamaro and His Five Women* (*Utamaro o meguru gonin no onna*), a film that treats both art forms and that thematizes all three of John Berger's chief concerns: the mechanical reproduction of art, the artistic genius, and the female body. Despite his position as president of the first labor union organized at the Shōchiku Ofuna Studio, Mizoguchi had trouble launching this highly personal project, for he had to buck the censorship board of the American occupation authorities. Immediately upon taking charge of the administration of the country, the Americans banned all *jidaigeki* so as to cut short any reanimation of nationalist sentiments. Mizoguchi successfully argued that his script deserved to be treated as an exception, since it was concerned not with a warrior or a nobleman but with an artist and a man of the people. Furthermore, his film was to be decidedly feminist. Naturally, "feminist" in 1946 Japan meant something rather different from what it means to us today; but to the Americans in charge of rebuilding a defeated nation, *Utamaro and His Five Women* could be counted as one more offering in their broad effort to prepare the Japanese for Western-style democracy. Female suffrage was a high priority, and not only because of the vote. To the one million American military personnel stationed in Japan, local women were so foreign in their attitudes and behavior as to be either off limits or the cause of frightful and often tragic misunderstandings. By dramatizing the situation of women in Tokugawa Japan, Mizogu-

10.2 Mizoguchi Kenji, *Utamaro and His Five Women* (*Utamaro o meguru gonin no onna*, 1946) (courtesy of the Japan Film Library Council). The painting duel.

chi's film would implicitly call for understanding and respect (on the side of the occupiers) and for systematic change (on the side of the occupied).

But the film's real claim to modernism stems from its glorification of the popular arts at the expense of time-honored traditions of painting. In its opening sequence *Utamaro and His Five Women* deliberately opposes *ukiyo-e* prints to traditional court painting, specifically to the powerful tradition of the Kanō school. When a young member of that school named Seinosuke whimsically stops off at a *nishiki-e* shop just outside the pleasure district to pick up a print for the amusement of his patron, the great Kanō, he is insulted by a boast inscribed on one of the prints, claiming the superiority of woodblock art to painting. Challenging Utamaro to a duel over the insult, he finds himself fighting (and losing) with paintbrushes. Like the young Mozart of *Amadeus,* who spontaneously touches up a composition Salieri has slaved over, Utamaro "improves" the painter's rendition of the goddess of mercy with a few swift strokes. "There, that's better. Wouldn't you agree? I've put life into the figure" (figure 10.2).

Economy, spontaneity, and the lively representation of life are all on the side of the artist who eats, drinks, and sleeps with the people. To keep his studio and shop open, Utamaro has learned to be quick, prolific, and adapt-

I feel shut in, conforming to tradition.

10.3 "I feel shut in, conforming to tradition," says the aristocratic apprentice sitting before a traditional Kanō school screen. *Utamaro and His Five Women* (courtesy of New Yorker Films).

able. "Utamaro draws on flesh," the astonished Seinosuke cries out, whereas the venerable Kanō school, by its own admission, locks painters into rigid rules of form and color. And the social system that has supported it for over two centuries does the same to its subjects. In a turbulent scene at Kanō's beautiful home, Seinosuke opts to follow Utamaro, thereby relinquishing his samurai inheritance, including his fief and all the privileges of the class into which he was born, and including his right to the hand of Kanō's daughter (figure 10.3). An icy tableau concludes this domestic drama: Kanō, after expelling Seinosuke from the premises, turns his back on his daughter who cowers obediently and pathetically in the foreground. Brushes are handed Kanō and he bends forward to touch up the flowers on the very screen painting that Seinosuke had already pointed to in complaining that court artists spend their lives endlessly reproducing standard plants and birds.

Although the historical Utamaro first found recognition with detailed prints of plants and birds,[12] his fame rests with his "realistic" designs of stunningly vibrant women. Mizoguchi concentrates entirely on Utamaro's passionate attempt to frame the turmoil of the lives of these women and the inner turmoil of their reactions to their lives. In the film's denouement, Okita, Uta-

DUDLEY ANDREW

10.4 Okita's love is as passionate as Utamaro's art. "Doesn't your *nishiki-e* of me express the same thought?" *Utamaro and His Five Women* (courtesy of the Japan Film Library Council).

maro's favorite model, one to whom he has been romantically linked, returns to his studio utterly distracted, after having killed her lover and the woman who had taken him from her. While Utamaro listens horrified, she confesses with pride in having taken love to such a limit, a limit, she says, that Utamaro's devotion to his art taught her (figure 10.4). With an ethereal look on her face, doubtless thinking of her imminent suicide, she tells the artist, "Be kind to the woodblock print of Okita" and then she rushes past the camera and out the door. Mizoguchi's tracking camera leaves her at the threshold; in fact it spins back to find Utamaro in a state of equal, perhaps greater, distraction. Watching her go off to her death, he is overcome with the need to render the scene on paper, yet his hands are shackled for having offended the *daimyō*. "I want to draw. I want to draw so much," he cries out pathetically.

This scene restates in its frightful consequences the film's insistence on the equivalence of popular art and passionate life, by having life imitate the excesses of art. What else could be meant by the fact that the woman whom Okita stabbed, Takasode, became famous and alluring because Utamaro had drawn a cartoon on her flesh? Having seduced Okita's lover with the art of (and on) her flesh, she now dies an artistic death. Art instigates the passions

10.5 Oran, the model. *Utamaro and His Five Women* (courtesy of New Yorker Films).

of life which it then sets about expressing. Thus mounts up the spiral of the erotic imagination.

Although it was motivated by one of the most famous incidents that have come down to us about Utamaro's life, the fifty-day punishment by handcuffs proves an inspired metaphor to carry this linkage of eroticism, repression, and art. Throughout the film Utamaro's hands manipulate women on paper while leaving them alone in their lives. With a nearly psychotic tone of anticipation Utamaro asks a new model to take her hands away from her shy face (figure 10.5). He then arranges her garments and her skin just so with his own hands before returning to his properly artistic distance. "I leave myself in your hands," says this girl, making it clear that to draw a woman is to possess her in another way (figure 10.6).

This fetish reaches its limit early in the film when Utamaro cannot keep himself from drawing on Takasode's naked back (figure 10.7). Here the sharp implement, the tattooer's needle, that will penetrate her skin and permanently fix his image, ties down the significance of the paintbrushes Utamaro wields in moments of excitement throughout the film. And it links these to the ornamental combs the women around him push ever so gently into the trusses of their magnificently coiffured hair.[13] The film helps us imagine that

DUDLEY ANDREW

10.6 Oran puts herself in Utamaro's hands. *Utamaro and His Five Women* (courtesy of New Yorker Films).

10.7 Utamaro designs cartoon for tattoo. *Utamaro and His Five Women* (courtesy of New Yorker Films).

it was less the final shape of the coiffeur, nor the social distinction hairstyle signaled, than the sensual playing with it that excited him and that might be seen as a model for his own work. Okita, plying her ornamental comb in front of her mirror, matches Utamaro who sits behind her with his pen (figure 10.8). When she finishes, she leans up against him, pouting and looking away. But her hair (her sex, that is) is in his face (figure 10.9). Shall we call this the use of models for art or the misuse of women for perversion? Artists have always pleaded exemption from such charges. After all Utamaro repeatedly renounces all claims on the women he draws. He may give advice but he never interferes in their affairs. Drawing them at their toilet, he could be counted as another of their servants. He shelters the pitiable Yukie when she runs away from her domineering father, Kanō (figure 10.10). He refuses to send Oran back to the *daimyō,* who, with the flick of his hand, had forced her and a score of "purebred beauties" to disrobe, then dive into his bay to bring him the slithery fish they catch. Undoubtedly women in the Tokugawa era were the playthings of their fathers and of male potentates. And in such a system, Utamaro appears to assert the rights of women and of his class against the aristocracy that controls them both.

But Mizoguchi's Utamaro is concerned first with his art and second with the well-being of those he portrays. The new ideas to which he subscribes all concern aesthetics, not social change. His enemy is not Kanō the aristocrat so much as Kanō the artist. He may excoriate the *daimyō* for sexually exploiting Oran, but he coaxes this same woman into sitting as a model for the glory of art. Shamelessly his colleagues beg Oran to expose herself so the artist can draw, saying, "It isn't for his own pleasure or gain but for the art of colored woodblock prints."

In fact, Utamaro's need for women does amount to a cultural shift in Japanese aesthetics. Crassly we might say that women initiate a circular flow of value from the beauty of their flesh to the artist's erotic imagination, to pictorial style, and finally to hard cash, when pieces of silver are exchanged for a finished print. More sympathetically, we can exalt Utamaro as a realist who pulled out brush and paper when the occasion presented itself, living off the incidents he witnessed.[14] Utamaro interprets more than creates. Like a critic, he requires an eloquent text in front of him to which he can respond. So that whether or not he genuinely held advanced views, his respect for women is first of all a precondition of his way of making art.

Mizoguchi reveres Utamaro precisely because he abjures the role of creator (father or progenitor), by subordinating self-expression so as to become the devoted scribe of the beauty and the sentiment around him. Even here his personal contribution is limited, for he depends on the printers, cutters, and

10.8 Okita plays with her ornamental combs and her coiffeur in front of Utamaro. *Utamaro and His Five Women* (courtesy of New Yorker Films).

10.9 Utamaro and Okita. *Utamaro and His Five Women* (courtesy of New Yorker Films).

Ways of Seeing Japanese Prints and Films 229

10.10 Utamaro comforts Yukie. *Utamaro and His Five Women* (courtesy of the Japan Film Library Council).

DUDLEY ANDREW

colorists whose contribution to woodblock prints was, we know, cocreative. Utamaro's name appears on the prints, but Mizoguchi is careful to show a team of more than a dozen artisans laboring to bring that name and those prints to the public.

Perhaps Mizoguchi's attraction to the period of the *ukiyo-e,* and to Utamaro in particular, stems from his own peculiar status as the supreme auteur in the Japanese film system, yet a director whose methods were especially dependent on the independent contributions of his collaborators. Mizoguchi was the director who refused to instruct his writer, camera operator, designer, or actors in what he wanted. "Do it until it is proper," he would say, and say repeatedly, driving his associates to produce their most intense version. I have described this sadistic method as based on an aesthetic of response, for Mizoguchi claimed to have created nothing in his life, rather to have responded, in the full and sacred sense of that term, to the creations and the passions of others.[15] Like the helpless tattoo artist before the naked torso of Takasode, Mizoguchi's genius could be aroused only by a design (a script, let's say) worthy of the subject. Then he could begin digging deeply into the flesh of that subject. Here we arrive at the heart of a paradox that continues to confuse critics of Mizoguchi concerned with gender.[16] He wields the phallic brush or tattooing needle, but the artist needs first to be possessed himself by a passion that comes over him from elsewhere and that then forces itself onto the body of the woman (figure 10.11).[17] Mizoguchi's men—in the tradition of the weak *kabuki* hero, known as the *nimaime*—come alive only under what is sometimes a fatal masochism. Shōzaburō, Okita's irresistible lover, begs her: "Hit me, kick me, you can even kill me if you like," and she playfully replies, "I'll shut you in and torture you." Later she plunges her knife into his stomach. The very next scene transfers such masochism to Utamaro. The artistic frenzy he feels after Okita's passionate suicide speech grows unbearable as it struggles against the handcuffs that block its release.

The tortured-genius syndrome infects Utamaro, Mizoguchi, and the auteur systems that nurtured both men. How can we revere the "genius" who needs the violence of modern life to produce his work? Mizoguchi recognized in *ukiyo-e* material conditions similar to those at work in the industry of filmmaking, and he recognized in Utamaro a man rising above those conditions to join himself to the sacred spirit of art. Recall the film's final scene: unshackled at last, Utamaro spurns the feast his friends have prepared. While they carouse in the background, he calls for paper, brushes, and ink, and he gleefully prepares to draw "Oran fishing, the spirit of Okita," and all the other moments he has committed to memory. In a final shot, print after famous print cascades onto the screen, prints that we recognize from further,

10.11 The helpless tattoo artist, impotent before the beauty until inspired by Uta-maro's cartoon. *Utamaro and His Five Women* (courtesy of New Yorker Films).

degraded reproductions, on postcards and playing cards. Because Utamaro's "originals" are themselves reproductions and therefore multiple, we can value whatever versions of his drawings we encounter as more than tokens of sacred objects guarded in some museum. At no matter what remove, in-cluding these images reproduced here, they refigure the impress of his imagi-nation on the wooden blocks where they were first transferred. In expressing the values of life that flowed around him, Utamaro immortalized himself be-yond the dreams of religious and classical painters, because the medium of his expression allowed at the outset the indefinite proliferation of his ideas in time and space. Mizoguchi wanted no less for this film, indeed for all his films.

III

With Mizoguchi's film in mind, let us return to John Berger's theses about the cultural context of Western art. As in the West, the technological repro-duction of the graphic arts amounts to the insurgent aesthetics of an insur-gent class. For the first time, fine art circulated among the people and for the first time the people were involved, however indirectly, in their own self-representation.

Mizoguchi flattered this hope by portraying Utamaro as a witness to the daily life around him, but he fell back on a more noble conception of art when he had filmed that same Utamaro in fanatical pursuit of sublimity. Here the notion of genius that Berger has never given up takes a different turn. For Berger, genius operates within a retrograde aesthetic system—that of oil painting. In his view, Rubens and Rembrandt (his preferred examples)[18] overcame the flatulent ideological system that oil painting signified and within which they were obliged to work. Through tortuous aesthetic experimentation, these "greats" starkly presented their society with the consequences of the ideology governing it.

Utamaro's case is, then, very different because, given the class conflict that informs Berger's judgments, his medium was part of the solution, not the problem. We have already noted his anger at the power of a perverse *daimyō* who misuses his subjects; yet whenever Utamaro stands before the authorities, he does so obsequiously, virtually thanking them for punishing his transgressions. How can we credit such deference, except to see in his immense artistic output a displacement of class rage? His shackled hands would, from this perspective, stand synecdochically for the situation of the middle class of the era. And his triumphant artistic productivity would then measure the energy, imagination, and resistance of this underclass alive within a decaying feudal system.

But if *ukiyo-e* is seen as a weapon of an insurgent class, one that promotes its self-definition, its values, and its power, then the rebellious artistic genius can only be redundant. Berger's thesis suggests to other scholars, though not to him, that the need for genius ended when technological reproduction put artists back into their own society through artisanal cooperation and through contact with the class within which they labored. Thus, Berger, were he presented with the case we have laid out, ought to accuse Mizoguchi of harboring a nostalgia for the recovery of aristocratic values within the technology of modern-day life. Moreover, his artistic pretensions may lead Mizoguchi to a sadistic stance before the women on whom he doted. Here we reach a variant of Berger's third and most famous thesis: that in the era of oil painting, an era in which wealthy men effectively owned the artists and the artworks, females were depicted by males as complicit in their own commodification.

Whether or not Berger's thesis has effectively held up over the past fifteen years, the examples he brings to bear, especially the "Vanitas" topos,[19] must

10.12 Oran (courtesy of the Japan Film Library Council).

affect our scanning of prints by Utamaro. Nearly all of Utamaro's hundreds of prints of women show them outside the company of men. The male viewer (Utamaro, first of all) stands alone in their presence. Their beauty or passion vibrates for the viewer alone, unhampered by competition (figure 10.12).

DUDLEY ANDREW

Furthermore, and this corresponds to one of Berger's greatest insights, these women turn inward, conning their own appearance, and keeping the circuit of desire within the frame of the print. Mirrors double the image of many of these women, giving us two views and the right to judge what the subject herself is measuring. Other women groom themselves, bend over their toes, lacquer their teeth, or work on their abundant hair, all for the unseen male viewer, all for Utamaro hovering in front of them. They never look up at the artist or at us, leaving themselves open to the erotic imagination (figures 10.13, 10.14). Their thoughts, in contrast, are fully absorbed within the print. We see one reading a love letter; another wistfully meditates on her absent lover. Utamaro, and subsequent male viewers, stand by to imagine comforting these women.

In the social system ruling the Occident during the heyday of oil painting, this economy of art based on gender and possession was indeed indecent. That it crops up so strongly in the Japan of 1790 would seem to spoil Berger's belief that it represents a specifically Western pathology, traceable to the material history of European culture. Either we consider the Japanese socioeconomic system to be a replica of that of early European capitalism or we must question our "way of seeing" women portrayed in Japanese prints: that is, we must question our understanding of Japanese aesthetics and of the Japanese imagination.

Unqualified to speculate on comparative socioeconomics, I am anxious to pursue the second hypothesis (a suspicion, really) based on comparative cultural aesthetics. Complicating any proposal of equivalence between the gaze of the Western male before oil paintings of nudes and the gaze of the Japanese male before *ukiyo-e* that display the beauty of courtesans, is another genre of prints by Utamaro, this one featuring a pair or group of women catching fish, washing clothes, playing games. This genre, which Utamaro may be said to have made his own,[20] finds the artist closed off from what appears to be a self-sufficient company of women. No matter that their activities have been allotted to them by a paternalistic authority, these women have reached an equilibrium within their work or play of which male artists and viewers can only be jealous. They stand before us as undistractible, and therefore they really do not stand before us at all.

Mizoguchi hints at just this during the long scene of Okita's confession in Utamaro's studio (note figure 10.4). Five minutes pass with but a single cut. The camera delicately tracks and pans to keep Okita in frame and to fill the rest of the frame with what matters to her. At first it takes in Utamaro, silent on screen left; but as her speech develops we track in to cut him completely out of the picture, leaving Okita with women in the background. In this in-

10.13 Kitagawa Utamaro, a bust study of a beautiful girl, *ukiyo-e* (courtesy of the Cleveland Museum of Art, Bequest of Edward L. Whittemore, 30.219).

DUDLEY ANDREW

10.14 Kitagawa Utamaro, *Courtesan Hanaogi of Ogiya Tying Her Sash*, *ukiyo-e* (courtesy of the Cleveland Museum of Art, The Kelvin Smith Collection, given by Mrs. Kelvin Smith, 85.359).

timate company, Yukie is able at last to blurt out: "Now I know the path a woman must follow." She will rush out after Okita, along with the other women, leaving Mizoguchi alone with the helpless and pathetic Utamaro. After filling the frame without him, his women have vanished. Their hell is a shared hell from which he is cut off except by imaginative projection.

Mizoguchi makes much of this projection. We might even say that Utamaro's obsession with the predicament of women displaces his interest from his own predicament. At the mercy of the *daimyō*, indeed of the whole unjust social system that constricts him, he turns to the women whom he and his oppressed class have in turn oppressed.[21] Playthings of men, these "five women around Utamaro"[22] have nevertheless achieved the kind of sublimity Utamaro sought in his art. He may have been subject to the authorities, but his prints would outlive them. Here we have reached something quite opposite Berger's characterization of Western art: here the society of prints and printmakers, like that of women, sequestered though both may be from the center of political power, ignores that power altogether.

A final genre of print ratifies this view. At the very end of his career, sometime in the first years of the new century and just after his punishment at the hands of the authorities, Utamaro daringly created a three-volume set of *shunga* (explicitly pornographic prints) entitled *The Merry Drinkers* (*Ehon waraijōgo*). Because new censorship laws proscribing erotic topics had been enacted a decade earlier, "the difficult and bold venture of publishing *shunga* required a considerable anti-establishment and treasonable spirit on the part of painter and publisher."[23] In taking the genre to new limits, Utamaro stands before us once again as a genius bucking the social system;[24] but by taking up a genre that had belonged to *ukiyo-e* from the beginning, his final *shunga* permit us to recognize how different Japanese prints are in cultural function from the Western pictorial traditions Berger describes. Unlike the *Playboy* centerfolds that Berger claims derive from oil painting, these prints all depict women taking their pleasure with men who are actually represented within the pictorial space. More or less responsible for the pleasure of both partners, some of these women clearly use the men whose backs are to us, while others, utterly disinterested, nonchalantly read books while being "entertained," or while pretending to "entertain." Mizoguchi and his Utamaro remained fascinated by such self-possession. It served as a model for them in their own dealings with the *daimyō* or with the SCAP (Supreme Commander, Allied Powers). And it can help us rethink the various meanings of "possession" that Berger's book raises so troublingly in the context of modern art: possession of the gaze, possession of an artwork, and that "possession" artists have felt when entranced.

1. Claude Blouin, *Dire l'éphémère* (Quebec: Hurtbuise, HMH, 1983), p. 131.

2. John Berger, *Ways of Seeing* (London: Pelican Books, 1983). Also note Walter Benjamin, "The Work of Art in the Age of Mechanical Reproduction," in his *Illuminations* (New York: Schocken Books, 1969), esp. p. 224.

3. The fourth section of *Ways of Seeing* concerns art in the age of advertising. I scarcely touch on this issue, despite its evident importance given the consumer culture that has come to dominate Japan.

4. Peter Fuller, *Seeing Berger* (London: Writers and Readers Press, 1980). This text takes up most of the arguments against Berger. Fuller is sympathetic to his subject's project, but in a qualified manner. His monograph is evidence of the notoriety and influence of *Ways of Seeing*.

5. Benjamin, p. 224.

6. Blouin, p. 62, citing the work of L. Hajek, *Les Estampes japonnaises* (Paris: Belfond, 1976), p. 34.

7. Frank Whitford, *Japanese Prints and Western Painters* (New York: Macmillan, 1977), p. 30.

8. Hishikawa Moronobu (1625–1695) is generally regarded as the first great master of *ukiyo-e* prints.

9. First of all, *ukiyo-e* manufacturers manipulated market conditions by creating a hierarchy of prints and even by reestablishing the relative uniqueness of certain prints (called *suronobu*) which came out in very limited editions, produced on exquisite paper and with enhanced colors. In the cinema one might liken this to the color and widescreen processes that announced themselves just after the Second World War as a way to differentiate the cinema from television, as a way to charge higher prices for special films, and as a way to attract to itself a wealthier theatregoing public that valued the distinction of "unique," or at any rate "scarce," experiences not available to everyone.

10. Benjamin, section IX.

11. The actual number of artists working in the golden age of *ukiyo-e* is generally put at between six hundred and seven hundred. See Harold Osborne, ed., *The Oxford Companion to Art* (London: Oxford University Press, 1970), p. 1171.

12. Indeed he was trained by a Kanō school artist. See Richard Lane, *Masters of the Japanese Print* (New York: Doubleday, 1962), p. 220, or Maurizio Bonicatto, *Ukiyo-e* (Rome: Instituto Giapponese de Cultura, 1971), p. 59.

13. Even those art critics who throughout the years have labeled Utamaro decadent agree that his technical mastery is incontestably evident in his ability to discern, and to render, an extraordinary variety of hairdos.

14. Significantly for us, Mizoguchi was careful to include newspapers in his film; a street hawker blurts out "Extra, Extra. Read all about the elopement of . . ." to sell the Edo version of the *National Inquirer*. Utamaro will in due time chronicle the same events, selling them no doubt in more limited editions but on the same streets and to

many of the same people fascinated by the stories and pictures of life in the floating world.

15. This view is developed at length in my *Film in the Aura of Art,* pp. 172–192.

16. See, for example, Joan Mellen, *The Waves at Genji's Door,* pp. 100–103. Mellen's remarks on this film are among the most sensitive written in English. Nevertheless, she errs, in my opinion, when she claims that Utamaro renounces passion in life so as to attain something greater in art. I believe, on the contrary, that Utamaro required passion in his life as a prerequisite to creation. It is to relieve his torpor and creative impotence that his friends take him to observe the perverse fishing ritual of the *daimyō,* where the sight of Oran excites him so.

17. It is worth noting that one of Tanizaki Jun'ichirō's most celebrated stories concerns a tattoo artist. Mizoguchi was in awe of Tanizaki and would adapt *The Reaper of Rushes* (*Ashikari*) shortly after the Utamaro project, giving it the name *Oyūsama.* Mizoguchi surely had meditated on this story.

18. Berger, pp. 61, 110.

19. Ibid., p. 51.

20. See Lane, p. 221.

21. We can push this notion of replication to its limit: the handcuffs that, in preventing him from drawing, only make Utamaro want to draw so much more could just as likely be used to tie a woman to a bed in the perverse hope of increasing her sexual desire. Thus, the artist, finding his own imaginary escape from authority in art, imagines the masochism of women over whom his art holds power.

22. "Five Women around Utamaro" has served as an alternate English translation of the film's title.

23. Introduction to *The Merry Drinkers* (USA: Sei Sei Doh, 1980), trans. Peter Dale.

24. Of supplemental interest to us, the introduction to *The Merry Drinkers* describes these prints as protocinematic, "stop action" moments of erotic encounter, complete with dialogue supplied.

KOBAYASHI'S WIDESCREEN AESTHETIC

BY CYNTHIA CONTRERAS

The seemingly sudden emergence of anamorphic cinematography in 1953 was actually the culmination of a lengthy technological process which, in turn, spawned a plethora of widescreen offspring and provided filmmakers with several aspect-ratio options. However, unlike sound and color, innovations which have become basically standard in the commercial cinema, the anamorphic format remains but one possibility. Its introduction served to displace the standard film ratio of 1.33 : 1 with the 2.35 : 1 process that Twentieth Century Fox trademarked as CinemaScope[1] and to prepare the industry for the multiple formats of 1.66 and 1.85.

A variety of technical processes, such as Vistarama, Franscope, and Tohoscope, were developed, most of which were derivations of CinemaScope; and viewers were treated to a number of widescreen innovations throughout the 1950s and 1960s, including VistaVision, Technirama, and Todd-AO. The multifaceted Panavision finally emerged as the preferred technology, since it could yield a print in several formats and thus helped make systems more compatible.

CinemaScope and its imitators were not only part of a technological and commercial revolution, however; they also contributed to the aesthetic evolution of the film medium, primarily by substantially elongating the cinematic canvas.[2] Directors and cinematographers quickly, though sometimes grudgingly, adapted to the different proportions and developed suitable compositional conventions appropriate to the wider screen.[3]

Yet, as David Bordwell has pointed out, the widescreen formats did not radically challenge the established norms of the classical Hollywood model, but rather "offered only trended changes in the classical style."[4] Nevertheless, from Otto Preminger to Sergio Leone the general tendency among filmmakers shooting in the 'Scope format has often been to emphasize its expansive properties and to suggest even greater spaces beyond the frame line.[5]

A notable exception to this norm can be found in Kobayashi Masaki's 1962 film Seppuku (Harakiri), in which, for the sake of social commentary, Kobayashi worked against the naturally expansive qualities of the frame to create a contracted sense of enclosure. Drawing upon artistic and dramatic precedents in Japanese traditional culture, he explored the compositional possibilities of widescreen in this and his other 'Scope films. In so doing, Kobayashi developed an appropriate canvas for his distinctive aesthetic vision.

In his nine-hour saga The Human Condition (Ningen no jōken, 1959–1961) and in Kwaidan (Kaidan, 1964), the director also emphasized the expansive properties of the frame and evoked offscreen space, but in Seppuku, and later in Samurai Rebellion (Jōiuchi, 1967), he favored self-contained compositions. In these films, Kobayashi created an enclosed, imprisoning world of social constraints, through geometrical arrangement of characters within architectural structures.

Before analyzing and illustrating the specific characteristics of this approach in Seppuku, I will first briefly discuss the defining significance of the frame itself, the peculiarities and problems associated with composing for the anamorphic lens, and Kobayashi's varied use of this format in several of his other films. In considering these films from the perspective of compositional format, the emphasis throughout will be on the concept of contextuality: how it relates to widescreen in general and to Japanese film in particular. In the discussion of Seppuku, the counterposing of the static and the dynamic through Kobayashi's approach to anamorphic composition will also be considered.

The first decision in composing a picture has to do with limits. An artist wraps an image/idea in a frame, the shape of which is determined by the contours of the envisioned forms. Water falls vertically; it flows on a twisting horizontal or diagonal plane; it rests as a lake within a golden rectangle. Flowers grow upwards from the earth, sunsets flare out. Then there are the people: seated, reclining, walking; people within nature, within architecture, in groups, alone; the head and bust can be isolated from the rest of the body. Material reality imprints itself on the imagination. The physical metamorphoses to the plane of imagination where it is filtered, distilled, and returned to physical form, composed, arranged, extracted, perhaps abstracted, and often placed within a frame.

Instead of duplicating the holographic expanse of creation in which the living human is enmeshed, the creation of the artist is generally separated and enclosed. We tend to frame our theatre, our paintings, and our films to set them apart as the mind's interpretation of experience. The shape originally favored by filmmakers was almost a square and eventually became fixed at the academy aperture of 1.33:1. When the contracting little television screen became the hearth of 1950s homes, the movie moguls offered grandeur in order to save their industry, and widescreen supplanted the square. CinemaScope in America was greeted with awe by audiences and, initially, concern by cinematographers, who were unaccustomed to the odd 2.35:1 dimensions.

Not so in Japan. According to Anderson and Richie, widescreen did initially present some problems for Japanese filmmakers "because the proportions did not lend themselves well to Japanese sets. The rooms of Japanese houses are small and hence difficult to photograph, the wide angle always wanting to take in more than is actually there."[6] Floor or cushion seating, rather than chair seating as a cultural norm, did lend itself to this format, however, by diminishing the verticality of the human figure. When there are several characters seated on the floor, the camera with a 2.35:1 frame can draw closer to them—without cutting off heads or feet—than it could if they were standing or seated Western style. This close-to-the-earth characteristic of Japanese culture is especially compatible with a wide format.

The Asian visual legacy is decidedly different from the framing traditions and individualistic, one-point perspective derived from the European Renaissance. In Japan, the story of the group has long been told on horizontal scrolls and on the laterally elongated stage areas of both the *kabuki* and *nō* theatres. Through *emakimono* (scrolls), *byōbu* (folding screens), and decorative *fusuma* (sliding screens), the painters have prepared both set designers and cinematographers.

In these paintings, emptiness was alive, a foil to space inhabited. In Japanese drawings the entire "canvas" did not have to be covered as it often did in traditional Western painting. Line, shading, and color found their counterparts in no-line, no-shading, no-color. A powerful dynamic existed between the medium of rice paper or silk and the inked forms inscribed thereon (figure 11.1).

Fortified by these artistic precedents for organizing space, Japanese directors quite readily accepted the compositional shape of CinemaScope and its variants. Since *The Hidden Fortress* (*Kakushi toride no san akunin*) in 1958, Kurosawa Akira has worked primarily in the 2.35:1 ratio, as have Imamura Shōhei, Kobayashi, and Ōshima Nagisa. Kinoshita Keisuke used it exclusively from the 1958 *Ballad of Narayama* (*Narayama bushikō*), as did Ichikawa Kon, especially from 1958 through 1965. When Itami Jūzō in *A Taxing Woman* (*Marusa no onna*, 1987–1988) narrows the screen to 1.33:1 to make the audience squirm before a tax collector's bureaucratic incursions, the effect is all the stronger by contrast with the current widescreen norm of 1.85:1, especially since Itami crams a lot of visual information into a narrow canvas.

In his famous essay "CinemaScope Before and After," Charles Barr states that "the natural subject for film is man-in-situation."[7] With a narrow frame, this becomes translated into human figure plus situation through editing and the close-up. In CinemaScope, contextuality becomes preeminent and transforms even the close-up, which need no longer be isolating and disorienting since the environment occupied by the character is still evident and situates the viewer throughout. The actor can be brought closer to the frame without eliminating the ambience or cutting the subject off from another character who might also be presented close to the camera. Barr suggests that "the interaction of people with each other and with their surroundings is much more subtly expressed by showing them simultaneously."[8]

Contextuality has long been considered the defining characteristic of the CinemaScope format.[9] Characters and their surroundings can be shown simultaneously, and cause and effect can be encompassed within the same shot rather than revealed through editing. The possibility of suggesting relationships through the spatial arrangement of characters is enhanced, and multiple centers of interest are possible. The human form is central in film, since the cinema is a narrative/dramatic as well as a visual medium, and the two basic environments for the human form are architecture and landscape, person in society and person in nature.

Japanese filmmakers have imaginatively adapted the 2.35:1 ratio to a variety of genres, as if the complex problem-solving involved in composing for this format was a welcome aesthetic challenge and a natural manifestation of human perception. As François Truffaut once asserted, human perception is,

CYNTHIA CONTRERAS

after all, horizontal and panoramic.[10] Perhaps widescreen is the ideal shape for expressing an innate sense of being part of a people, of being defined by participation in a group effort, of identity through contextuality. It is noteworthy that when CinemaScope was first introduced in America, the most frequently heard complaint from both technicians and critics involved the close-up.[11] At that early stage, one of the first problems to be solved was how to effectively isolate the individual on a wide screen, because the spaciousness of the screen seemed best filled by landscape or by the group. Kobayashi, a student of Asian art for many years before becoming a filmmaker, quite thoroughly explored the varied spatial possibilities of widescreen composition in all nine of his films since the 1959 Part 1 of *The Human Condition,* with the exception of the made-for-TV *Kaseki* (1975) and the 1983 documentary *Tokyo Saiban.*

The Human Condition uses the wide screen to depict the enormous obstacles that threaten to dehumanize the film's hero. Yet, despite the size of the screen, the panoramic settings, and the huge war epic cast, the film is distinguished by the spareness of its compositions: brushstrokes over empty space without a touch of romantic flourish. Beyond the already expansive frame lies the vast foreign terrain of Manchuria, engulfing a people who have unwisely strayed too far from home. In this film, Kobayashi also experiments with the possibilities for extending the frame into the implied space around

11.1 Kusumi Morikage, *The West Lake* (ca. 1700), Tokugawa period, six-fold screen, ink and slight color on paper (courtesy of The Metropolitan Museum of Art, Purchase, 1972, Joseph Pulitzer Bequest, 1992, 199.1). All rights reserved, The Metropolitan Museum of Art.

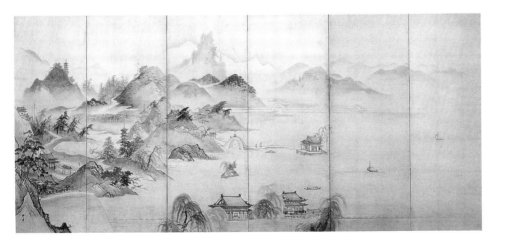

it, particularly through camera movement which frequently discloses ever more people and landscape. Although there are certainly Western precedents for doing this, the most striking correlation with the Japanese art world can be found in the tradition of scroll painting, about which Dietrich Seckel has noted that the

> all-uniting "framelessness" does not allow the picture to stop short at the edges of the scroll but, by playing on the viewer's imagination, extends it far beyond. Here, as in all Far-Eastern painting, the "suggested" pictorial area is considerably larger than the actual. [12]

In *Kwaidan,* Kobayashi also emphasizes offscreen space. Here, however, it provides the dramatic tension of the various stories, since ghosts inhabit the space outside and the camera occasionally assumes their point of view. The exquisite beauty of the settings, especially in the "Woman of the Snow" episode, depicts a shamanistic fairy-tale world in which mortals and immortals intermingle across the seemingly permeable membrane of matter.

In the "Hōichi the Earless" episode, Kobayashi refers directly to scroll painting depictions of the decisive Minamoto and Taira battle at Dan no Ura in 1185 and counterposes these images with a stylized theatrical reenactment. These juxtaposed images are accompanied by the narrating voice of a *heikyoku* singer, the traditional singer-storyteller who recalls the exploits of past heroes such as these. *Kwaidan,* which was made after *Seppuku,* makes frequent use of the bird's-eye and the omniscient or, one might say, the floating perspectives associated with traditional Japanese art.

In art which favors the one-point perspective, on the other hand, one can look at a landscape painting and easily situate the painter vis-à-vis the subject. The presence of the artist on a hillside gazing across a meadow or standing at the edge of a country lane is clearly delineated through perspective and point of view. Often in Chinese and Japanese landscapes, the painter is situated in a location which would be an impossible one for a spectator to inhabit. The point of view is that of a hovering bird or disembodied spirit. Rather than the subjective "I" of the landscape participant, there is the omniscient eye of the detached observer, thereby fulfilling the Buddhistic ideal of viewing life from a position deeper than that of the ego.

When translating angled artistic perspective into cinematic compositions, shot designations are generally referred to as high angle and low angle. These terms can be full of content implications as the viewer looks down upon or up to the subject. Yet the bird's-eye perspective of the Japanese painter does not carry the same connotations as the high-angle shot any more than the

CYNTHIA CONTRERAS

©TOHO 1967 上意討ち 拝領妻始末

11.2 Kobayashi Masaki, *Samurai Rebellion* (*Jōiuchi,* 1967) (courtesy of the Japan Film Library Council). The controlled geometric patterns of the closed form underscore the social constraints.

tatami position of the camera is equivalent in meaning to the low-angle shot. For instance, director Shinoda Masahiro likes to refer to the placement of the camera close to the floor—the tatami shot—as the position of the reclining Buddha.[13] It is the eye of the detached observer rather than that of the editorializing artist.

When exploring the horizontal dimension, particularly in *The Human Condition* and *Kwaidan,* Kobayashi suggests ever more space beyond the already elongated screen; but in *Seppuku* and *Samurai Rebellion,* he experiments with a closed form of controlled geometric patterns. Through careful compositional structuring, Kobayashi manages to use the contextual implications of the wide screen while creating an atmosphere of constraint as a comment upon rigid social structures (figure 11.2). Self-contained and favoring interiors, *Seppuku* places its characters, who are often situated at opposite ends of the screen, within hierarchical social constructs, which creates a sense of confinement despite the expansive screen size.

The theme of *Seppuku* is one that is repeated throughout Kobayashi's work: injustice and retribution. Chijiwa Motome (Ishihama Akira), a young *rōnin* with no financial resources, requests permission to commit *seppuku,* or ceremonial disembowelment, at the Iye clan compound in the hope that he will be given money instead and told to go away. The cruel courtiers, however, decide to make an example of him in order to discourage others from this practice. Permission is granted and, even though he has sold his weapons to provide for his ailing wife and son, he is forced to perform the ritual with his bamboo sword.

His father-in-law, Tsugumo Hanshirō, visits the Iye manor, ostensibly with the same request. But when the household is assembled for his ceremony, he slowly reveals his true intent. He unmasks the hypocrisy of the clan and the unyielding social structures which sacrifice human feeling—and life—to rigid protocols. The story is told in a series of flashbacks framed by the ongoing dialogue between Tsugumo Hanshirō (Nakadai Tatsuya) and Saitō Kageyu (Mikuni Rentarō), the chamberlain.

As Noël Burch has pointed out, Japanese art and literature often involve several simultaneous modes of discourse. For instance, handscrolls recount already known tales both in script and in image.[14] One might say that Tsugumo's narrating voice supplants the calligraphic texts, which usually guide the pictorial flow, as the camera frames and reframes discrete compositions of the unfolding images. Like the *heikyoku* singer retelling the exploits of archetypal heroes (e.g., Hōichi in *Kwaidan*), Tsugumo recounts and comments upon the fate of an unknown young *rōnin* and his less than heroic demise.

In telling this story, Kobayashi does use Western, linear perspective, since filmic images are conventionally deep rather than flat, as in traditional Japanese art, but he also explores the steeply angled perspective of the bird's-eye shot and the oblique angle generally associated with Japanese painting. On several occasions, the camera looks down upon an open courtyard. It is positioned at a corner of the roof of the surrounding buildings, and the rooftops create a sense of flattened, parallel perspective. This bird's-eye view into rooms through missing roofs, called *fuki-nuki yatai,* is illustrated in early scrolls and prints, such as those of the *Tale of Genji,* and is used by Kobayashi in several of his other films as well (figures 11.3, 11.4).

The cinematography in *Seppuku* is characterized by a propensity for reframing the 2.35:1 aspect ratio into 1.85:1, 1.33:1, or vertically arranged rectangles, and triangles. Often the screen is divided into three distinct vertical or horizontal segments; but a single center of interest is consistently maintained through lighting, line, and the attention of characters to a particular focal area. Since this film is less about an inner struggle than about coming

CYNTHIA CONTRERAS

to terms with social structures, angled viewpoint and parallel perspective are sometimes used, but the subjective point of view is not. As the director himself has stated:

> If my films have any meaning, I feel it lies in my depiction of human problems created by the powerful historical framework. Historical interpretation always plays a very fundamental, important part in my films. The relationship of an individual's consciousness to his setting is my main theme.[15]

The locations are interiors, and the few outdoor settings in the final flashback vengeance scenes serve as a release from the stifling social constraints which are emphasized throughout most of the rest of the film. Lighting is used to focus attention, "reshape" the screen, delineate character, and suggest the passage of time. Formal distances are generally observed between characters and are accentuated by their placement within the widescreen space. In this way, sociological structures are made visible.

One of the outstanding characteristics of this film is the interplay between long static shots and movement, between composition and choreography. Through the counterposing of the static and the dynamic, movement and stillness, *Seppuku* embodies key concepts of Buddhism which, in turn, characterize the *bushidō* code of the samurai. At the intersection of time and space, the perfect balance between the active and the passive, the *yin* and the *yang* create the possibility for realizing the Buddhist ideal of spiritual equilibrium and enlightenment. These philosophic and aesthetic ideals manifest themselves within the dramatic structure of *Seppuku* and, in the narrative, are invoked by Kobayashi, who argues for balance between the needs of the individual and those of the social group. As mentioned before, Kobayashi referred directly to this interplay between the static and the dynamic in *Kwaidan* by literally juxtaposing photographs of paintings depicting a historical event with a theatrical performance of it.

This blend of influences from theatre and art is particularly significant in *Seppuku*. Like the *nō*, the film is ritualistic in style. This is fitting since it is about social rituals, as the title *Seppuku* suggests.[16] It is through beliefs and rituals that groups define themselves. In *Seppuku*, the panning of the ensemble or isolation of an individual by a zoom or dolly shot is often done to suggest a connection between the group and the individual, between ancient, fossilized forms and immediate, vital reality; and the camera movement comments upon the linkage as well as the tensions between these two. The use of oblique angles, diagonal lines, and movement is dynamic and often suggests

11.3 Kobayashi Masaki, *Kwaidan* (*Kaidan,* 1964) (courtesy of the Japan Film Library Council). The *fuki-nuki yatai* perspective associated with scroll painting.

spatial depth. These techniques are used principally when the actions of an individual threaten to upset the fixed social order, which is depicted throughout by static, painterly compositions.

In contradiction with the usually expansive implications of the anamorphic format, Kobayashi carefully structures his frames to suggest enclosure, confinement, and stasis, not unlike the self-contained, geometric world of a Buddhist mandala, which, however, is generally square rather than rectangular (figures 11.5, 11.6). The aim of the mandala is to teach through symbols, and the flat compositions are densely packed with carefully arranged deities and their retinues in hierarchical arrangements within precise spaces.[17] Kobayashi's dramatization of the tensions between the individual and his highly codified social environment is illustrated throughout the film by the way he arranges his characters in relation to one another and the surrounding physical structures. The order which is intended to create harmony and serenity becomes rigid and oppressive instead. By working against the expan-

CYNTHIA CONTRERAS

11.4 *Genji Kokagami,* 1657, woodblock print (courtesy of the Museum of Fine Arts, Boston, Denman Waldo Ross Collection, 22.228-30).

11.5 *Ryokai mandara,* Japan, post-Ashikaga period, late seventeenth century (courtesy of the Museum of Fine Arts, Boston, William Sturgis Bigelow Collection, 11.7119). An illustration of formal geometric grouping.

sive tendencies of the frame, he underscores the ironies and contradictions within the social structure itself.

The widescreen format allows Kobayashi to emphasize visually the highly structured codes of behavior of the feudal society. The formal placement of characters within the same shot in relation to one another, determined by rank and propriety, and the confinement of characters within the squares and rectangles of surrounding architectural forms create an oppressive atmosphere despite the wide aspect ratio.

CYNTHIA CONTRERAS

11.6 Kobayashi Masaki, *Kwaidan* (courtesy of the Japan Film Library Council). The child emperor, framed by pillars, is the central, most distant, figure.

When it becomes Tsugumo's turn to perform the *seppuku* ritual, Kobayashi makes full use of the Mondrian-like squares, rectangles, and rhomboidal spaces of traditional Japanese architecture (figure 11.7). The scene of the ceremony is located in the courtyard, which is composed of raked sand and surrounded on three sides by a covered porch. On the two facing sides, there are *shōji* screens which can be opened and closed for easy exits and entrances. On the third side, there is a raised area beyond the walkway, and the clan insignia is on the wall behind this space.

Characters are seated strictly according to rank. Saitō, as the chief retainer, sits on a stool in front of the insignia with his senior advisors seated on the floor at either side of him. Behind them is a servant who, like a *nō* stagehand (*kōken*), is always present in the background to perform functional tasks, such as to adjust a stool. Also seated on stools placed along the sides of the courtyard itself are ranking members of the clan hierarchy, while lesser figures and attendants sit on the floor on both sides of the portico. These many figures, so static and formally arranged, reinforce the sense of enclosure of the space. The eaves of the portico roofing frame the sun into a rhomboid, the size of which becomes an indicator of time passing. At first this rhomboid creates a wide frame which encloses the oblique rectangle of the ceremonial pallet. As the story progresses, the lighted area is gradually reduced until, like an hourglass almost run out of sand, it is only a small piece of sunshine between Tsugumo and Saitō.

Tsugumo is seated in the center framed by the sides of the courtyard, the

11.7 Kobayashi Masaki, *Seppuku* (*Harakiri*, 1962) (courtesy of the Japan Film Library Council). Tsugumo Hanshiro (Nakadai Tatsuya) calmly debates with Saitō Kageyu (Mikuni Rentarō) before the *seppuku* ritual. Multiple geometrical forms isolate Tsugumo at the bottom of the frame.

seated men, the rhomboid created by the sun, and the white pallet. Saitō sits in the elevated area in front of the clan insignia, framed as if on a stage. Although respected as a samurai who once had status, Tsugumo is visually in an inferior position in relation to Saitō. Yet, as the dialogue ensues, it becomes apparent that, unlike his son-in-law Chijiwa, Tsugumo is the controlling force behind events. There are visual and verbal overtones of a law court proceeding as Tsugumo portrays the plight of the individual caught in the system, and Saitō defends the code and his role as administrator of it.

The hero of *Seppuku* is a believer in the ideals of the *bushidō* code, which governs samurai behavior and provides the forms of self-definition within the feudal structure. However, these codes are administered by self-interested samurai lords, who mask their power struggles by invoking these established ideals.

The reverse-angle shots which dominate most of the courtyard scenes are sweeping long shots, since they encompass not only the back of one character and the facing character in the distance but also many of the other seated figures and the framing architectural forms. Saitō is generally seen from the

CYNTHIA CONTRERAS

11.8 Kobayashi, *Seppuku* (courtesy of the Japan Film Library Council). The medium shot of Saitō Kaguyu is equally weighted with the long shot of Tsugumo Hanshirō, seated in the center and enclosed by architecture and character arrangement.

low-angle perspective of the courtyard, while Tsugumo is usually seen from
a high angle, emphasizing the fact that Saitō has hierarchical power, although Tsugumo retains moral authority (figure 11.8).

Figures placed in the background of a shot often provide narrative information. For instance, Tsugumo's appointed *kaishaku,* or second, is often included in the background in full or medium shots of Tsugumo as a reminder
that this issue of the second will be Tsugumo's device for delaying the pro-
ceedings and for making his indictment. In front of Tsugumo are his swords,
and beside him the pragmatic bucket which will be used for cleaning up
afterward.

As frequently happens within the widescreen context, narrative and descriptive information are given simultaneously. For example, in other scenes
recounted by Tsugumo and shown as flashbacks, we learn of the financial
distress which drove Chijiwa to his act of desperation. Objects in the mise-
en-scène tell a story of their own without being singled out by close-ups. Bit
by bit, the few household objects begin to disappear as, we assume, they are
sold, and the rooms become barren.

Kobayashi's Widescreen Aesthetic

Even the outdoor scenes—which depict Tsugumo's revenge upon Omo-daka, Kawabe, and Yazaki, the three men who have rejected Chijiwa's pe-tition—reflect Kobayashi's controlled approach to setting. Omodaka and Tsugumo's journey to the plain of Goyu-in is the only time Kobayashi re-moves the characters from enclosing buildings, courtyards, and streets to a purely natural location. Typically in Kobayashi's films, nature becomes a finely honed abstraction of line and movement. The frame is more open, but the images remain austere. Precedents for these film images can be found in traditional Japanese landscape paintings. As Alain Silver describes,

> The pen-and-ink simplicity of terrain, a fondness for mists, and line drawings which emphasize the interfacing of earth, sky, and sea are other qualities of traditional Japanese landscapes which often find equivalents in film images.[18]

There is a tracking shot from in front of them with Omodaka in the fore-ground, walking briskly toward left of center in light-colored clothing, and Tsugumo, a dark figure in the lower right background, following him. It is sunrise, and the diffused lighting is soft and impressionistic. The mythic qual-ity of these iconic characters is evoked as they journey to the ritual sword fight. They represent all warriors preparing to test their skills as they seem to glide through a netherworld of graves and morning mist. The widescreen, mobile camera, and sense of depth allow the spaces through which they pass to comment upon the nature of this journey and provide epic proportions befitting the timeless reenactment of the duel ahead.

As in his next film, *Samurai Rebellion,* the stylized duel between samurai swordsmen takes place among wind-blown grasses against a stark, open landscape. On the hillside behind the two characters are the silhouettes of grave markers. Diagonal forms are emphasized throughout the scene in the line of the sloping land behind them, a sword slanted across the frame, the placement of characters in opposite corners of the screen, and in the frequent use of oblique angles. The diagonal line as a compositional force has long been significant in Japanese painting (figure 11.9) and can be found as early as the *Tale of Genji* scrolls. Danielle and Vadime Elisseeff have noted that "in that scroll the composition was arranged along diagonal axes which af-forded views from below as well as from above; the height and position of figures along these axes not only indicated their nearness or remoteness, but also subtly corresponded to their importance in the unfolding narrative."[19]

A particularly dramatic instance of the diagonal line comes during a series of shots in which Omodaka is advancing on Tsugumo and is suddenly taken aback by the sight of his fierce demeanor as Tsugumo approaches. An

CYNTHIA CONTRERAS

11.9 Kanō Tsunenobu (1636–1713), album, Edo period, color and ink on silk (courtesy of The Metropolitan Museum of Art, Gift of Mr. and Mrs. Harry Rubin, 1972 [1972.213(25)]).

oblique angle is used, and Tsugumo is seen in a medium-full shot in the center of the screen with the horizon cutting a diagonal from the lower left to the upper right corner. The camera moves slightly closer as Tsugumo extends his arm so that the sword reaches horizontally across and beyond the screen frame on the left (figure 11.10). He then raises the sword into a diagonal line with the tip touching the upper left corner. This diagonal is completed by the downward line of his other arm toward the lower right corner. The background diagonal, the line of his arms and sword, and the oblique angle combine to suggest an invincible warrior. This shot makes full use of the widescreen dimensions.

Finally, because of his challenge to the Iye clan, Tsugumo must die in battle with them. The sequence which begins with Saitō's command to kill Tsugumo and ends with the actual shot of muskets being fired at him is carefully structured on the juxtaposition of the static and the dynamic. The fighting scenes, filmed with fluid camera movements and fast-paced editing, are coun-

11.10 Kobayashi, *Seppuku* (courtesy of the Japan Film Library Council). Tsugumo Hanshirō, sword extended diagonally, prepares for a duel with Omodaka Hiko-kurō. Note the cemetery markers in the background.

terposed with shots of Saitō quietly awaiting the results of the conflict going on outside of his room. Like the *waki* in the theatre, his function is to balance the activity by remaining perfectly still. Saitō is shown seated alone in a large, empty room as fighting is heard offscreen. The frame for once is open and unencumbered. The camera may slowly move around him, but he remains motionless. Yet the offscreen sounds of conflict impose themselves on this serene order.

For the most part, the full or long shot is employed, and the screen is filled with men rushing into view, at various times, from different offscreen direc-tions in order to block Tsugumo's escape. The widescreen is crowded with people, emphasizing the impossibility of victory by one man over so many aligned against him. When he manages to break through on several occa-sions, the others sweep across the screen after him, usually in a horizontal movement. As he evades one group, another laterally arranged group ap-pears in front of or behind him. Just as in the static shots, the bodies of these

CYNTHIA CONTRERAS

men, along with the architectural forms, serve to enclose him many times within the frame.

Metaphorically speaking, one could say that the frame itself seems to be a source of oppression. Tsugumo is trapped within it by the enclosing compositional forms. Yet when he breaks through to escape from the confines of the space, he finds himself once again enclosed within similar constraining forms in the subsequent shot. Before he dies he commits *seppuku* as he had promised to do. In adherence to the *bushidō* code, he keeps his word and fulfills his duty.

Set in the samurai era of the *chambara* genre, *Seppuku* is about the ritual expression of that highly codified world. The cruelty masked by elegant forms is revealed as the narrative slowly unwinds, and the tension between *giri* (duty, social demands) and *ninjō* (personal feelings) guides the dramatic action to its climax.

Favoring simple, restrained compositions, Kobayashi divides the screen into discrete areas and uses the geometric forms of the architecture to enclose and separate his characters from one another. Just as there are stories within stories, there are frames within frames. Within the widescreen format, formal distances between characters can be maintained while, at the same time, the architectural enclosure of individuals can suggest how tightly controlled the society is and how few options are available to the individual.

The relationship between the individual and his setting is central to this film. The historical context is clearly delineated, and the spaces the characters will occupy are shown first as empty rooms. Time will pass, individuals will meet and pass on, but the spaces will endure. Ultimately, this film is about the interaction of time and space. Just as the images of the *emakimono* are fixed yet are given life by the viewer's act of unrolling the scroll, so too in the film, space becomes the stable context for people and objects. It is given three-dimensional depth through architectural arrangements and through the movement of the characters and the camera. Dynamism is provided by the temporal forces of movement and montage, which penetrate and alter the serene spaces. Like a *nō* play, the film is structured according to patterns of tension and release, contraction and expansion.

In all his widescreen films, Kobayashi skillfully organizes the elongated frame as a canvas whose dimensions offer unique expressive possibilities for social criticism through presenting characters in context. Drawing upon the artistic precedents for horizontally based composition within his cultural heritage, Kobayashi uses this format powerfully to shape his aesthetic vision of life.

1. Initially, the proposed ratio was 2.66 : 1, but it was reduced to 2.55 : 1 to accommodate the four-track, magnetic stereophonic sound that Fox had intended to be an integral part of the CinemaScope system. Finally the ratio was reduced to 2.35 : 1, which was the maximum width most conventional theatres could project. John Belton points out that, by the end of 1956, there were 41,000 theatres around the world in which CinemaScope films could be shown, but only 10,000 of them had magnetic capability to accommodate the multiple-track stereo magnetic sound. Note John Belton, "Fox's Development of CinemaScope, 1953–54" (Paper delivered at the 129th SMPTE Technical Conference, Los Angeles, California, October 31–November 4, 1987), p. 18. Also see John Belton, "CinemaScope: The Economics of Technology," *Velvet Light Trap* 21 (Summer 1985): p. 35.

2. "If CinemaScope is a commercial *revolution*, it is also an aesthetic *evolution*" (François Truffaut, "A Full View," in *Cahiers du cinéma*, ed. and trans. Jim Hillier [Cambridge: Harvard University Press, 1985], p. 274; originally published as "En avoir plein la vue," *Cahiers du cinéma* 25 [July 1953].

3. For a composite of initial reactions to CinemaScope by Hollywood directors and cinematographers, see Cynthia Contreras, "The Elements of Anamorphic Composition" (Ph.D. diss., City University of New York, 1989), pp. 19–23.

4. David Bordwell, Janet Staiger, and Kristin Thompson, *The Classical Hollywood Cinema: Film Style and Mode of Production to 1960* (New York: Columbia University Press, 1985), p. 363.

5. Subject matter can be a major factor in determining aspect ratio choice. The 2.35 : 1 ratio has often been considered most appropriate for epic films, such as David Lean's *Lawrence of Arabia* (1962) or Bernardo Bertolucci's *Last Emperor* (1987), although more intimate subjects have also been filmed in this format. Ōshima Nagisa used it for his 1969 film *Boy* (*Shōnen*) and Jean-Luc Godard regretted not shooting in widescreen for *Breathless* (1959). Note Jean Narboni and Tom Milne, eds., *Godard on Godard* (New York: Viking Press, 1972), p. 183.

6. Joseph L. Anderson and Donald Richie, *The Japanese Film: Art and Industry*, (Princeton: Princeton University Press, 1982), pp. 253–254. David Desser argues that 1958 films like Kurosawa's *The Hidden Fortress*, Kinoshita's *The Ballad of Narayama*, and Ichikawa's *Conflagration* (*Enjo*) disprove Anderson and Richie's contention that widescreen was a problem for Japanese filmmakers. David Desser, *Eros plus Massacre: An Introduction to the Japanese New Wave Cinema* (Bloomington: Indiana University Press, 1988), pp. 7–8.

7. Charles Barr, "CinemaScope: Before and After," *Film Quarterly* 16, no. 4 (Summer 1963): p. 20.

8. Ibid., p. 21.

9. For a discussion of inclusiveness as the distinguishing characteristic of widescreen, see Karel Reisz and Gavin Millar, *The Technique of Film Editing*, 2d ed. (London: Focal Press, Butterworth and Co., Ltd, 1981), p. 283.

10. "The cinema is a visual art, and our natural vision is panoramic: our eyes are one beside the other, not one on top of the other—they complement one another along the horizontal axis and are no use at all to each other along the vertical" (Truffaut, "A Full View," pp. 273–274).

11. Fritz Lang quipped that CinemaScope is "a format for a funeral, or for snakes, but not for human beings: you have a close-up and, on either side, there's just superfluous space" (Charles Higham and Joel Greenberg, *The Celluloid Muse* [London: Angus and Robertson, Ltd., 1969], p. 122).

12. Dietrich Sekel, *Emakimono* (London: Jonathan Cape, 1959), p. 60.

13. Shinoda Masahiro referred to this concept during an interview with me in Tokyo on August 21, 1990. Audie Bock also notes that Shinoda spoke about this during an interview with her. Audie Bock, *Japanese Film Directors* (Tokyo, New York, and San Francisco: Kodansha, 1978), p. 344.

14. Noël Burch, *To the Distant Observer: Form and Meaning in the Japanese Cinema* (Berkeley: University of California Press, 1979), p. 98.

15. Joan Mellen, *Voices from the Japanese Cinema* (New York: Liveright, 1975), p. 139.

16. The word "*seppuku*" is much more suggestive of a ceremonial act than "*harakiri*" (literally "belly-cutting"), the title under which the film was distributed in the West.

17. Danielle Elisseeff and Vadime Elisseeff, *Art of Japan,* trans. I. Mark Paris (New York: Harry N. Abrams, Inc., 1985), pp. 121–123.

18. Alain Silver, *The Samurai Film* (Woodstock, N.Y.: The Overlook Press, 1983), p. 39.

19. Elisseeff and Elisseeff, p. 276.

PLAYING WITH FORM:
Ichikawa's An Actor's Revenge
and the "Creative Print"

BY LINDA C. EHRLICH

C
H
A
P
T
E
R

12

When writing of the relationship between the Japanese visual arts and that nation's cinema, the tendency is to look to the classical forms of pictorial art. One points, for example, to the similarities between *sumi-e* paintings and the muted quality of the black-and-white cinematography in films like Mizoguchi Kenji's *Ugetsu* (*Ugetsu monogatari*, 1953). Or note Donald Richie's perceptive description of Kinoshita Keisuke's *Fuefuki River* (*Fuefukigawa*, 1960) as a story recounted "in a period manner: partial colouring of scenes in the manner of early *ukiyo-e* prints, long scroll-like dollies and asymmetrical compositions—a self-conscious reconstruction of a Japanese style."[2]

Often overlooked is the relationship between certain Japanese films that feature a formalistic playfulness and daring, and the aesthetics of the more contemporary "creative print" (*sōsaku hanga*). This new art form originated during the Meiji and Taishō periods (1868–1926), as another manifestation of the enthusiasm for Western ideas the

That kind of artistic sincerity [of painting in the twentieth century] has never been present in printmakers from the very nature of their work. They work in reverse; they create obliquely . . ." (FRANK AND DOROTHY GETLEIN)[1]

Japanese displayed during those tumultuous years, following over two hundred years of virtual isolation. Many Japanese artists rushed headlong to learn about Western artistic techniques and sense of expressiveness.[3] It is well known that artists like Vincent van Gogh, Theophile Alexandre Steinlen, and Henri de Toulouse-Lautrec, among others, were influenced by Japanese art, but it is equally true that many Japanese artists of the Meiji period were inspired by Western art toward their own brand of modernism.

In the catalogue to the exhibition entitled "Paris in Japan: The Japanese Encounter with European Painting," Takashina Shūji and Thomas Rimer identify a central problem which faced Japanese artists during this period of great change: the need to project an air of difference from others—a sense of individualism, which went against standard artistic practice and social conditioning in Japan.[4] Scott Nygren notes: "Insofar as Japanese artists sought in Western modernism's borrowing of Japanese tradition a modernism to position against Japanese tradition, they became caught in mirrors within mirrors, an aporia, or collapse of meaning."[5] While some Japanese artists flourished in this bohemian milieu and served as role models for a new generation of Japanese artists, the strain of individual assertion proved too much for others.

One group of Japanese artists from this period chose more of a middle ground. Reacting against the limitations of the traditional *ukiyo-e* woodblock print, the *sōsaku hanga* artists also turned away from the more ponderous qualities of Western oil painting, maintaining a closer affinity (but not a blind allegiance) to characteristically Japanese themes and printmaking techniques. In the words of one contemporary printmaker, Hiratsuka Un'ichi: "Western art gave me my technique but Japanese art gave me my approach."[6]

The formalistic boldness found in *sōsaku hanga* was one outgrowth of the interest in a Western-style individualism that developed in Japan during that early period of contact with the West. The exploration of that individualism was one component of the "technique" of the prints, while a renewed exploration of traditional Japanese themes could be considered a common "approach" (to use Hiratsuka's terms). This resembles the two tendencies in Japanese art described by Joan Stanley Baker: an "outward-looking" mirroring of the external world through imitation, and an introspective, poetic nature which takes into consideration human qualities of imperfection.[7] *Sōsaku hanga* artists looked outward for new skills, such as those of perspective and foreshortening, but they also turned inward to reexamine indigenous aesthetic values.

It is important to view the *sōsaku hanga* movement against other trends in

LINDA C. EHRLICH

12.1 Kinugasa Teinosuke, *An Actor's Revenge* (*Yukinojō henge*, 1936) (courtesy of the Japan Film Library Council).

the art world of the Meiji and Taishō periods. Western-style paintings (*yōga*) remained more bound by techniques and theories imported from abroad, particularly those of impressionism. Through this European influence, some Japanese painters showed a concern with such new avenues of expression as the depiction of light and shadow, and the visual interpretation of current political affairs. In contrast, the "creative print" artists tended to use more indigenous materials and techniques, drawing on the Japanese genius for flat, two-dimensional abstraction.

Also in the Taishō period, there was the "new print" (*shin hanga*) movement of such artists as Hashiguchi Goyō, Itō Shinsui, and Kawase Hasui. In general, this movement, whose prints often featured the traditional themes of landscapes, beautiful women, and *kabuki* actors, was more closely aligned with the aesthetics of *ukiyo-e* and lacked the thematic and formalistic boldness displayed by the work of the *sōsaku hanga* artists. Lawrence Smith notes that the *sōsaku hanga* artists have "the intensity, inwardness and obliqueness of much traditional Japanese art; they also have the direct humanity which it has often lacked."[8]

These same tendencies are true of experimental films like Ichikawa Kon's *An Actor's Revenge* (*Yukinojō henge*, 1963), a remake of Kinugasa Teino-suke's 1936 film of the same name (figure 12.1), based on the story of a *kabuki onnagata*, a male actor who plays female roles.[9] In Ichikawa's film, the black-and-white stylistics from the 1930s are taken over by a widescreen perspective in which formalistic boldness and traditional subject matter combine to produce an unforgettable visual experience. Ichikawa's *An Actor's Revenge* draws on the same modernist tradition found in the *sōsaku hanga* movement, which aims at highlighting the individual as artist.

Japanese "creative prints" and films share similar successes: both are (relatively) widely distributed and exhibited, and both have enjoyed great international appeal. The success of print artists like Munakata Shikō in the 1955 São Paulo Bienal and the 1956 Venice Biennale helped raise the stature of the *sōsaku hanga* artist in Japanese eyes as, paradoxically, the successes of film-makers like Kurosawa Akira and Mizoguchi Kenji in the Venice film festivals of the 1950s helped the Japanese consider their own films a serious art form. It is unfortunate that both "creative print" artists and Japanese film directors have often had to rely on foreign approval to convince Japanese critics and viewers that their work is worth taking seriously. As Oliver Statler explains: "In Japan, [*ukiyo-e* prints] had long been regarded as plebian trifles, vulgar souvenirs of the vulgar crowd. A print was a print, in Japanese eyes, and modern print artists suffered decades of scorn and neglect because of this attitude."[10]

This ambivalent attitude toward new forms of art mirrors the ideological debates of the late Meiji and the Taishō periods, when the nation moved from a period of national isolation (*sakoku seisaku*) to a national policy of "civilization and enlightenment" (*bunmei kaika*) and "opening of the country" (*kaikoku-ron*). During the 1920s, for example, "radical restorationists" and nationalistic groups reacting against Western influence became embroiled in "desperate and even violent resistance against the West."[11] This love/hate relationship began before the period under study in this essay, and continues into the present time. As Carl French noted in his introduction to an exhibition entitled *Through Closed Doors: Western Influence on Japanese Art, 1639–1853*, there is a "strong element of paradox in the Japanese response to the outside world," a response which runs the gamut from conservative nationalism to an abundant fascination with novelty.[12] Perhaps it would be helpful to look at this relationship between Japan and the West, and at ourselves, with more of a sense of humor.

LINDA C. EHRLICH

While the status of "creative prints" as serious art has now been well established, the playful nature of these works of art and, one may add, of many Japanese films has often eluded the critic's glance. As critics and scholars, we have tended to consider play and fun too trivial or as something "without limits, rebellious, radically other."[13] It may only be through the comic, through playfulness, however, that we can learn of the pastiche of images that make up the modern consciousness—images like the geisha consuming a Baskin-Robbins ice cream cone, or the young samurai, glimpsed through cherry blossom, tying on jogging shoes in screens by the contemporary artist Teraoka Masami.

The essence of play, as described by J. Huizinga in his *Homo Ludens: A Study of the Play-Element in Culture,* is something which lies outside seeming dichotomies of wisdom and folly, truth and falsehood, good and evil.[14] This disinterested, yet ordered, activity, as described by Huizinga, also invokes a sense of freedom and secrecy to achieve its effects. Following the line of least resistance, playfulness serves as a force for *building* community through a playful indulgence in "exaggeration, inversions of the common order, depictions of vanity," to cite Henri Bergson's definition.[15]

In the theatrical and pictorial arts, the traditional Japanese sense of comedy lacks the satirical or moralistic tone often associated with the comic in the West. In the performance style known as *kyōgen,* comic interludes, frequently featuring an inversion of the common order, are interspersed between the more serious *nō* performances. Junko Berberich adds to the definition of *kyōgen* the idea of individual or collective "rapture" (absorption, the act of being carried away by an intensifying emotion).[16] In his *Playfulness in Japanese Art,* Tsuji Nobuo states that he considers the idea of playfulness a third category to be added to the two categories of Japanese art elucidated by Sherman Lee (decorativeness and realism).[17] Tsuji considers this Japanese artistic playfulness to be simple and life-affirming, influenced by Chinese Taoist antecedents but lacking the large-scale quality of much Chinese art. According to Tsuji, examples of playfulness in Japanese art include the naiveté of *haniwa* figures, the *haboku* splashed-ink paintings, the *karakuri-e* (mirage, or trick, painting), the Kamakura-period *Scrolls of Frolicking Animals (Chōjū giga),* which feature metaphoric animal caricatures of priests, and the works of Edo-period "eccentric" artists like Itō Jakūchū, Ike-no Taiga, and Shōhaku.

In her article on "The Parameters of Play," Liza Dalby points out how traditional forms of play in Japan, such as moon viewing or catching fireflies, have now been transformed into solitary hours at pachinko and other mechanized amusements, and how the traditional value placed on pilgrimage has been transformed into the group honeymoon tour and other such modern excursions.[18] In the same (but more visually pleasing) manner, the *sōsaku hanga* converted the traditional modes of playfulness to a new and bold level of visual incongruity.

The *sōsaku hanga* movement aimed at establishing the printmaker as an artist, not merely as a craftsman. Unlike the *ukiyo-e* print which was a popular (and therefore stigmatized) art in Japan, the *sōsaku hanga* movement was born of a sense of individual difference, where the depiction of personal impressions was considered paramount. Rapid reproductions of the print marked the *ukiyo-e* movement, while the *sōsaku hanga* artists stressed the uniqueness of each design and each artist. At least three people (what Statler referred to as the "time-honored artist-artisan-publisher team"[19]) were involved in making a traditional print; but with the *sōsaku hanga*, the printmakers were responsible for all aspects of their work, from design to execution. Although *ukiyo-e* artists tended to belong to a stylistic school, the same was not true of the "creative print" artists, despite the formation of small professional societies of such artists.[20] Smith describes how the main unifying force of the *sōsaku hanga* artists was "devotion to the idea of the print as a primary, creative work of art which was not a reproduction of something else."[21]

In general, the *sōsaku hanga* has tended toward a joyful celebration of life, and toward the uncluttered line suited to the nature of the woodblock itself. Kawakita Michiaki compares the natural resistance of a block of wood to the Japanese ability to react "with sensitivity and flexibility to an obstacle and produce something decorative."[22] Examining the relationship between the *sōsaku hanga* and certain free-verse Japanese poetry from the early twentieth century to the present, Thomas Rimer points out that, no matter how abstract they became, the "creative prints" still maintained a sense of "muted realism" and "a sense of craft rooted in instinctive apprehension of the power, the wholeness, of nature itself."[23] This sense of "muted realism," in which the wholeness of nature and the everyday are joyfully celebrated, can be seen in the prints of artists like Iwami Reika, which draw on the natural grain of the wood (even incorporating actual pieces of driftwood in the composition [figure 12.2]), or in Noda Tetsuya's large-scale diary pages based on family photographs, with their seemingly mundane, yet resonant, themes. Kuroda Shigeki's etchings of figures on bicycles speeding along also provide a perfect "moving pastiche" of the traditional and the rush of modernity (figure 12.3). Although the press of modern life is not usually considered a comic

LINDA C. EHRLICH

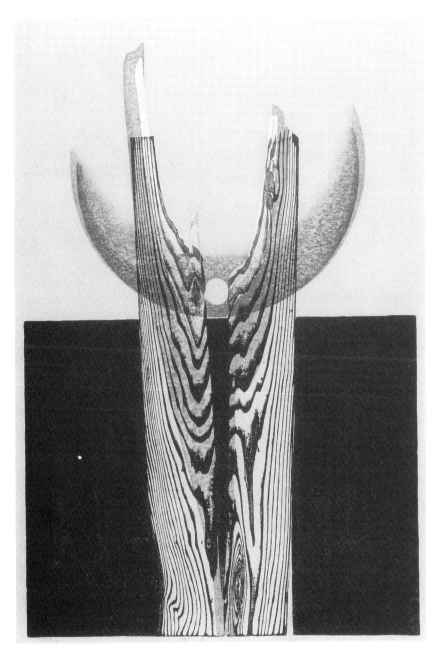

12.2 Iwami Reika, *Song of Water A*, 1970, color woodcut with mica and gold leaf (courtesy of the Cincinnati Art Museum, The Howard and Caroline Porter Collection, 1983.170).

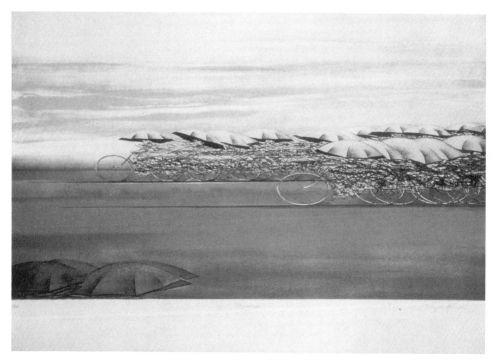

12.3 Kuroda Shigeki, *Sky Course* (courtesy of the Mitzie Verne Collection of Japanese Art).

or playful topic, the sheer mass of Kuroda's bicyclists illuminates the "mechanical encrusted on the living," to borrow Bergson's phrase for a source of comedy in everyday life.

Writing of printmaker Ay-O's use of the rainbow as a leitmotif, Joseph Love notes how that artist (like many other *sōsaku hanga* creators) "rejects that serious artistic moralism which would remove the play element from art" (colorplate 8).[24] Ay-O's exuberant, almost flamboyant, celebration of exaggerated form infuses his prints with a pulsating flow of energy that plays with the borders of the frame as if to draw the observer within. As we shall see, Ichikawa employs similar techniques in his highly eclectic remake/transformation of *An Actor's Revenge*.

Playfulness in An Actor's Revenge

In Ichikawa's *An Actor's Revenge,* the viewer is made aware of the humanity of the actor, as both character and self, through the fact that Hasegawa Kazuo appears both as an *onnagata* and as a ruffian, as well as playing him-

LINDA C. EHRLICH

self—the consummate actor who had performed the same roles in the earlier film version.[25] The story, set in the mid-1800s, is itself full of conventional melodramatic touches—a festering desire for revenge against the three Edo-period merchants who had driven Yukinojō's father to suicide, a manipulation of innocence, evil brought to justice—but this "melodrama of triumph" as presented by Ichikawa is primarily a pretense for a grand visual and theatrical display which modifies the sense of melodrama. As David Williams points out in his review, the "idiosyncratic visual style" is both "the key to the film and in a way part of its theme."[26]

"Stylized realism" and "naturalistic spectacle" may seem to be contradictory terms, yet it is exactly the tension in these apparent contradictions that marks the power of *kabuki* and the beauty of this film. Noted Japanologist Donald Keene writes that the dramatists of the eighteenth century felt they could depict life realistically *through* stylization, not in opposition to a stylization that also included the supernatural or transcendental.[27] In avant-garde films like Ichikawa's *An Actor's Revenge,* the traditional and the melodramatic are points of entry, not destinations. The formulaic provides a comfortable base from which we can see beyond the formulas. Commenting on the "bizarre mixture of the realistic and theatrical" in *An Actor's Revenge,* Keiko McDonald writes: "One might say that [Ichikawa's] replay of Hasegawa's earlier triumph takes the form of an affectionate look at traditional *kabuki* conventions, even as it parodies them."[28]

This postwar treatment of a popular prewar hit foregrounds the contemporary nature of cinema rather than the original spirit of the Edo-period tale. Ichikawa's frequent division of the frame into various geometric sections in which figures are highlighted and then "erased," reminds the viewer over and over of the theatrical nature of the tale. Miyagawa Kazuo, cameraman for such Ichikawa films as *Conflagration* (*Enjō,* 1958) and *The Key* (aka *Odd Obsession; Kagi,* 1959), reported in an interview that Ichikawa used fragmentation of the screen more than other directors with whom Miyagawa had worked. "He thought that the camera should be more 'involved' in the film, almost like an actor."[29]

As in prints by artists like Ida Shōichi and Ay-O, the use of vibrant, symbolic colors and unnatural proportions are logical, not as reproductions of some outer reality, but within the closed world of the work itself. On stage (in the film), a snow scene dissolves into what appears to be a real scene of snow falling—delighting, and yet mystifying, the viewer. Actors enter scenes in the film in the manner of *kabuki* actors approaching the stage on the *hanamichi* walkway that traverses the audience space. In one scene a seemingly endless rope is tossed across the screen to an unseen destination, playing

12.4 Shinoda Tōkō, *Saga,* 1982. Lithograph with red and silver ink (courtesy of the Cincinnati Art Museum, The Howard and Caroline Porter Collection, 1990.120: 1–3).

on, and defying, the limits of the CinemaScope screen, as in calligrapher-lithographer Shinoda Tōkō's print *Saga* (1982, figure 12.4) in which the image extends beyond the edges of the frame. Although this is a common trait of Japanese composition, it is carried to an extreme in *An Actor's Revenge,* in which the black background within the 'Scope format high-lights figures in the corner or along a horizontal axis. In the same way, the light and heavy elements of Shinoda Tōkō's design expressively interact with the white background. These are worlds at once in harmony with tra-ditional Japanese aesthetics, and yet separated from the sphere of ordinary life—worlds in which reality becomes play.

As Ichikawa denies the viewer the expected image in this melodramatic tale, he allows for a new range of narrative and visual meaning to emerge, especially through the use of comic touches.[30] Hasegawa in the dual roles of Yukinojō and a Robin Hood (or the *kabuki* character Nezumi Kōzō) type of thief, Yamitarō, comment about each other, and even "flirt" with each other, with obvious delight at the self-reflexive punning (figure 12.5).[31] "I somehow feel like you're my brother," one declares to the other (i.e., to himself). David Desser identifies this as a source of "distancing humor, a kind of 'in' joke."[32] Just when we think we have discerned a visual pattern to the film, the next sequence begins in a new area of the screen—figures suddenly emerge from a corner or rooftop, as if defying gravity—causing the viewer both surprise and amusement. Like the revolving stage on which the *onnagata* performs,

LINDA C. EHRLICH

12.5 Ichikawa Kon, *An Actor's Revenge* (*Yukinojō henge,* 1963) (courtesy of the Japan Film Library Council). A mirror image of self-admiration.

the director whirls us from one scene to another, capitalizing on the element of surprise.

Through this sense of the comic, we as viewers are prevented from taking the narrative of *An Actor's Revenge* (and ourselves) too seriously. Cartoon-like aspects—for example, the appearance of faces in the theatre audience within "bubbles"—remind us of inserts in Japanese prints or of comic-strip aesthetics. In true melodramatic fashion, a young woman puts her hand over her heart, sighing deeply out of love for the *onnagata* performing on stage. Ichikawa himself began his training as an animator, and many of his films, like *Mr. Poo* (*Pū-san,* 1953, based on two serial comic strips by Yokoyama Taizo) and *Being Two Isn't Easy* (*Watashi wa nisai,* 1962), display the director's skill in this art form.[33] In many ways the characters in *An Actor's Revenge* also seem to be viewing, rather than precipitating, the development of the story. Suspense is maintained, but the performers are primarily engrossed in playing with the play itself.

The artificial nature of many of the sets reminds one of the presentational aspect of this tale of revenge, and helps to foreground the human factor. A similar technique is employed in the print *Mountaineer* by Azechi Umetarō (figure 12.6), in which the stylized mountains in the background seem to

Playing With Form

12.6 Azechi Umetarō, *Mountaineer,* 1952, color woodcut (courtesy of the Cincinnati Art Museum, The Howard and Caroline Porter Collection, 1984.249).

LINDA C. EHRLICH

12.7 *An Actor's Revenge* (*Yukinojō henge*, 1963) (courtesy of the Japan Film Library Council). Playing with gender.

recede, causing the figure of the mountaineer to assume larger-than-life proportions. Although this could potentially appear grim and heroic, the actual effect is one in which objects assume the charming proportions that one might expect from a child's drawing. Like the odd forest in which the female pickpocket Ohatsu declares her love for Yukinojō, stylized Nature announces, and indulges in, its own artifice.

An Actor's Revenge alternates rapidly between scenes of breathtakingly clear color, scenes in which mist and uncertainty predominate (like the shot of the half-hidden moon), and a darkened screen ("stage") in which close-ups of objects or of parts of the human body add a subtext to the unfolding tale of revenge. In fact, the entire film is a study of incongruous juxtapositions—in its striking visual compositions, in the mixture of traditional Japanese music and nondiegetic contemporary jazz and "lounge music" on the soundtrack, in the movement from old-fashioned full-body "proscenium" shots to zoomed-in close-ups, and in the nature of characters like the "masculine" aggressive female thief Ohatsu and the "feminine" actor Yukinojō.

Another factor which adds a note of wry comedy to the story of *An Actor's Revenge* is the gender-switching inherent in the *onnagata* role.[34] This gender-switching is further highlighted by Hasegawa Kazuo's playing not only the *onnagata* (a man playing a woman) but also Yamitarō (a man playing a

12.8 *An Actor's Revenge* (courtesy of the Japan Film Library Council).

man), and the actor par excellence (a man playing himself). We marvel at the intertextuality of this elegantly dressed man who remains an idealized woman both on and off stage, while at the same time maintaining the inner nature of a virile fighter (figure 12.7). This kind of gender-switching provides a Brechtian alienation effect which allows the viewer a chance to relax rigid preconceptions about the nature of personal identity, while it also clearly points to the division between the actor and the character.

Ichikawa daringly highlights the sexual nature of the *onnagata* by focusing on this character's complex love relationship/manipulation of the beautiful Namiji (Wakao Ayako), daughter of one of the evil merchants (figure 12.8). (This love affair is itself not without a touch of absurdity, or painful reality, as actor Hasegawa Kazuo was then a somewhat "over-the-hill," pudgy fifty-five-year-old, while Wakao Ayako was yet an ingenue in her twenties.) In the role of the beloved, Yukinojō is unmasked and also is the one who coldly carries out the unmasking of others. As the two main female characters (Namiji and Ohatsu) profess their love to the *onnagata* in turn, we cannot help but laugh at the parodies of the *nureba* love scenes from traditional *kabuki*, and at the pitiful countenances of the "macho" men these women are scorning for this mixed-gender character.

LINDA C. EHRLICH

12.9 Tajima Hiroyuki, *Stone Cutter and His Apprentice*, 1971, color woodcut (courtesy of the Cincinnati Art Museum, The Howard and Caroline Porter Collection, 1990.121).

12.10 Saitō Kiyoshi, *Clay Image* (*Haniwa*), 1952, color woodcut (courtesy of the Cincinnati Art Museum, The Howard and Caroline Porter Collection).

LINDA C. EHRLICH

In "The Secret Ritual of the Place of Evil," Hirosue Tamotsu addresses the fact that, to the audience, the *onnagata,* as female surrogate, was both an object of aspiration and a scorned outcast (like the courtesan whose roles the *onnagata* frequently played).[35] Hirosue's thesis is that both the actor and the courtesan were viewed in an arena, based on ancient animistic/shamanistic beliefs, in which "nobility and debasement, beauty and wretchedness, were indivisibly mixed." In Edo-period Japan, the official reaction to *kabuki* was one of disdain, yet there was also a sense of fascination with the demimonde of which it was a crucial part.

Hirosue classifies the eroticism associated with the *onnagata* as a recon-struction of a "predifferentiated eroticism,"[36] but it is important to remem-ber that this is an eroticism based on fiction, just as the *onnagata* represents a basically fictitious ideal of "feminine perfection." Ichikawa plays on this ambiguity in his film by transforming, in the words of the *kyōgen* master Okura Toraaki, "the real into the unreal."[37]

The formalistic simplicity of line of many contemporary *sōsaku hanga* also allows for this kind of ambiguity. Tajima Hiroyuki's *Stone Cutter and His Apprentice* (1971), for example, abstracts the figures into an amorphous body, of undetermined gender, a human form that merges with the element it is meant to control (figure 12.9). These figures, like that of the Mountain-eer, or like the *haniwa* figure in Saitō Kiyoshi's print of the same name (fig-ure 12.10), are both monumental and objects of light amusement.

The ending of Ichikawa's version of *An Actor's Revenge* shows the *onna-gata*—his revenge completed—performing on stage to the admiration of Ohatsu (the female pickpocket), Yamitarō (Hasegawa Kazuo's alter charac-ter), and others. The protagonist, dressed as always in the garb of the *onna-gata,* appears to have given up on acting as he wanders off alone into a field of pampas grass, disappearing from sight. At this point, Yukinojō has be-come both individual and nonindividuated form. Is this last highly stylized scene a merging with nature or the beginning of yet another play? We as viewers are left with a sense of having seen something eclectic and refreshing, a playful dialogue between form and content, between the traditional and the modern, so apparent in Japanese arts like the "creative print" which pre-sent an image of the modern age.

Notes

1. Frank Getlein and Dorothy Getlein, *The Bite of the Print: Satire and Irony in Woodcuts, Engravings, Etchings, Lithographs, and Seriographs* (New York: Clark-son N. Potter, Inc., 1963), p. 14.

2. Donald Richie, *Japanese Cinema: An Introduction* (Oxford: Oxford University Press, 1990), p. 58.

3. For a detailed discussion of painters like Fujita Tsuguji, Kuroda Seiki, and Umehara Ryūzaburō, note Takashina Shūji and J. Thomas Rimer, eds., *Paris in Japan: The Japanese Encounter with European Painting* (St. Louis: Washington University Press, 1987).

4. Takashina and Rimer, p. 75.

5. Scott Nygren, "Reconsidering Modernism: Japanese Film and the Postmodern Context," *Wide Angle* 11, no. 3 (July 1989): p. 13.

6. Ibid., p. 38.

7. Joan Stanley Baker, *Japanese Art* (London: Thames and Hudson, 1984), pp. 7–8, 11.

8. Lawrence Smith, *The Japanese Print since 1900: Old Dreams and New Visions* (New York: Harper and Row, 1983), p. 28.

9. The *onnagata* was not originally an essential entity of the *kabuki*. With the banning of female performers (of *onna* or *yūjo kabuki*) in 1629, and of male performers (of *wakashū kabuki*) in 1652, the *onnagata* developed as a necessary invention. The *onnagata* distills essential aspects of womanly speech and movements, and its artistic goal is to portray the decorative essence of womanhood, rather than its reality.

10. Introduction, catalogue, "Japan's Modern Prints—*Sōsaku Hanga*" (Chicago: Art Institute of Chicago, 1960), p. 2.

11. Tetsuo Nàjita and H. D. Harootunian, "Japanese Revolt against the West: Political and Cultural Criticism in the Twentieth Century," in *Cambridge History of Japan*, vol. 6, ed. Peter Duus (Cambridge: Cambridge University Press, 1988), pp. 711, 713. Note D. William Davis's discussion of the conscious use of tradition by Japanese ideologues in "Back to Japan: Militarism and Monumentalism in Prewar Japanese Cinema," *Wide Angle* 11, no. 3 (July 1989): pp. 16–25.

12. Rochester, Mich.: Oakland University/Meadow Brook Art Gallery, 1977–1978, p. 1.

13. R. L. Rutsky and Justin Wyatt, "Serious Pleasure: Cinematic Pleasure and the Notion of Film," *Cinema Journal* 30, no. 1 (Fall 1990): p. 7.

14. J. Huizinga, *Homo Ludens: A Study of the Play Element in Culture* (London: Routledge and Kegan Paul, Ltd., 1949), p. 6.

15. Henri Bergson, "Laughter," trans. Fred Rothwell, in *Comedy*, ed. Wylie Sypher (New York: Doubleday and Co., 1956), p. 748. Bergson describes these exaggerations and inversions as "something mechanical encrusted on the living."

16. Junko Sakaba Berberich, "The Idea of Rapture as an Approach to *Kyōgen*," *Asian Theatre Journal* 6, no. 1 (Spring 1989): p. 32.

17. Tsuji Nobuo, *Playfulness in Japanese Art*, trans. Joseph Seubert (Lawrence, Kansas: The Spencer Museum of Art, 1986). Note, in particular, pp. 9–15, 34, 61–86.

18. Liza Dalby, "The Parameters of Play," in *Tokyo: Form and Spirit,* ed. Mildred Friedman, (New York: Harry N. Abrams, Inc., 1986), pp. 201–218.

19. Oliver Statler, *Modern Japanese Prints: An Art Reborn* (Rutland, Vt.: Tuttle, 1956).

20. By 1918, there was an organization devoted to the *sōsaku hanga,* the Nihon sōsaku hanga kyōkai (reorganized in 1931 as the Nihon hanga kyōkai). Early journals devoted to the *sōsaku hanga* included *Hōsun* (started in 1907) and *Tsukubae* (in 1914).

21. Smith, p. 13. In his catalogue to a 1972 exhibition of contemporary Japanese prints at the Los Angeles County Museum of Art, George Kuwayama divides the *sōsaku hanga* artists into three generations: the early generation of artists like Onchi Kōshirō and Hiratsuka Un'chi, who tended to move between abstraction and representation, focusing on naturalistic themes; the second generation of artists like Munakata Shikō, Saitō Kiyoshi, and Azechi Umetarō, whose works tended toward a more abstract, reductive sense of natural forms and an experimentation with new techniques and materials; and a third generation, exemplified by works of a highly decorative or fanciful nature, by artists like Mizufune Rokushū and Hagiwara Hideo. One can now add a fourth generation of artists like Ay-O [Ijima Takao], Noda Tetsuya, and Arakawa Shūsaku, who play with what could be termed a postmodern montage of elements from both "high" and "low" culture. These latter generations frequently move from the woodblock medium to employ intaglio techniques, the silk screen, or even photographic images. (Of course, none of these generational divisions are absolute, as there are also variations within the works of the artists mentioned in Kuwayama's general categories.) Statler adds one more generation to this list in a catalogue from an earlier *sōsaku hanga* exhibition: the pioneering "first generation" of artists like Yamamoto Kanae, Tobari Kogan, and Minami Kunzō.

22. Kawakita Michiaki, *Contemporary Japanese Prints,* trans. John Bester (Tokyo: Kodansha, 1967), p. xx.

23. J. Thomas Rimer, "A Lyric Impulse in Modern Japanese Prints and Poetry," *Asian Art* 11, no. 1 (Winter 1989): pp. 48, 53.

24. Joseph Love, "The Radical Artist and the Print," *Japan Quarterly* 20, no. 2 (1973): p. 187.

25. Hasegawa Kazuo (whose original name was Hayashi Chōjirō) entered the Shōchiku Kyoto film studios in 1926, while still a young performer in the *kabuki* theatre. Appearing in many of Kinugasa Teinosuke's silent films, Hasegawa became known for portraying a quiet kind of savoir faire and a gentleness within strength, which marked a new style for Japanese actors. Ichikawa's *An Actor's Revenge* was commissioned by Daiei Studio to commemorate Hasegawa's three hundredth film appearance. Hasegawa actually plays *three* roles in the film, as he makes a brief appearance in a flashback as Yukinojō's mother.

26. David Williams, "*An Actor's Revenge,*" *Screen* 11, no. 2 (March–April 1970): p. 5.

27. Donald Keene, "Reality and Unreality in Japanese Drama," *Landscapes and Portraits: Appreciations of Japanese Culture* (Tokyo: Kodansha, 1971), p. 52.

28. Keiko McDonald, *Japanese Classical Theatre in Film* (Rutherford, N.J.: Fair-

leigh Dickinson Press, forthcoming). The author would like to thank Professor McDonald for sending this (yet) unpublished essay.

29. Max Tessier and Ian Buruma, "Japanese Cameraman: Kazuo Miyagawa," *Sight and Sound* 48 (1978–1979), p. 189.

30. This sense of playfulness is related to the kind of playfulness elucidated in David Bordwell's *Ozu and the Poetics of Cinema* (Princeton: Princeton University Press, 1988). Bordwell describes Ozu's exact, and yet unpredictable, sense of playfulness regarding such formalistic devices as eyeline (mis)matches and color links. Bordwell also points out the playful nature of Ozu's narration which "teases, equivocates and deflates. By appealing to unity, the narration sets up a rigorous, self-contained system and then undermines that through withheld information, flaunted gaps, and self-conscious asides" (p. 72). Ichikawa's more flamboyant film does not set up such a unified, subtle system, although the director does tease the viewer with the unexpected.

31. Nezumi Kōzō (whose name can be translated as "rat thief") is the main character of a *kizewamono*-style *kabuki* play by Kawatake Mokuami (1816–1893). The *kizewamono* were written in the latter part of the Edo period and reflect a society in crisis. Thieves like Nezumi Kōzō are outlaws who help the poor as a means of atoning for their past evil deeds.

32. David Desser, *Eros plus Massacre: An Introduction to the Japanese New Wave Cinema* (Bloomington: Indiana University Press, 1988), p. 179.

33. As in the subsequent *An Actor's Revenge*, physical humor abounds in *Mr. Poo*, the story of a timid man who attempts to rise above his lowly station but is continuously "tripped up."

34. Of course, this myth of androgyny is not limited to artistic forms like *kabuki*. It can also be seen on the Western stage in the boy actors and breech roles of the Restoration Theatre, in cross-gender casting in the modern stage and screen in works like *M. Butterfly* (1986), and *Victor/Victoria* (1982), and in the Linda Hunt character (Billy Kwan) in Peter Weir's *Year of Living Dangerously* (1983).

35. Tamotsu Hirosue, "The Secret Ritual of the Place of Evil," *Concerned Theatre Japan* 2, no. 1–2 (1971): p. 20.

36. Ibid., p. 17.

37. Ueda Makoto, *Literary and Art Theories in Japan* (Cleveland: The Press of Western Reserve University, 1967), p. 103. In Okura's five-volume set of writings entitled "For My Successors" (*Warabe Gusa*, 1660), translator and editor Ueda quotes the lead actor of the Okura *kyōgen* troupe Okura Toraaki (1597–1662) as saying that "the *nō* transforms the unreal into the real; the Comic Interlude [*kyōgen*], the real into the unreal" (p. 103). Okura is referring to comedy's ability to present stereotyped characters in a somewhat unreal world; that is, to "make true things funny and funny things true" (p. 105).

PLAYING WITH SPACE:
Ozu and Two-Dimensional
Design in Japan

BY KATHE GEIST

CHAPTER 13

In their seminal article on Ozu Yasujirō's un-conventional use of space, Kristin Thompson and David Bordwell argued Ozu's modern-ism.[1] Joseph Anderson and Loren Hoekzema countered with the reminder that the treat-ment of space in traditional Japanese theatre, painting, and music is similar to a modernist treatment in the West in considering space "as an element separate from the narrative space."[2] This article will probe further the problem of distinguishing between Western modernism and Japanese traditionalism, and focus on the similarities between Ozu's use of space and that of Japanese traditional artists working in two-dimensional media.

From early times, Japanese painters devel-oped a different attitude toward space from that of their Western counterparts. The con-cept of an inviolable narrative space devel-oped in the West during the Renaissance, primarily in response to the invention of one-point perspective, which made classical illu-sionism possible. But one-point perspective was merely a symptom of an underlying philosophy that caused artists in the West to approach art quite differently from their counterparts in China and Japan. For the Greeks, the human being was the measure of all things, and space was something to be dominated by man. This philosophy worked itself out not only in the expansionist imperative of both Greece and Rome, but in two-dimensional design as well. In temple friezes, vase painting, mosaic, and wall painting, Greek and Roman designs were geometrical, centered, symmetrical. There was a tendency to fill up all available space, known as *horror vacui;* but where empty space remained, it was evenly distributed, no more in one place than in another. Designs usually contained human figures, and these were generally placed at the center of the composition.

European medieval art continued these design strategies. God was now the measurement and the measurer and became the subject of most painting, but God generally appeared in a manlike form or, conveniently, as His Son, Jesus Christ. Excepting the work of a few notable painters in the seventeenth century and after, nature was a secondary subject in Western painting and was usually rendered with an Aristotelian, scientific scrutiny. This collaboration between science and art led, during the Renaissance, to the development of one-point perspective, which soon replaced the multipoint perspective systems through which narrative space up to that time had been less convincingly created.

By contrast, the Taoist and Buddhist traditions of China and Japan saw the human being as merely an element in nature; they celebrated the void (*mu*) and tended to see space and time as relative and interdependent intervals (*ma*) rather than fixed measurements that could be pinned down and controlled. As a result, the Japanese painter approached space very differently from the Western painter. Nature rather than the human being was the dominant subject matter and was rendered impressionistically rather than exactly. There was no "horror vacui." Nature contains a lot of vacant as well as unseen spaces, and traditional painters apparently felt no need to either lay bare or fill up all this space when rendering it two-dimensionally. Instead they used empty space as an active design element. Moreover, the Japanese painter seldom treated narrative space as a unified whole, separate from the surface on which it was rendered, but generally acknowledged the surface of the screen or scroll containing the painting. A single scene, for example, might be painted over several folding screens and would, therefore, be broken into segments, often separated by lacquer frames. Confronting a similar problem (in architectural painting, for example), Western painters would almost always paint separate scenes within each framed area to preserve the unity of their narrative space.

The formula for one-point perspective was never discovered in Japan but was introduced by the Dutch in the seventeenth century and found its way into traditional Japanese art by the late eighteenth century. Traditionally, narrative space was constructed using various kinds of intuitive perspective systems much as in Western medieval painting; but it was never an inviolable space, for writing in the form of calligraphy frequently shared the space and made the two-dimensional nature of the surface obvious. Western medieval painting, which appeared mainly in the form of manuscript illumination, shared this dual spatial percept, but later ages would rule it out in the West. In Japan, however, painters did not shift from a dual-purpose narrative space to a unified one, but became increasingly sophisticated in exploring and exposing the contradictions inherent in creating an illusion of three dimensions on a two-dimensional surface. A similar exploration would not take place in the West until the advent of modernism.

In his monumental work on Ozu, David Bordwell reminds us that we cannot simply link Ozu's work to the "outer circle" or broadest configurations of Japanese history and culture but must contextualize these configurations within the periods in which Ozu worked.[3] Even so, Bordwell cannot resist comparing Ozu's lifelong study of Tokyo and his many views of the city to Hiroshige's *One Hundred Famous Views of Edo* (1857). Yet the comparison is justified, for traditional Japanese art remained pervasive in twentieth-century Japan.[4]

Since the Meiji period, two distinct schools of painting have coexisted in Japan: *yōga,* or Western-style painting; and *nihonga,* or Japanese-style painting. Despite the popularity of *yōga* in the Meiji period and Japan's fascination with Western modernism in the 1920s, traditional painting maintained a strong presence in Japanese society. Works from previous centuries were frequently on exhibition, and new works, *nihonga,* were created by artists who founded vital schools, clubs, and publications.[5] The traditional *toko-noma* alcove in Japanese homes required a Japanese-style painting and insured a continued consciousness of this painting style. Discoveries in the late Meiji period of art objects from pre-Edo times housed in tombs and temples fed a growing interest in earlier schools of Japanese art. As Japan turned inward and nationalism increased in the 1930s, interest in classical Japanese art grew even greater.

Ozu's *There Was a Father* (*Chichi ariki,* 1942) evidences the link between national policy and art appreciation when the father remarks to his son, "Traditional Japanese art is profoundly beautiful." One assumes, however, that the father's sentiment was not merely a sop to the censors but was shared by Ozu, who, during the war, asked a Chinese monk to write the word "*mu*" for him in calligraphy. He is said to have kept the painting all his life.[6] After the war his interest in traditional arts surfaced in his films, particularly *Late Spring* (*Banshun,* 1949), which showcased temple and garden architecture, tea ceremony, and *nō. Mu,* a fundamental concept in Japanese aesthetics indicating the positivity of empty space, was the only epitaph chosen for Ozu's tombstone.

Like many twentieth-century Japanese artists, Ozu combined elements of traditional Japanese and modern Western aesthetics. Such combining is apparent in *nihonga* artist Kawabata Ryūshi's *Music of Spring Trees* (1932), in which a traditional Japanese landscape has been placed against the traditional flat, gold background but has been abstracted and geometricized in accord with modern Western aesthetics.[7] In 1965 artist Isobe Yukihisa created a scandal by combining Sōtatsu's famous *Wind God* with "contemporary signs and symbols: Coca-Cola, imported whiskey labels . . . Olympic badges, and so forth." Influenced perhaps by Duchamp's "Mona Lisa" and Andy Warhol's pop art, Isobe elaborated, "Great masterpieces of art are easily seen and available in reproduction on calendars, stamps, magazines, and books; they are no different from spoons, instant foods, comic strips, or TV's."[8] One is reminded of Ozu's *Late Spring,* in which the camera contemplates a Coca-Cola sign in one scene and the Ryōanji garden in another. Ozu's point, however, is not that traditional art had been overcommodified but that it coexists with the commercial and the mundane; and these, as Duchamp had already shown and Warhol, Robert Rauschenberg, and Jasper Johns would later demonstrate, can be turned into art simply by putting them into the context of art.

In creating narrative space in his films, Ozu was clearly conscious of traditional two-dimensional art forms in Japan, for he frequently extrapolated the implications of traditional attitudes toward space into the time medium of cinema. Of the many ways in which Ozu imitated traditional spatial constructions, the most obvious and obviously conscious of these imitations is the view into deep space framed by objects in close-up. For example, a high shot from *End of Summer* (*Kohayagawa-ke no aki,* 1961) is framed on the left and above by an extreme close-up of a tree while looking down on the tiny figures of two women walking by a river (figure 13.1). For comparison, the composition of a Hiroshige print of the Kinryūsan Temple (1856) is framed on the left and above by an "extreme close-up" of the temple gate with its huge lantern, then shoots into deep space along a snowy path to the main temple buildings (figure 13.2). (The shot from Ozu's *Walk Cheerfully* [*Hogaraka ni ayume,* 1930] which Bordwell compares to a Hiroshige print is based on the same compositional strategy.[9])

KATHE GEIST

The two compositions also illustrate the same use of empty space as a positive compositional element (*mu*). Apart from the large, off-center lantern and gatepost, nothing appears in the fore- and middleground of Hiroshige's print. Similarly Ozu's composition makes generous use of empty space, the two small figures displacing only a small amount of it. Ozu's composition is not as radical as Hiroshige's, for his figures are centrally placed, not relegated to the edges like Hiroshige's temple visitors. On the other hand, Ozu's figures are not anonymous bystanders, but are rather two of the film's central characters. Although the shot is set up as a point-of-view shot, it is nevertheless unusual to introduce an intimate conversation with an extreme long shot as Ozu does here. By doing so, Ozu was flaunting conventional film style while imitating traditional Japanese pictorial style.

Ozu's use of empty space as a compositional element is not confined to the single shot, but expands into the edited sequence where he uses what are sometimes called empty shots as transitions between scenes. The empty shot is not, of course, completely empty, but in terms of classical film style it is empty of reference: no characters from the film appear in them, and the location and/or purpose of these shots is often unestablished. I have demonstrated elsewhere that the so-called empty shots frequently have a narrative or symbolic significance, but one that is by no means readily apparent.[10] At the same time, the empty shots often invite the viewer to read meaning into them much as the empty spaces in Japanese painting do.

The *mu* concept implies that empty space contributes actively to a composition, and in traditional painting the empty space is used to suggest a world lying beyond what the painter shows us. These splashed ink paintings by artists like Sesshū and Shūgetsu represent mountains rising out of the mist behind the rocks in the foreground—the mist represented by empty space. Horizontal washes suggest the river, but no shoreline is shown, and we are left to imagine the point at which the river touches land. Three brushstrokes represent a housetop, four or five the house behind it. The rest of each house and the houses behind are left to our imagination. The same is true of the little boats in the lower right, each composed of about three strokes.

In Ozu's *End of Summer*, the youngest daughter, Noriko, accompanies the man she loves to the local commuter station in downtown Ōsaka. In a few days he will be leaving for Sapporo—they have come from his office farewell party—and the two sit sadly in the station, too shy to express their feelings of affection for one another. The sequence ends with a shot of the empty station platform. Although we see no train, its presence is obvious from the shadows it throws against the wall and the sound effects that accompany the shot. Like Sesshū's brushstrokes that suggest two houses, the implied pres-

13.1 Ozu Yasujirō, *The End of Summer* (*Kohayagawake no aki*, 1961) (courtesy of the Japan Film Library Council). View of Arashiyama with Akiko and Noriko.

ence of the train tells us that the two young people will now take their separate trains. This in turn suggests the much greater distance that will soon separate the would-be lovers. The empty platform suggests the impending absence of the young man and the emptiness or loneliness that both he and Noriko will feel.

Perhaps the most evocative empty shot in an Ozu film is the shot of the clinic that appears in *End of Summer* after the patriarch Kohayagawa Manbei collapses. Noriko runs to call a doctor. Ozu cuts from her telephoning to the telephone ringing over a shot of the empty clinic. A shot of the clock in this same empty room follows, and the phone keeps ringing. Where is the doctor and why doesn't someone answer the phone? We imagine the worst. Five empty shots inside the Kohayagawa house follow until finally we see the doctor, his arrival unexplained, kneeling at Manbei's bedside. Using no overt drama whatsoever, only sound over empty though identifiable space, Ozu reveals the power of emptiness, of a lack of information, to suggest a multitude of dramatic possibilities.

KATHE GEIST

13.2 Utagawa Hiroshige, *Kinryūsan Temple, Asakusa*, 1856, Japan, Edo period, woodblock print (courtesy of the Brooklyn Museum of Art).

In addition to utilizing the power of empty space, Ozu frequently evoked the tendency found in Japanese prints and paintings to flatten a space rendered three-dimensionally, and often he used the same devices as the painters to achieve this flattened effect.[11] Traditional painters flattened space by using white, gold, or gridded backgrounds, which tend to push forward and deprive three-dimensionally rendered figures in the foreground of a deep space to inhabit. Such backgrounds appear most frequently in screen painting or in prints. In Hiroshige's *Wild Geese Alighting by Moonlight*, three geese plunge earthward in front of a huge white moon. Although the clouds below the moon suggest depth, the moon itself pushes forward and denies the geese the space suggested by their energetic movement. Screens with gold backgrounds create a similar effect: objects painted three-dimensionally, such as the bird in Kanō Sanraku's *Plum Tree and Pheasant,* seem to have no space in which to exist. Instead of suggesting space in Harunobu's *Climbing Temple Steps,* the three-dimensionally rendered stairs create a grid which flattens the geisha against the surface plane of the painting. The flattening, gridlike effect of the stairs is enhanced by the high, raking angle from which they and the geisha are viewed. Such high, raking angles with similar flattening effects had a long history in Japanese painting and were most notably used by the twelfth-century painters of narrative scrolls (*emakimono*).

For his shots inside the Kohayagawa house in *End of Summer*, Ozu utilizes all of these visual devices to flatten the space. In one shot, for example, white morning light comes through the back doors and windows, a gold light comes through the matting around the doors, the modular units comprising the back wall form a grid pattern, and a raking angle, low here instead of high, helps to further flatten the space. In this shot we look from one room into a second, behind which is a small ledge surrounding a garden—potentially a very deep space, which has been rendered essentially flat.

Seventeenth-century artists of the *Rimpa* school seemed particularly intrigued by the tension between a two-dimensional surface and a three-dimensional rendering. In his *Tale of Ise (Ise monogatari)* scroll, Sōtatsu copied the twelfth-century *emaki-e* style. In one scene (figure 13.3), he completely flattened the dollhouselike space of the earlier *emaki-e*, creating a patterned grid against which the figures interact. In *End of Summer*, Ozu creates a similarly patterned grid as background for the office assistant, Rokurō, who is caught spying on his boss Manbei (figure 13.4).

Implicit in the examples of flattened space cited above is an ambiguity created by the presence within each composition of objects and figures which are rendered three-dimensionally and yet are denied a three-dimensional

KATHE GEIST

space in which to exist. With the exception of Sōtatsu's figures, which are themselves rather flat, these subjects tend simply to be pushed forward, almost into the viewer's space. The tension between two- and three-dimensionality becomes more pronounced when there is an obvious recession into space, in which case it is no longer possible simply to push an object forward. In Kōrin's famous *Plum Trees,* for example, a blue stream filled with highly patterned gold eddies recedes into space, that is, gets narrower as it goes "back" (actually up). The space into which this stream recedes, however, is denied by the flat gold background of the screen and the decorative patterning on the stream. The receding stream cannot be simply pushed forward and still be read as a stream receding into space. Instead, the viewer alternates between seeing a stream receding into the background and seeing a two-dimensional design. A push/pull effect is created, in which we read space first one way and then another. Such an effect was also evoked by Ozu in a number of ways.

Similar to those of the traditional painters, Ozu's flattened spaces are articulated by the individuals that move through them. A *ma* sense of space not existing in its own right but as the creation of time, of the action that takes place within it, is thus created. But Ozu moves beyond this to play deliberately with our perception of flat versus deep space. In *End of Summer,* he shows the front door and back door of a noodle restaurant in succession (figures 13.5, 13.6) followed by the shot of an alleyway (figure 13.7). Deliberately matched, the shots are all very similar—a light area in the center surrounded by grid patterns belonging to the walls and doorways of traditional Japanese architecture. Space in the first two shots is quite shallow, however, while in the third it is deep. Yet because of the matches, we tend to read all three shots as flat until suddenly old Manbei walks into the back of the third shot (figure 13.8), and our eye is pulled into a space several houses deep. Just as in the Kōrin painting, surface design dictates one reading of these shots while spatial cues (e.g., the old man) dictate another.

The ambiguity experienced by a viewer wondering whether to read two-dimensional space as being flat or as conveying depth was carried to greater extremes by *ukiyo-e* artists who created ambiguities regarding size and distance relationships. In Kiyonaga's *In the Bathroom* we see a woman coming out of the bath while another woman still bathes. If we look at the bottom of the print, the woman on the left clearly stands in front of the cubicle in which the second is bathing. If, however, we look at the middle of the painting, we become insecure in this knowledge and find it difficult to tell exactly how far from one another the two women are. The confusion arises from the flatten-

13.3 Tawaraya Sōtatsu, scene from *Tale of Ise* scroll (*Ise monogatari emakimono*) (courtesy of the Tokyo National Museum).

13.4 *The End of Summer* (courtesy of the Japan Film Library Council). Rokurō in the restaurant.

ing of space via the grid lines and the white background, from the parallel perspective systems used in the painting, and from the fact that the women are the same size.

Ozu has created a similar composition in *End of Summer* (figure 13.9). The Ozu frame is not as difficult to read because the two figures are clearly of different sizes—which tells us that one is farther back—and there is, of course, a single-point perspective. Nevertheless, the distance between the two figures is somewhat difficult to judge for several reasons. First, the woman stands behind a screen, which blurs her figure slightly and makes her seem farther away than she actually is. Second, space has been flattened via the grid lines, the gold tones in the background, the low camera angle, and the size discrepancy in the plants. The small plants in the foreground appear to be the same size as the much larger plants in the background, and this tends to bring the back plane forward and squeeze out the middle ground.

Deliberate, playful ambiguities can be found in the early work of Ozu and in that of *ukiyo-e* artists. In Kiyonobu I's *Painting the Screen*, the lady appears to be painting on a screen (figure 13.10). A close look at Kiyonobu's

13.5 *The End of Summer* (courtesy of the Japan Film Library Council). Front door of restaurant.

13.6 *The End of Summer* (courtesy of the Japan Film Library Council). Back door of restaurant.

rendering of the floor, however, indicates that the lady's lover lies between her and the screen, and that being the case, she could not possibly reach the screen with her brush.

A similar playfulness occurs in a sequence of Ozu's *Dragnet Girl* (*Hijōsen no onna,* 1933) in which a boy wanders through a record shop with variously sized RCA Nipper dogs, most of them about a foot high. In one shot we see a dog that looks quite large, but we do not know if it is a small dog that has been foregrounded and stands well in front of the boy or a large dog standing next to him. Finally the boy reaches out and touches the dog, and we realize that in contrast to the other dogs, this one stands about four feet high.

Kristin Thompson has described the Nipper-dog sequence in *Dragnet Girl* as an example of Ozu's modernism, defined as an interest in space for its own sake.[12] Certainly Ozu was modern in flaunting the fact that film is a two-dimensional medium in the face of the dominant Hollywood film tradition, which, like Western Renaissance art, demands a coherent illusionism. But in challenging the spatial assumptions of the dominant film tradition, Ozu had no need to look to Matisse and Picasso, for he had in traditional Japanese painting an alternative model to classical illusionism. Centuries before Matisse and Picasso explored the tension between a flat, two-dimensional sur-

13.7 *The End of Summer* (courtesy of the Japan Film Library Council). Alley near Sasaki's house.

13.8 *The End of Summer* (courtesy of the Japan Film Library Council). Manbei enters alley near Sasaki's house.

13.9 *The End of Summer* (courtesy of the Japan Film Library Council). Sasaki and Manbei.

KATHE GEIST

13.10 Torī Kiyonobu, *Painting the Screen,* woodblock print, ca. 1711, 27 × 37.1 cm. (courtesy of The Art Institute of Chicago, Clarence Buckingham Collection, 1942.61). Photograph © 1992, The Art Institute of Chicago. All rights reserved.

face and illusionistic, three-dimensional space, Japanese painters had done so both intuitively and deliberately. Bordwell has noted that Ozu's play with space and image seldom intrudes upon or interrupts the narrative flow of Ozu's films.[13] Unlike the modernism of Jean-Luc Godard or even Sergei Eisenstein or Jean Cocteau, Ozu's films, while often teasing the audience, flow undisturbed by a need to forcibly break with tradition. Similarly, traditional Japanese painting is always accessible, sparing us the broken, distorted images of Picasso, while at the same time probing related issues. Undoubtedly, Ozu knew modern Western painting as he knew both classical and modern film. But insofar as his assaults on classical Hollywood concepts of space were inspired by, or similar to, two-dimensional media other than film, those media appear to have been Japanese and traditional rather than Western and modern.

Notes

1. Kristin Thompson and David Bordwell, "Space and Narrative in the Films of Ozu," *Screen* 17, no. 2 (Summer 1976): pp. 41–105.

2. Joseph Anderson and Loren Hoekzema, "The Spaces Between: American Criticism of Japanese Film," *Wide Angle* 1, no. 4 (1977): pp. 2–6.

3. David Bordwell, *Ozu and the Poetics of Cinema* (Princeton: Princeton University Press, 1988), p. 17.

4. Ibid., p. 49.

5. National Committee of Japan on Intellectual Cooperation, *The Yearbook of Japanese Art, 1927* (Tokyo: 1928).

6. Kazuo Inoue, *I Lived, But . . .* (Tokyo: Shōchiku, 1983 [film biography of Ozu]).

7. Hugo Munsterberg, *The Art of Modern Japan: From the Meiji Restoration to the Meiji Centennial, 1868–1968* (New York: Hacker Art Books, 1978), p. 49.

8. David Kung, *The Contemporary Artist in Japan* (Sydney: Angus and Robertson, Ltd., 1966), p. 65.

9. Bordwell, p. 49.

10. Kathe Geist, "Yasujiro Ozu: Notes on a Retrospective," *Film Quarterly* 37, no. 1 (Fall 1983): pp. 2–9; "The Role of Marriage in the Films of Yasujiro Ozu," *East-West Film Journal* 4, no. 1 (December 1989): pp. 44–52.

11. Noël Burch, who sees all traditional Japanese painting as tending toward a flat surface design, sees all of Ozu's filmic techniques as likewise augmenting the flattening of space (*To the Distant Observer: Form and Meaning in the Japanese Cinema* [Berkeley: University of California Press, 1979], pp. 117ff., 174). This is far too simplistic a view, however; for both traditional painters and Ozu frequently worked with deep space and, when they flattened space, were interested not merely in the flat surface, but in the play between the flat surface and the illusion of depth.

12. Kristin Thompson, "Notes on the Spatial System of Ozu's Early Films," *Wide Angle* 1, no. 4 (1977): p. 17.

13. Bordwell, p. 74.

GATE OF FLESH(TONES):
Color in the Japanese Cinema

BY DAVID DESSER

CHAPTER

14

About two-thirds of the way into Ozu Yasu-jirō's *Ohayō* (1959), a very drunk Mr. Tomizawa stumbles into what he takes to be his own house. When we see little Isamu coming over to sneer at the older man, we realize, as Tomizawa does not, that he has entered the wrong abode. When Isamu's mother, Mrs. Hayashi, tells her drunken neighbor what has occurred, he laughs and exits. The film follows Isamu back to his room before returning to Mr. Tomizawa. However, in cutting from the Hayashi house to the Tomizawa house, Ozu's camera is already inside before Mr. Tomizawa enters. He comes in, reeling, and when his wife, sitting in the next room, scolds him for his drunkenness, he laughingly says, "Right this time! My own home!"

There is a complexity behind this gag which initially seems to result solely from the typical pattern of spatial confusion that Ozu's vaunted cinematic style brings forth. In his refusal to build scenes with master shots, the row houses and the families within that are the focus of *Ohayō* remain spatially some-

A large part of what has been written about painting, it is fair to say, has been written almost as if paintings were works in black and white. (ALLEN POTTILLO)[1]

what vague (even the family relationships require much time to sort out), a vagueness solidified by Ozu's insistence on filming through houses, on looking from the room of one house across alleyways into another. Early in the film, for instance, Mrs. Haraguchi greets her returning son while standing in an alley that separates her house from the Ōkubo household. In the first shot she greets her son looking offscreen left; in the second shot of her looking (interrupted by a shot of her son coming desultorily down the street), she watches offscreen right. While this is an instance of Ozu's refusal to maintain Hollywood-style screen direction, a careful viewing of this scene demonstrates that Ozu took the first shot of Mrs. Haraguchi from within her apartment looking out, and the second from inside the Ōkubo household directly opposite, thus cutting directly 180 degrees.[2] Many other shots in the film deliberately confuse the spatial arrangements of the row houses, with a baffling series of exits and entrances from front doors and back doors, from the street which bisects the neighborhood, to the alleys that are perpendicular to the street. Thus in this mistaken-household scene, to the confusion of the audience Ozu seems to add the confusion of the inhabitants, like the drunken Mr. Tomizawa.

Yet there is more to this gag than an aging man's drunken inability to find his home, more than the amusing confusion of spatial relationships typical of Ozu. For another element is present here, an element of subtle similarity that exists solely for the audience to appreciate: color. Perhaps only retrospectively, or from repeated viewings, do we glean that the interior door of the Hayashi house is blue and that so, too, is the Tomizawa door. This is the significance of Ozu's anticipatory angle inside Tomizawa's house, awaiting his drunken entrance—that we see a similarity between these doors, a similarity of color. Even more careful viewing reveals that, as it happens, the Tomizawa household is the mirror image of the Hayashi one, at least from the interior angle perpendicular to the main doorway. For we note that while the doorknob of the Hayashi house is screen left, the doorknob of the Tomizawa's is screen right; moreover, a teakettle screen in the left foreground of the Hayashi house is balanced by a teakettle screen in the right foreground of the Tomizawa residence. This mirroring of the Hayashi household by the Tomizawa interior could have been handled just as well in black and white, but it is precisely the use of color that gives us the basis for noting the comparison in the first place. Since we never actually see the exterior of the doorways in question we do not know how much Mr. Tomizawa's confusion is due to color and how much to other factors (and since he comes home at night, one wonders how much color he can see in any case). The point of this gag, we then realize, is not to poke fun at the character's confusion, but to tease the attentive audience, which recognizes, if only subliminally, the similarity between the two households based on the color blue of the doors, doors seen only from the inside—precisely the vantage point not seen by the inhabitants themselves as they enter the house.

Color is used in *Ohayō*, as it is in other of Ozu's color films, mainly for its graphic patternings, and not for any narrative or symbolic purposes, unless we allow similarity of colors (like blue in the door scenes) to stand in for similarity of families (colorplate 9). For instance, can we claim any analogies based on the use of red in a juxtaposed scene between the Haraguchi family and the Hayashi family at breakfast? First we see the Haraguchi family sitting at breakfast, where a red bowl is prominently seen in the center of the table. Ozu then cuts to the Hayashi household at breakfast, where we see a red bowl on the right side of the table and a red bowl in front of each seated person. We would have to go some way to make the case that the use of red bowls in each household indicates a similarity of familial relationships, though, as it happens, each family is experiencing some sense of strife. But this strife is spelled out clearly in the narrative, and familial relationships are juxtaposed, in any case, by the predominant narrative strategy of this film, which gives a handful of scenes to six different households. More significantly, we do not expect red bowls to disappear when the respective family's problems are resolved. Further, a noticeable use of red appears in a scene in which any symbolic content, of the scene or of the color, is simply not possible. At one point, in a transition sequence to take Mrs. Haraguchi from one household to the next, Ozu frames her in the alleyway outside her home by using a red picture on a wall calendar in the middle foreground screen left, a red bowl in the center of the apartment across the alley in the background, and a red bowl in the middle foreground screen right. Color here separates parts of the frame: its use is graphic. In the drunk scene of Mr. Tomizawa, color is used discursively, that is, beyond its graphic functioning, but not narratively or symbolically.

Another instance in the Japanese cinema where color and its confusion is used to generate humor may be found in a film released a little more than a decade following *Ohayō*: Kurosawa Akira's *Dodeskaden* (*Dodesukaden*, 1970). Drunkenness is also a feature of Kurosawa's gag, although the color confusion within this gag is far more noticeable than in Ozu's more subtle effort. Early in *Dodeskaden* we are introduced to two day laborers, best buddies, whose clothing is coordinated to their respective wives and houses. One workman wears yellow: a yellow vest and a yellow headband to complement the yellow (and black) blouse of his wife and the horizontal yellow slats of his house. The other workman is coded as red: his red pants and red headband complement his wife's red skirt and the red stripes on his house. As we see shortly after this introductory scene, the workmen use this color coordination to identify their homes: the yellow worker checks his vest against his house upon his drunken return. Later, they will switch wives and houses, and we will see that the interior of the homes matches the color coordination, so that when they switch, the red workman looks out of place in his buddy's yellow interior. Later still, again staggering home, the yellow worker will experience some confusion as he heads for the red house (this following the swap) but checks his colors at the door and stumbles across the way to the yellow house, his original abode. The color coordination of these characters (bright yellow and bright red) works both for the characters and for the audience, and is played strictly for laughs.

Yellow and red, however, predominate, along with blue, throughout *Dodeskaden*. This first film in color for Kurosawa is strongly patterned around the primary colors. Katsuko, raped by her uncle and made pregnant, spends much of her time folding paper flowers of yellow, red, and blue. A high-angle shot of the rape scene shows Katsuko lying amidst a sea of primary colors. Primary colors also predominate in the pictures of trains painted by Roku-chan, the "trolley crazy" (*densha bakka*) youth. The primary colors are most obviously associated with the shantytown wherein the day laborers and Katsuko dwell, and in which the trolley crazy youth drives his imaginary train (figure 14.1). The opening scene of the film shows an exterior of a modern street in Tokyo, lit in realistic style; but when the youth crosses into the shantytown, swatches of color, especially red and blue, appear on the exterior wall of the first house he comes to. The primary colors, then, in addition to their humorous usage to code the day laborers, may be said to represent symbolically the abstracted, purified world of the shantytown. The simplicity and childlike aspects of Rokuchan are reproduced in his paintings, whose use of the primary colors reflects the well-accepted theory that children see and respond first to bright colors, especially the primaries. By extension, then, this simplicity of vision extends to the entire shantytown where the extensive use of primary colors may symbolize the basic innocence of the dwellers.[3]

As *Dodeskaden* was Kurosawa's first full use of color, he clearly attempted to experiment with color, to use it in noticeable ways.[4] Thus, when the trolley crazy youth returns home from his workday, the sky, sun, and moon are clearly painted inserts (with yellow, blue, and orange predominating). Similarly, the fantasizing of the homeless father and his doomed son is visualized for us: the gate, fence, home, and pool they construct in their imaginations is delivered in rich pastel shades. Beyond this, as we have seen, the dominant

14.1 Roku-chan's fantasies help animate the colors of *Dodeskaden* (courtesy of Tōhō Productions).

production design relies on the primary colors for symbolic purposes. However, color, as the model of Ozu's films reminds us, should not necessarily be reduced to symbolic or narrative purposes. Especially in *Dodeskaden*, the model of abstract expressionism should also be applied. As Kurosawa ably demonstrates, the narrative tendencies of film should not blind us to its graphic potential.

These two examples, drawn from two masters of the Japanese cinema, may be taken as the poles of a continuum of the *creative* use of color within the Japanese cinema, from the basically realistic to the obviously expressionistic. For, of course, most color films use color simply because it is expected, because it is industrially demanded. However, even within a more strictly commercial context—that is, outside of the "art cinema" mold into which Ozu and Kurosawa have been fit in the West—a patently unrealistic, stylistically excessive, and obviously creative use of color may be found: the work of Suzuki Seijun. Yet to appreciate Suzuki's particular take on the question of color, it is necessary to frame in some detail the history of color in the Japa-

Gate of Flesh(tones)

nese cinema, which also means a foray through the Hollywood cinema, due to its enormous normative pressures on other national cinemas.

Most historians now agree that "in the early twenties, 80–90 percent of American films were tinted in some manner."[5] Tinting involves washing a part of a release print of a film, not the negative, in a chemical bath, which renders the entire frame a single color. Thus films could have some tinted scenes, the rest remaining in black and white; or a single film could have scenes in different tints. For example, a film might boast nighttime scenes in blue, battle scenes in red, and so on. (This is the pattern in D. W. Griffith's 1915 masterpiece, *The Birth of a Nation*.) The rather large number of films in "color" might seem surprising to the film student or scholar used to seeing silent movies strictly in black and white. But just as an older generation of filmgoers mistakenly believed that the fast and often jerky motion of the silent cinema was a function of silent technology instead of the once common practice of running silent films (meant to be projected at 18 fps) at sound speed (24 fps), so, too, our image of silent movies represents our contemporary inability to recreate a bygone era.[6]

Tinting was by no means the only color process available to filmmakers before 1932. Just as sound experimentation accompanied cinema from its inception, so, too, color was associated with pioneering efforts at moviemaking. Georges Méliès, for instance, relied on a veritable army of young women to hand-paint, frame by frame, a number of his more imaginative vehicles. That it would be Méliès who was early interested in color should come as no surprise, since his conception of the cinema was essentially a theatrical one—film to reproduce the magic and spectacle not just of his theatre, but of the world of his humorous imagination. Thus, on the one hand, color came to be associated with spectacle, as against the "realistic" black-and-white-life scenes of the Lumières.[7] On the other hand, color *is* realistic; it was the black-and-white film which the new invention of the cinema relied upon that was inherently unrealistic, and so early filmmakers eagerly awaited the invention of color cinematography to accompany the increasingly lifelike art of the cinema.[8] That U.S. camera operators were particularly concerned with the inability of photography to match life, and desired ever-greater attempts to match the real, may be gauged by the fact that "there have been over one hundred major color processes [in still photography], about half of which originated or were used in the United States."[9] What is true of photography is no less true of cinematography. Therefore, hand-painting or tinting were always seen as second best, and as no substitute for a photographic color process. This explains the origins of Kinemacolor, the earliest and most influential photographic process in the prefeature period, 1909–1915. And

　　　　　　　　　　　　　　　　　　　DAVID DESSER

this equally explains the continued search for a photographic color process that would meet the criteria of realism, and at the same time remain flexible enough to maintain standards of artful cinematography, that Hollywood continually developed and refined.

Although Kinemacolor was, in fact, a process invented in England, it found its greatest use in the United States. The massive light levels it required made it awkward for studio filmmaking, however, which became ever more desirable as feature films came into vogue. (In Germany in the 1920s it was the rare film that was *not* shot in the studio, and German émigré directors making their way to Hollywood in the twenties brought this preference with them.) Because of the high light levels necessary, Kinemacolor was unsuited to the developing "glamour style" of cinematography, which relied on more diffuse lighting and soft focus. Tinting kept its popularity as a color process, whereas Kinemacolor faded. Other photographic color processes were both invented and utilized in the United States during the early part of the twentieth century, the most important of which was Technicolor. Invented by Herbert Kalmus at MIT prior to 1920, Technicolor first introduced to Hollywood filmmakers a two-strip process which appeared in 1928, followed, more importantly, by the three-strip process introduced in 1932. Three-strip Technicolor, which relies on three negatives in the production process and on a permanent dye for the positive film (i.e., the release print) called imbibition printing (or IB-Tech), was the dominant color process for twenty years. Not until 1950, when Eastman-Kodak introduced a monopack color process called Eastman Color (one negative instead of the necessary three with Technicolor), would Hollywood use another color process. Technicolor hung on for the next two decades, until Eastman Color gradually replaced it entirely; since 1970, Technicolor has become merely another laboratory processing motion picture film in Hollywood. But those twenty years in which three-strip held sway have rightly been called the years of "Glorious Technicolor."

The cost of Technicolor (which required a bulky, expensive specially adapted camera, high light levels, and a "Technicolor consultant" on every picture) kept the number of color features relatively low in the 1930s.[10] By the middle of the 1950s, this number grew exponentially as Hollywood, in an effort to compete with television, turned to newer film technologies. In addition to an increased use of color, Hollywood experimented with different aspect ratios (CinemaScope being the most famous and useful) and with stereophonic soundtracks. For all of the realistic impulse behind the desire for color cinematography, the particular qualities of Technicolor, combined with the expense to utilize it in the first place, meant that color became associated with specific genres, especially with bigger-budget forms: "Musicals, histori-cal spectacles and exotic adventures tales, comedy, romance in an exotic lo-cale."[11] In the 1950s, we must add the Western to this list. The realistic im-pulse that gave rise to color cinematography was thus partially deflated by Technicolor, with its saturated hues—themselves a function of the com-pany's desire to associate Technicolor with spectacle. Eastman Color, much cheaper to use, also had less-saturated tones, and could be lit with little change from black-and-white models. (Even Technicolor pushed its film speed over the years to accommodate Hollywood cinematographers.[12]) Thus Eastman Color replaced Technicolor as a matter of both commercial practice (it was cheaper) and aesthetic desires (it looked more realistic). That the East-man Color stock (i.e., the release print) faded rather quickly compared to the permanent dye of IB Tech was a compromise film companies were willing to live with. Eventually, to meet the demands of major Hollywood directors, like George Lucas and Martin Scorsese in the late 1970s (and a quirky turn to black-and-white cinematography, by such directors as Peter Bogdanovich, Scorsese, and Woody Allen), Kodak introduced a low-fade film stock.[13]

This breathless discussion of color in the cinema indicates, if nothing else, that color is implicated not simply in technological contexts, but equally in aesthetic and commercial contexts as well. Color must, first of all, be desired on the part of filmmakers. The desire for color in the cinema was, as indi-cated, both a scientific and a commercial one—color belongs to the realm of realism and the realm of spectacle (fantasy). In order to add color to movies, a technological process needed to be invented, but having been in-vented, it remained a question whether or not it would be adopted. Techno-logical, commercial, and aesthetic constraints affected the adoption of color throughout the 1930s and after. Increased use of color in the 1950s, which was enabled both by Technicolor and by Eastman Color, was spurred on by commercial pressures (competition from television) and aesthetic concerns (the qualities of the color process associating it with certain genres). The his-tory of the use of color in the Hollywood cinema is a complex one, still in need of further analysis. The same is even truer of Japan, much of whose cinematic history has yet to be explored.

It is true, unfortunately, that so many of the primary documents in the history of Japanese cinema have disappeared or were destroyed.[14] Neverthe-less, historical analyses of the Japanese cinema must proceed. The question of color, for instance, little dealt with in published histories, is problematic. The ubiquitousness of color (tinted) films in the United States in the 1920s, as we indicated above, is not reflected in circulating prints of the surviving films (a considerable number compared to the Japanese cinema). Thus we may not judge the Japanese situation on the basis of surviving prints. More-over, as studio records and film journals have also either not survived or sig-nificantly been consulted with regard, at least, to color, our judgments about the use of color must be tentative.[15]

One striking, if highly tentative, conclusion one may come to is that color was little desired in the Japanese cinema compared to other national cinemas. U.S. film companies, as we have noted, were interested in color almost from the inception of the cinema until the near-total use of color by the mid-1960s. Early French cinema, inspired by the fantasies of Méliès, was highly moti-vated toward color until the 1920s when the industry declined and avant-garde filmmakers, with an essentially noncommercial agenda, began to dominate the French output. The British cinema was as highly motivated to utilize color as the Hollywood cinema, although it segregated color along generic lines, as did Hollywood, while the perpetual weakness of the British film industry made color a commercially risky proposition. Even in the 1930s and into the 1940s, when color appeared significantly in other national cine-mas, like the German cinema under the Nazis (utilizing the German-invented Agfacolor), the Japanese cinema was little disposed to color. Even through-out the late 1960s, when color became the standard in worldwide film-making and black and white the exception, the latter maintained a palpable presence in Japan, as it still does today.

This is not to say that early color experimentation was absent from Japan. Anderson and Richie report that the practice of hand-painting films in the prefeature period was "not unknown" due to the fact that "labor was cheap and delicate hand-painting a highly developed skill."[16] How prevalent it was is left vague. Tinting similarly was used in Japanese films, although the par-ticular color schemes differed from the West: orange for night scenes (com-pared to blue in Hollywood), and a preference for pink in spring scenes to emphasize the seasonal blooming of cherry blossoms.[17] Again, how preva-lent tinting was is left open, although a phrase like "little experimentation with color" certainly implies its lack.[18] Kinemacolor, the photographic pro-cess that initially seemed so promising, also found its way to Japan. Anderson and Richie discuss the Tennenshoku Katsudō Shashin (whose name trans-lates as the Natural Color Movie Company), which came to be known as Tenkatsu, which was formed specifically in 1914 to utilize the British color process in its films. Although Anderson and Richie do not state the situation so explicitly, we may conclude that the exclusive use of Kinemacolor was a commercial strategy on the part of Tenkatsu founder Kobayashi Kisaburō to compete with the dominant company of the time, Nikkatsu. Thus color be-comes associated with its potential commercial appeal, while the initial film that Tenkatsu produced, *Yoshitsune and the Thousand Cherry Trees* (*Yoshitsune sembon zakura*), associated color, as did Hollywood, with historical spectacle. Anderson and Richie attribute the decline in the use of Kinemacolor by Tenkatsu to the vicissitudes of World War I, but do not take up the question of color in the Japanese cinema until they survey postwar developments. Must we conclude, therefore, that color was of no import in the massive creativity which otherwise characterizes the Japanese cinema of the 1930s? Only further research will confirm this.

Assuming that color experimentation was quite limited in the prefeature era and almost absent from the otherwise hugely active and creative 1930s, we might venture some conclusions about this absence. The realistic impulse that underpinned Western desires for color was likely less a factor in the Japanese cinema on the basis that realism is not a particular characteristic of any traditional Japanese art form. It is arguable that just as Japanese cinema diverged from the dominant Hollywood model in terms of its editing patterns, shot lengths, and spatial configurations, not to mention character and narrative types, so, too, the desire for color based upon an ideology of the real would not be a factor.[19] We may take this further, and claim, along with Rudolf Arnheim in his early writings on the cinema, that art is a function of limitation. The art of the cinema, in this notion, relies precisely on its two-dimensional, silent, black-and-white image.[20] We may note the way in which much traditional Japanese art is not simply nonrepresentational, but highly geared around incorporating both the limitations and the particular characteristics of the medium into the artwork. Thus, wooden sculpture in Japan does not hide its "woodenness" but uses the grain of the wood as part of the gestalt of the artwork. Ink painting emphasizes the qualities of both the black (and shades of gray) of the ink and the brush itself. As Sherman Lee says about a handscroll by Sesshū: "the brush strokes are no longer really functional in a representational sense . . . certain elements of the brushwork have become an end in themselves."[21] Ink painting even uses both the characteristics and the space of the paper on which the brushstrokes are applied (the famous "empty spaces" of Zen paintings). Similarly, as Lee points out with regard to the *haniwa* figures of early Japan: "true to its name, a circle of clay [*haniwa*], the legs of the Japanese sculpture [of a horse] are simply cylinders of clay; the body is almost a cylinder; the head is clearly based on a cylinder." Even, or perhaps especially, traditional Japanese theatre emphasizes the "theatricality" of its presentation. Filmmakers may work in the same aesthetic mode, emphasizing the cinema's particular characteristics: durational possibilities (the long take) or, alternately, decoupage; the qualities of light, shades of gray, and empty spaces within the mise-en-scène; narrative paradigms drawn from theatre or literature, and so forth.

Yet, as we have seen, color is implicated not just in aesthetic patterns, but equally in industrial ones as well. We might therefore note that the expense of Technicolor was all but prohibitive to the Japanese film industry which, especially in the early to mid thirties, relied strictly on the home audience for profit. Moreover, the tensions between Japan and the United States which later in the decade made trade unfavorable limited even the possibility of importing Technicolor into the country; eventually in the 1930s Japan stopped the importation of Hollywood films, a move that had a huge (although not dominant) impact on Japanese screens. The war economy would have had a still further impact on Japanese filmmakers' ability to utilize color, whatever the process.[22] Thus, on the basis of both aesthetic and commercial constraints we may hypothesize the relative lack of color in prewar Japanese cinema.

When the Japanese did return to color experimentation in the postwar world, they did so, at least according to Anderson and Richie, with its potential commercial appeal in mind. Shōchiku, in 1951, produced Japan's first color feature, *Carmen Comes Home* (*Karumen kokyō ni kaeru*), on the basis of desiring to compete with color foreign films. Shōchiku produced a second color film in 1953, *Natsuko's Adventures* (*Natsuko no bōken*), and that same year saw Tōei come out with *The Sun* (*Nichirin*). Shōchiku's films were shot on a Japanese color process called Fujicolor, while Tōei's effort was filmed in Sakuracolor, another Japanese attempt at a color process. These films were not especially successful technologically, aesthetically, or (except for *Carmen*) commercially.[23] It was at Daiei, however, that color experimentation was both highly desired and successful.

Daiei, in the immediate postwar era, was still a new and struggling studio. (It was formed in 1942.) Its strategy for success relied on a combination of technological innovation and international appeal—especially the latter, with the company's "films for export" policy. The surprise success of *Rashomon* (1951) at the Venice Film Festival and the less surprising, but no less gratifying, success of Mizoguchi Kenji's *Ugetsu* (1952) led Daiei to produce *Gate of Hell* (*Jigokumon*, 1953). Using Eastman Color, Kinugasa Teinosuke's otherwise routine *jidaigeki* demonstrated to the West that color could at least add to the exoticism, the spectacle, of the already exotic period films suddenly pouring out of Japan. Following *Gate of Hell*, Daiei then "launched a regular program of color-film productions and thus became the first Japanese company to go in for color on more than an experimental basis."[24]

By the early 1960s, color, if not ubiquitous, was at least routine, with Nikkatsu, Shōchiku, Tōei, and Tōhō regularly releasing color films. Many of these films were also in the anamorphic widescreen ratio commonly known as CinemaScope, whose adoption by the Japanese industry came about even more quickly than did its turn to color. (Introduced in the West in 1952, by 1958 widescreen cinematography was routine in Japan, and even dominant in films by individual directors, like Kurosawa and Ichikawa Kon, and by studios, like Shōchiku, Nikkatsu, and Daiei.[25]) But if color was routine in the early 1960s (though not an industry requirement), the specific use of color, its qualities, was often highly idiosyncratic, and nowhere more so than in the films of Suzuki Seijun at Nikkatsu.

The notion of an "idiosyncratic" use of color presupposes a standard use of color by which one may judge, or at least notice, a film which diverges from this norm. In terms of style, in which the use of color is only one factor, and around which Suzuki's reputation is beginning to cohere, we need a definition, one which recognizes that style is to some extent a matter of choice, but which choices at any given instance, are constrained either by technology, budget, or a system (industrial, generic, ideological). David Bordwell provides a most apt definition of style in the terms just outlined: "a system of technical choices instantiated in the total form of the work, itself grasped in its relation to pertinent and proximate stylistic norms."[26] Thus we must recall that both color and CinemaScope were quite the norm by the early 1960s, especially for Nikkatsu studios, which already had been specializing in youth melodramas and male action films for some years. Moreover, color norms for Nikkatsu were by Western standards "garish," the hues (density) typical of Eastman stock but their selection and combination extreme by standards of cinematic realism and contemporary fashion. In this respect, the use of color by Nikkatsu, and by Shōchiku's New Wave directors with whom Suzuki may be linked, might be said to reproduce the traditional Japanese proclivity Sherman Lee characterizes as "exaggeration." This conception of exaggeration extends to either end of a spectrum from restraint to excess: "One remembers the restrained grace and elegance of the tea ceremony and the uninhibited wild and noisy activities of some festivals."[27] So, too, one might point in the Japanese cinema's use of color to the excessive restraint of *Gate of Hell* and the overdetermined presence of color in the works of Suzuki.

In most instances, however, the narrative and editing style otherwise prevalent at Nikkatsu come right out of Hollywood's book of patterns. Indeed it is the case that just as the so-called Classical Hollywood Cinema virtually codified an approach to cinematography and editing, so, too, the

American industry discourses on color created a virtual set of rules. Mary Beth Haralovich clearly outlines these rules in her observant article on the use of color in Douglas Sirk's *All That Heaven Allows*.[28] These rules reflect the notion of "invisibility" that pervades Classical Hollywood film style. Thus "color should be emphasized only when it carries specific meaning," and the production design should ensure that color should not create distracting focal points, such as by using "fewer and less saturated colors."[29] What one might call the primary directive, however, is the following standard, which is Hollywood's ideological watchword in all of its devices: "Color should contribute to unobtrusive realism."[30] Color in the Hollywood cinema, used creatively, would remain caught between the twin poles of realism and of spectacle, and thus the generic differentiation between color and black and white. In later years, when color became the norm, a differentiation would be made between filmmakers who subscribed as fully as possible to the color norms and those who held these norms in tension: the films of Michelangelo Antonioni and Federico Fellini; the Hammer Studios horror films; and in some Asian traditions, such as the Chinese cinema, for instance, whose adoption of three-strip Technicolor in the late 1960s created a new tradition of color usage. In these instances, notions of realism, and certainly of "unobtrusiveness," do not apply.

Of course, other models of filmic construction were available to directors like Suzuki. Aspects of traditional Japanese narrative practice—with its stops and starts, hesitations, elisions, disruptions, and stylistic practices, like the ludic passages Bordwell isolates in his article on 1930s decorativeness in Japanese cinema—are among the range of choices from which Suzuki might borrow. In *Eros plus Massacre*, I mention particular instances within Suzuki's films for the way in which color suddenly comes to the fore in highly theatrical ways in scenes from *Tokyo Drifter* (*Tōkyō nagaremono*, 1966) and *The Life of Tattoo* (*Irezumi ichidai*, 1965). Yet it is worth noting that the theatricalization of these scenes is not a Japanese-style theatricality. Though the color scheme in the climax of *The Life of Tattoo* seems drawn from the *kabuki* canon, the sudden *switch* in lighting and color are not found in traditional *kabuki* which, while it certainly relies on color (and on the coded use of color), does not rely on colored lights or other shifts in lighting patterns. This theatricalization of color and lights is more obviously drawn from Western theatre (or so-called modern *kabuki*, which was influenced by modern Western theatre), which routinely relies on both lighting cues to reflect dramatic shifts (e.g., spotlights, often with colored gels over them), and on the spectacular use of lighting cues, as in the Broadway musical or other stylized genres. In an odd way, the sudden, obviously "unrealistic" shift in colored lighting in, for instance, *Tokyo Drifter,* recalls nothing so much as Joshua Logan's attempt to use color and lighting creatively in the film version of *South Pacific* (1958). Indeed, *South Pacific* is credited for breaking the ban on symbolically colored lighting within the Hollywood cinema.[31] Especially in preparation for the musical numbers, Logan's realistically lit film shot on location shifts its lighting scheme through the use of colored gels of a single hue. Whether or not one feels Logan's efforts to be truly creative, one term rarely applied to his adaptation of *South Pacific* is "Brechtian." Yet Brechtian is precisely what both Satō Tadao and Noël Burch claim for Suzuki.[32] Perhaps we may argue that Logan's film contains its color excesses within genre (the spectacle of the musical) and as a deliberately theatrical model. Logan attempts to create a tension between location shooting and the theatricalization of the story within the location. Suzuki, on the other hand, does not contain his stylistic excesses, but rather makes these excesses the center of attraction of his film. The clearest example of this is his adaptation of the influential, and now oft-filmed, novel by Tamura Taijirō, *Gate of Flesh* (*Nikutai no mon,* 1964).[33]

Tamura's *Nikutai no mon,* published in 1946, inaugurated a literary movement in the immediate postwar era termed "*Nikutai-ha,*" which might be translated as "Carnal Desire school." Tamura's *Gate of Flesh,* and his *Desertion at Dawn* (*Akatsuki no dassō*), must be understood as an ideological rejection of the militarist and feudal ideology. Perhaps it was felt that eroticism, understood as a kind of thinking with the body, might replace feudalism. This erotic potential in the arts was made possible by the freedom of expression mandated by the American occupation. This story of postwar prostitution was part of two developing film cycles under occupation aegis: women's liberation films and "kissing" films. It is worth noting that Tamura's *Desertion at Dawn* was also filmed in this period (the screenplay was written in late 1948), but was subjected to numerous revisions by the Occupation's delaying its production and eventual release until early 1950. The focus on prostitutes in both *Gate of Flesh* and *Desertion at Dawn* was part of the critique of militarist-feudalist ideology which the Occupation actively encouraged.[34] However, that Suzuki should remake not just *Gate of Flesh* in 1964 but also *Desertion at Dawn* in 1965—under the title of *Shunpu-Den,* or *The Story of a Prostitute* (aka *Joy Girls*)—must be reckoned as significant.

We might claim, on one hand, that the 1960s remakes of Tamura's novels in some sense wish to return us to the flush of democracy and the promise of liberation that characterized the early Occupation period. On the other hand, we may also note that the Tamura adaptations, imbricated in the kissing films cycle, were subject to some serious discussions for their exploitative tendencies. Indeed, this first appearance of kissing films (which inspired a variety of discussion about kissing in Japanese culture and inaugurated a wave of soft-core pornographic magazines) quickly deteriorated into what were called "*ero-guro*," or erotic-grotesque, productions. Thus the focus on prostitutes was an excuse for *ero-guro*, whereas the cycle of striptease films similarly appearing had no veneer of political validity whatsoever. Suzuki's films, especially *Gate of Flesh,* are linked to the beginning of another cycle of exploitation films, the so-called "*pinku eiga*" (pink films) which Nikkatsu would allow to dominate its output in the next years.

More to the point, however, Suzuki's film is critical of the Occupation in ways both the novel and Makino Masahiro's 1948 film version would neither have dared to be nor perhaps have desired to be. The smattering of English on the soundtrack and the U.S. soldiers who desire either to purchase the services of Japanese women or arrest petty Japanese male criminals implicates the Occupation in the cycle of exploitation Suzuki sees as uninterrupted from the militarist era. For it is equally the case that the Pacific War is clearly no less guilty for the current state of exploitive affairs than is the Occupation.

Yet for all of the transgressive aspects of Japanese cinema, most Japanese films are remarkably comprehensible to us. Only in the rarest instance is a work "incomprehensible for the public," as Hori Kyūsaku said when he fired Suzuki Seijun after the latter made *Branded to Kill* (*Koroshi no rakuin,* 1967). While it is the case that a great many Japanese films actually do possess a more complex or diffuse narrative pattern, and do have a tendency toward overt stylization, their basic aesthetic system is entirely normative within a mainstream commercial context, and recuperable along the lines of stylistic flourishes, or what Bordwell terms the "decorative function of style," a technical device which exceeds its denotative, thematic or expressive function.[35] We might claim that stylistic excess became another norm, another possibility, and that such excessive moments do not entirely displace a coherent narrative line, but merely emphasize the decorative possibilities of film form.

Suzuki's *Gate of Flesh* is entirely comprehensible at the level of its story (unlike *Branded to Kill*), and some of its stylistic excesses are containable within established filmic norms for such excessive displays, as for instance, sequences which are clearly marked as fantasy. Thus we find here a scene in which Borneo Maya, watching a dancing Ibuki Shintarō, whom she very much desires, envisions him in slow motion, the frame around him becoming hazy. She then imagines seeing the nude form of Machiko (with whom Ibuki had earlier made love) standing next to him; this is transformed into an image of her and Ibuki embracing, the camera executing a series of fast 360-degree pans. Other stylistic excesses are containable by convention: as Maya and Ibuki later actually do make love, the camera pans down their prone forms and goes into soft focus. Yet much of the film's style is not contained by such conventions, not explicable as a character's fantasy or other symbolism. And this is most clearly seen in the film's use of color.

Gate of Flesh focuses on Maya, Komasa no Sen, Jeep no Omino, and Huten Oroku, a group of women prostitutes in occupied Japan, who have banded together in an uneasy form of friendship under the leadership of Sen. Each is specifically color coded, even more so than the workmen of Kurosawa's later *Dodeskaden*. Sen dresses exclusively in red. She is a positive vision of red when first seen in a red headband, dress, sweater, boots, even a red purse. As we see later, her slip is also red. Omino is coded as purple, although she has fewer pieces to her ensemble; the same is true of Oroku, who is almost exclusively clothed in yellow (red is detectable under her hat brim in some instances). Maya is coded as green, and she is initially given the full green treatment: headband, dress, boots, purse. Later, her outfit will simplify into just the green dress.[36] This color coding certainly visually separates the women from the rest of the players—other prostitutes wear typical prints or stripes; no other characters are coded by a single color. It similarly defines them against each other; moreover, another of their group, Machiko, is coded both by her style of dress (she wears the traditional kimono) and her lack of color, her kimono consisting of pleasing shades of gray.

Each woman's particularly insistent association with a single color pays off most spectacularly in a sequence in which each woman expresses a fantasy aloud. In four separate single-take shots, isolated from the rest in a medium long shot, each woman's address finds the frame surrounding her awash in the same color as her dress. These color changes are not marked specifically as fantasy, or containable by any diegetically motivated shift in narrative register. Instead, each color-coded woman stands forward and the entire mise-en-scène is given over to her shade.

One is tempted to read the colors as symbolic, particularly as a way of containing their deliberate obtrusiveness. Certainly the red of Komasa no Sen makes her stand out as befits her leadership role. As Bordwell and Thompson note, "Bright colors draw the eye more than do subdued ones. 'Warm' colors in the red-orange-yellow range seem to come forward to us, while 'cool' colors from purple to green recede."[37] If the red of Sen makes her stand out, then the green of Maya, which makes her recede, is similarly in keeping with her reticence, her youth, her essential fears in the climate of sexual violence and exploitation which surrounds her.

DAVID DESSER

Beyond a physiological analysis of how color draws the eye, we wonder if the color associated with each woman has an objective correlative to her character. Attempts have been made over the years to claim that individual colors possess meaning in their own right. Thus: "Red is said to be exciting because it reminds us of fire, blood, and revolution. Green calls up the refreshing thought of nature, blue is cooling like water."[38] Sen is certainly a firebrand whose actions also lead literally to bloodshed. The red of blood itself is utilized quite daringly in *Gate of Flesh* in a graphically documented sequence in which Ibuki slaughters a cow. Suzuki crosscuts between Ibuki's slaughtering the animal and the women's growing excitement at the sight. The red of blood also relates to the red sun of the Japanese flag. In one scene, a drunken Ibuki waves a Japanese flag, signed by his now-dead comrades in the recently ended war. Later, when Ibuki is betrayed to the American Military Police by a local *yakuza*, his gunshot wounds bleed into the red center of his flag. Similarly, the green that Maya wears contrasts with Sen's angry red, and her youthful innocence and pleasant complexion are indeed refreshing compared to Sen's cynicism and energetic hostility.

As Arnheim points out, however, there is a danger in assigning colors a universal characteristic, a meaning which cuts across cultures: "And when yellow symbolized imperial splendor in China but indicated shame and contempt in the European Middle Ages, can we be sure that, as Goethe assumes, the Chinese referred to a golden yellow, whereas the color of the prostitutes and the persecuted Jews had a mean, greenish tinge?"[39]

On the other hand, Suzuki himself speaks of his particular use of the four colors to code his female protagonists: "In my sense of symbols, green means peace and calm, yellow stands for kindness and compromise, red means dread and fear, and purple stands for loneliness and anxiety."[40] His analysis seems intended to contain his eccentric use of color, to tell critics and audiences the kind of thing he thinks they want to hear, for only by the most generous extension will his own reading of the color codes stand up. Maya is far from either communicating or experiencing peace and calm—quite the opposite—so at best, Suzuki's color patterning must be read as ironic in her case. The same is true of red, for although Sen's attitude of hostility and jealousy clearly speaks of emotional turmoil and repression, she does not overtly show much fear or dread.

Thus we may not necessarily contain the color scheme by recourse to a symbolic pattern, either universal or textually specific. Instead, we must allow the color scheme to act as an aesthetic text, separate from the narrative. This color text functions alongside other excesses of Suzuki's style, which similarly need not be reduced to narrative functions. We cannot, for instance, explain away his particular use of superimpositions of characters who are already present within the scene. When Ibuki hurriedly leaves Sen (after making love to her) to escape the military police, a superimposition of him being wounded by a gunshot may be read as either Sen's imagination of what has occurred or the narrator's deliberate imposition (so to speak) within the frame. But when we see a superimposed image of Maya, who is present in the scene, as she watches Machiko's beating, we are confronted by an eccentric, if understandable, stylistic panache. The same is true of a spotlight which highlights Sen as she lies on a bed after making love to Ibuki and then rises to dress. The light has no diegetic source—a stylized moment like those mentioned above in *Tokyo Drifter* and *The Life of Tattoo*. However, we may claim that if Suzuki's use of primary colors in this film does not have a reducible symbolic function, we may at least point to an extratextual *reference*, if only because such use of primary colors is not, as it were, native to Japanese style.

In an essay on traditional Japanese uses of color, Haga Tōru points out that colors are rarely used alone. "The articles of everyday life: kimono, fans, covers for books, even playing cards, combined several hues, producing an effect both striking and elegant. Almost every color was composed of some measure of gray, blue, or red, or toned down with brown." The Japanese aesthetic terms for the effects of these colors are *shibui* (rich sobriety) or *iki* (refined smartness).[41] This is the color patterning of *Gate of Hell,* for instance, whose Heian-era setting is mirrored in the traditional aesthetic flavor the film itself manifests. The costumes of the four Occupation-era prostitutes bear no resemblance to traditional wear, either in color or style—the women all wear dresses, Western shoes, and carry American-style purses. However, the primary colors they wear may be compared to another recurring image that features primary colors: the American flag, with its red, white, and blue. Three times Suzuki delivers a shot of the waving Stars and Stripes, including the film's final shot.

In the first two shots of the American flag, one wonders if Suzuki's framing of the flag is deliberately "wrong"—the flag seems to be flying right to left (i.e., the stars are screen right and the stripes move outward to the left in the breeze). Images of the American flag in the United States always have the stars on the left, with the stripes seeming to move toward the right, in the direction a Westerner reads print. We cannot account for this framing strategy by recourse to traditional Japanese ways of reading, for while the Japanese do read right to left, they also read top to bottom. When they do read horizontally, it is left to right in Western style. In the film's final image, Suzuki delivers the more standard (American) image of the flag, waving left to right in the breeze—the flag itself a clear synecdoche of the American occupation. Haga points out that many Japanese were repelled by the colors of Western flags when they were exposed to them at the end of the Tokugawa era:

> The people of Tokugawa Japan undoubtedly found the flags that began to fly in Europe and the United States . . . like the French *tricolore* and the American star spangled banner, either unattractive or glaring in coloring. In fact, in 1853, the year Japan enforced the opening of the country, a Bakufu governor involved in negotiations with the Western powers wrote, "the ships and flags we see in the harbor are too dazzling to look at." [42]

Surely the rejection of the color schemes of Western flags contained more than a hint of cultural resentment at the enforced opening of the country. So, too, Suzuki's commentary on the Occupation, as symbolized by the flag, uses primary colors to stand in for the West. But even if this is so, and it is clear from the narrative that the Occupation is crucial to the film's meaning, it hardly contains the color excesses, barely motivates the patently unrealistic, playful, obtrusive and above all, humorous uses of color that make the film memorable for its style. As in the films of Ozu and Kurosawa, Suzuki's use of color has precedents in traditional Japanese culture in its ludic qualities. Similarly, Suzuki's films reflect, as do Ozu's and Kurosawa's, the prevalence and particular qualities of color in Japanese daily life. Even in the realistic sections of *Dodeskaden*, as when the poor father goes begging for food for his dying son, the bright neon colors of modern nighttime Tokyo and the bright red dress of an unsympathetic bar hostess remind us of the playful postmodernism of contemporary Japan. By its seeming excesses of style and spectacle, *Gate of Flesh* poses a challenge to our notions of a normative use of color in the cinema and begs for further analysis of the notion of a deliberately decorative, excessive mode of film technique. At the very least, Suzuki's films demonstrate an original talent worthy of further study, which itself requires a continued analysis of color in Japanese art and cinema.

Notes

I would like to thank David Bordwell for generously discussing aspects of the use of color in the cinema, and Arthur Nolletti, Jr., for a critical reading of the essay.

1. Art historian Allen Pottillo, quoted in Rudolf Arnheim, *Art and Visual Perception: A Psychology of the Creative Eye* (Berkeley: University of California Press, 1974), p. 344.

2. The definitive definition of Ozu's film style and how it relates to the dominant Hollywood model may be found in David Bordwell, *Ozu and the Poetics of Cinema* (London: British Film Institute, 1988).

3. I am not overly concerned with analyzing the use of color in *Dodeskaden*, that is, with "reading" the colors as symbolic or representative of something else. Therefore, it may also be true that Kurosawa intended to make a film partially about pollution, and so the colors of the film "evoke a poisoned environment, glowing with radioactivity, weirdly colored by buried chemicals that have ruptured the ecosystem and returned to disfigure humans and dwellings alike" (Stephen Prince, *The Warrior's Camera: The Cinema of Akira Kurosawa* [Princeton: Princeton University Press, 1991], p. 258). And while I am inclined to reject this allegorical reading of the color scheme, Prince's take on the film marks one of the rare attempts to understand how color is used in Japanese cinema, at least in Kurosawa's case. One might go on to claim that if *Dodeskaden* is not the film on pollution Kurosawa intended to make, he would go on to make a film on this subject: *Dreams* (*Yume*, 1990), whose color scheme is equally worthy of discussion.

4. As is well reported (see, for instance, Donald Richie, *The Films of Akira Kurosawa*), Kurosawa desired to use one shot in color in *High and Low* (*Tengoku to jigoku*, 1963). He wanted pink smoke to rise out of a chimney in the climactic scene where the cops pick up the trail of the kidnapper/murderer; the color of the smoke is discussed narratively. Presumably, Kurosawa thought this touch of pink in the otherwise black-and-white film would possess a visual jolt for the audience to match the dramatic punch it packs for the characters. The videocassette version utilizes this touch of pink.

5. Edward Branigan, "Color and Cinema: Problems in the Writing of History," *Film Reader* 4 (1979): 20. See also David Bordwell, Janet Staiger, and Kristin Thompson, *The Classical Hollywood Cinema: Film Style and Mode of Production to 1960* (New York: Columbia University Press, 1985).

6. Because only the release prints of films were tinted, surviving negatives of silent movies have no "color." Thus, as the original prints wore out and eventually disappeared, the colors of silent movies disappeared along with them. Further, many silent movies (such as Charlie Chaplin's and Harold Lloyd's) were rereleased in later years with sound tracks; release prints of films with sound tracks may not be tinted, as the chemicals of the tinting process interfere with the optical sound track. Only well-preserved original prints, or specially printed rerelease versions, give some indication of the color that graced a large percentage of American (and other) feature films.

7. "As Steve Neale has shown in his discussion of the history of film industry discourses on color, color had two contradictory impulses: toward realism and toward spectacle" (Mary Beth Haralovich, "*All That Heaven Allows:* Color, Narrative Space, and Melodrama," in *Close Viewings,* ed. Peter Lehman [Tallahassee, Fla.: Florida State University Press, 1990], p. 62).

8. Sound and color would essentially have to await the 1930s to become stabilized in Hollywood. But the realistic impulse of the cinema was manifested in ever-faster

DAVID DESSER

film stock—from the monochromatic limitations of early film (sensitive only to the blue spectrum) to orthochromatic film (which added green to its repertoire), to panchromatic film (sensitive to the visible spectrum), which was introduced to movie-making in the mid-1920s.

9. Branigan, pp. 21–22.

10. Douglas Gomery reports that fewer than 5 percent of American films were made in color in the late 1930s (*Movie History: A Survey* [Belmont, Calif.: Wadsworth, 1991], pp. 286–287).

11. Bordwell, Staiger, and Thompson, p. 355.

12. See Branigan, p. 26.

13. The loss of color on the part of the release prints also affected the color negatives of Eastman Color, although storage conditions extend the life of color negatives compared to release prints. But viewing original prints of films printed on Eastman Color (or competing monopack systems, like Agfacolor on which *Ohayō* was shot) struck in the 1950s presents, in its own way, as many aesthetic problems as viewing silent movies projected at the wrong speed, lacking color, indeed lacking the sound that accompanied them during their original release. For instance, unless a new print is struck from a satisfactory negative, it is doubtful that our impression of the colors in Ozu's films is entirely accurate, despite my comments above! Hence the importance of a newly struck print of Suzuki's *Gate of Flesh* discussed in this essay.

14. One has in mind the devastating Kanto earthquake of 1923 and the saturation bombings of Tokyo and Osaka during the Pacific War, which destroyed, along with most of the cities, a good deal of film and film-related material. Another factor, one to which American films were also subjected, was simple neglect combined with technological limitations. Neglect meant that negatives were relatively little cared for and that prints were projected literally until they fell apart. (Japanese companies also tended to mix and match scenes from different films, especially *jidaigeki*, cutting up prints to make new combinations.) The industrial context in which films were produced and consumed provided little space for the notion of *preservation*. The concept of a film archive for public exhibitions was unknown until the 1930s with the Museum of Modern Art. Similarly, the nitrate film stock that was prevalent before the routine use of so-called "safety film" in 1950 is both highly flammable and subject to disintegration. Compounding the problem was the common practice, even in the United States, of destroying prints to recover the silver nitrate from the films themselves. Many silent movies that have survived have done so almost accidentally.

15. The lack of material about color within published sources in Japanese or in English does not necessarily reflect a lack of available information; instead, it may reflect the fact that historians of the Japanese cinema have had little interest in the question of color.

16. Joseph L. Anderson and Donald Richie, *The Japanese Film: Art and Industry*, expanded ed. (Princeton: Princeton University Press, 1982), p. 33.

17. Ibid.

18. Ibid.

19. That Japanese cinema diverges from the dominant Hollywood model, and that it does so on the basis of traditional Japanese aesthetic patterns which have an ideological dimension, is the argument put forth by Noël Burch in his highly influential and suggestive *To the Distant Observer: Form and Meaning in the Japanese Cinema* (Berkeley: University of California Press, 1979).

20. For a clear summary of Arnheim's notion of film art, see J. Dudley Andrew, *The Major Film Theories* (New York: Oxford University Press, 1976).

21. Sherman E. Lee, "Contrasts in Chinese and Japanese Art," reprinted in this volume.

22. See Donald Kirihara, *Patterns of Time: Mizoguchi and the 1930s* (Madison: University of Wisconsin Press, 1992) for a fuller discussion of the industrial practices of Japanese cinema during the complexities of the prewar era. A further intriguing area of historical research would involve the question of Agfacolor, the German color process frequently utilized by the Nazis. They would certainly have been inclined to provide the process to their trading partner and war ally, Japan. Did they? Did the request ever come up?

23. Anderson and Richie, pp. 233–234.

24. Anderson and Richie, p. 233.

25. I introduce both the question of color and that of CinemaScope in the 1960s in my *Eros plus Massacre: An Introduction to the Japanese New Wave Cinema* (Bloomington: Indiana University Press, 1988), pp. 7–8. I remain as hesitant about color now as I did then, noting the use of color in Ōshima Nagisa's early films, black and white some years later, and a return to color; the same is true of Imamura Shōhei, whose latest effort as of this writing, *Black Rain (Kuroi ame, 1989)*, is in black and white.

26. David Bordwell, "A Cinema of Flourishes: Japanese Decorative Classicism in the Prewar Era," in *Reframing Japanese Cinema: Authorship, Genre, History*, ed. Arthur Nolletti, Jr., and David Desser (Bloomington: Indiana University Press, 1992).

27. Lee, "Contrasts in Chinese and Japanese Art."

28. See note 7 above.

29. Haralovich, pp. 63–64.

30. Ibid., p. 63.

31. Bordwell, Staiger, and Thompson, p. 356.

32. Satō Tadao, *Currents in Japanese Cinema*, trans. Gregory Barrett (Tokyo: Kodansha, 1982), p. 227; Burch, p. 363.

33. There are no fewer than three film versions: the first by Makino Masahiro in 1948, Suzuki's in 1964, and a 1988 version directed by Gosha Hideo. However, on the package of the video version of Gosha's film (Tōei Video) it is claimed that Gosha's adaptation is the sixth film version of the novel. *Pia Cinema Club 90*, a reliable Japanese-language source, lists only the three by Makino, Suzuki, and Gosha.

34. For further discussion of Tamura's novels, these early film versions, and the Occupation's film policy in general, see Kyōko Hirano, *Mr. Smith goes to Tokyo: Japanese Cinema under the American Occupation* (Washington, D.C.: Smithsonian Institution Press, 1992).

35. Bordwell, "A Cinema of Flourishes," p. 331.

36. It is possible to read some of the scenes of Maya's dress as being blue, or blue-green. Similarly, violet would sometimes describe Omino's costume in different scenes. This may have to do with either the quality of the lighting of those specific scenes or the quality of the print I studied closely for this article—the home-video version from Nikkatsu Video. As I am not here concerned with the use of the camera or framing strategies, the fact that the film is pan-and-scanned instead of presented in the more typical letter-boxed format of Japanese videos for CinemaScope movies is of little concern in this context.

37. David Bordwell and Kristin Thompson, *Film Art: An Introduction*, 2d ed. (New York: Alfred A. Knopf, 1986), p. 136.

38. Arnheim, p. 368.

39. Ibid., p. 371.

40. Interview with Suzuki Seijun, *Eiga Hyōron*, January 1969, p. 20.

41. Haga Tōru, "Color and Design in Tokugawa Japan," in *Japan Color*, ed. Tanaka Ikko and Koike Kazuko (San Francisco: Chronicle Books, 1982), unpaged.

42. Ibid.

FILMOGRAPHY[1]

An Actor's Revenge (*Yukinojō henge*, Japan, 1936). Kinugasa Teinosuke.
An Actor's Revenge (*Yukinojō henge*, Japan, 1963). Ichikawa Kon.
Alexander Nevsky (USSR, 1938). Sergei Eisenstein.
All That Heaven Allows (U.S., 1956). Douglas Sirk.
Amadeus (U.S., 1984). Milos Forman.
Army Nurse (*Nǚérlóu*, PRC,[2] 1985). Hú Méi.
Ballad of Narayama (*Narayama bushikō*, Japan, 1958). Kinoshita Keisuke.
Ballad of Narayama (*Narayama bushikō*, Japan, 1983). Imamura Shōhei.
Being Two Isn't Easy (*Watashi wa nisai*, Japan, 1962). Ichikawa Kon.
Between Husband and Wife (*Wǒmen fūfù zhī jiān*, PRC, 1950). Zhèng Jūnlǐ.
The Birth of a Nation (U.S., 1915). D. W. Griffith.
Black Cannon Incident (*Hēipào shìjiàn*, PRC, 1985). Huáng Jiànxīn.
Black Rain (*Kuroi ame*, Japan, 1989). Imamura Shōhei.
Boy (*Shōnen*, Japan, 1969). Ōshima Nagisa.
Branded to Kill (*Koroshi no rakuin*, Japan, 1967). Suzuki Seijun.
Breathless (*A Bout de Souffle*, France, 1959). Jean-Luc Godard.
The Burning of Red Lotus Temple (*Huǒshāo Hóngliánsì*, China, 1928–1931). Zhāng Shíchuān.
Carmen Comes Home (*Karumen kokyō ni kaeru*, Japan, 1951). Kinoshita Keisuke.
A City of Sadness (*Bēiqíng chéngshì*, Taiwan [RC], 1988). Hou Hsiao-hsien (Hóu Xiàoxián).

1. All films are listed in the following manner: translated title, original title, country of origin, year, director(s). This filmography includes only the films mentioned in the essays in this anthology.
2. All mainland Chinese films made after 1949 are marked "PRC." Those made before 1949 are marked "China," as a point of distinction.

323

*Conflagration (Enjō, Japan, 1958). Ichikawa Kon.

*A Corner in the City (Dūshì de cūnzhuāng, PRC, 1982). Téng Wénjì.

Corner in Wheat (U.S., 1909). D. W. Griffith.

*Country Affections (Xiāngqíng, PRC, 1981). Hú Bǐngliú.

*Country Folks (Xiāngmín, PRC, 1986). Hú Bǐngliú.

*Country Voice (Xiāngyīn, PRC, 1984). Hú Bǐngliú.

A Crazy Page (aka *A Page of Madness; Kurutta ippeiji, Japan, 1926). Kinugasa Teinosuke.

*A Crowded Streetcar (Man'in densha, Japan, 1957). Ichikawa Kon.

*Crows and Sparrows (Wūyā yǔ máquè, PRC, 1949). Zhèng Jūnlǐ.

Death by Hanging (Kōshikei, Japan, 1968). Ōshima Nagisa.

*Dislocation (Cuòwèi, PRC, 1986). Huáng Jiànxīn.

*Doctor's Day Off (Honjitsu no kyūden, Japan, 1958). Shibuya Minoru.

*Dodeskaden (Dodesukaden, Japan, 1970). Kurosawa Akira.

*Dragnet Girl (Hijōsen no onna, Japan, 1933). Ozu Yasujirō.

*Dream of the Red Chamber (Hónglóu mèng, PRC, 1962). Cén Fàn.

*Dreams (Yume, Japan, 1990). Kurosawa Akira.

*The Drive to Win (Shā'ōu, PRC, 1981). Zhāng Nuǎnxīn.

*Early Spring (Sōshun, Japan, 1956). Ozu Yasujirō.

*The End of Summer (Kohayagawake no aki, Japan, 1961). Ozu Yasujirō.

*The Four-and-a-Half-Mat Room in Back — Soft, Secret Skin (Yojōhan fusuma no urabari-shinobi hada, Japan, 1974). Kumashiro Tatsumi.

*Gate of Flesh (Nikutai no mon, Japan, 1964). Suzuki Seijun.

*Gate of Hell (Jigokumon, Japan, 1953). Kinugasa Teinosuke.

*The Go Masters (Mikan no taikyoku, Japan/PRC, 1982). Satō Masahiro and Wáng Zhīmín.

*Harakiri (Seppuku, Japan, 1962). Kobayashi Masaki.

*A Hen in the Wind (Kaze no naka no mendori, Japan, 1948). Ozu Yasujirō.

*The Hidden Fortress (Kakushi toride no san akunin, Japan, 1958). Kurosawa Akira.

*High and Low (Tengoku to jigoku, Japan, 1963). Kurosawa Akira.

*The Human Condition (Ningen no jōken, Japan, 1959–1961). Kobayashi Masaki.

Ikiru (Japan, 1952). Kurosawa Akira.

*Judou (Júdòu, PRC, 1990). Zhāng Yìmóu.

Kaseki (Japan, 1985). Kobayashi Masaki.

The Key (aka *Odd Obsession; Kagi, Japan, 1959). Ichikawa Kon.

*King of the Children (Háizi wáng, PRC, 1988). Chén Kǎigē.

*Kwaidan (Kaidan, Japan, 1964). Kobayashi Masaki.

The Last Emperor (Italy/U.S./PRC, 1987). Bernardo Bertolucci.

*Late Spring (Banshun, Japan, 1949). Ozu Yasujirō.

Lawrence of Arabia (Great Britain/U.S., 1962). David Lean.

*Lieutenant Guan (Guān liánzhǎng, PRC, 1951). Shí Huī.

*The Life of an Actor (Geidō ichidai otoko, Japan, 1941). Mizoguchi Kenji.

*The Life of Oharu (Saikaku ichidai onna, Japan, 1952). Mizoguchi Kenji.

The Life of Tattoo (*Irezumi ichidai*, Japan, 1965). Suzuki Seijun.

The Life of Wǔ Xùn (*Wǔ Xùn zhuàn*, PRC, 1948–1950). Sūn Yú.

Long Live Missus (*Tàitai wànsuì*, China, 1947). Sāng Hú.

The Loyal Rōnin of the Genroku Era (*Genroku chūshingura*, Japan, 1941–1942). Mizoguchi Kenji.

Makioka Sisters (*Sasameyuki*, Japan, 1983). Ichikawa Kon.

Miserable at Middle Age (*Āi lè zhōngnián*, China, 1948). Sāng Hú.

Mr. Poo (*Pū-san*, Japan, 1953). Ichikawa Kon.

Muddy Waters (*Nigorie*, Japan, 1953). Imai Tadashi.

Myriads of Light (*Wànjiā dēnghuǒ*, China, 1948). Shěn Fú.

Naked General (*Hadaka no taishō*, Japan, 1958). Horikawa Hiromichi.

Natsuko's Adventures (*Natsuko no bōken*, Japan, 1953). Nakamura Noboru.

Neighbors (*Línjū*, PRC, 1981). Zhèng Dòngtiān, Xú Gèmíng.

October (aka *Ten Days That Shook the World*, USSR, 1928). Sergei Eisenstein.

Ohayō (Japan, 1959). Ozu Yasujirō.

Old Well (*Lǎojǐng*, PRC, 1987). Wú Tiānmíng.

On the Hunting Ground (*Liècháng zhásā*, PRC, 1984). Tián Zhuàngzhuàng.

Osaka Elegy (*Naniwa hika*, Japan, 1936). Mizoguchi Kenji.

Profound Desire of the Gods (*Kamigami no fukaki yokubō*, Japan, 1968). Imamura Shōhei.

Raise the Red Lantern (*Dàhóng dēnglóng gāogāo guà*, PRC, 1992). Zhāng Yìmóu.

Rashomon (*Rashōmon*, Japan, 1950). Kurosawa Akira.

The Realm of the Senses (*Ai no koriida*, Japan, 1976). Ōshima Nagisa.

Red Desert (*Deserto Rosso*, Italy, 1964). Michelangelo Antonioni.

The Red-Haired Girl (*Akai kami no onna*, Japan, 1979). Kumashiro Tatsumi.

Samurai Rebellion (*Jōiuchi*, Japan, 1967). Kobayashi Masaki.

Sansho the Bailiff (*Sanshō dayū*, Japan, 1954). Mizoguchi Kenji.

Sayuri Ichijo—Moist Desire (*Ichijō sayuri—nureta yokujō*, Japan, 1972). Kumashiro Tatsumi.

Serfs (*Nóngnú*, PRC, 1963). Lǐ Jūn.

Seven Samurai (*Shichinin no samurai*, Japan, 1954). Kurosawa Akira.

Sisters of the Gion (*Gion no shimai*, Japan, 1936). Mizoguchi Kenji.

Song of the Fisherman (*Yúguāng qǔ*, PRC, 1934). Cài Chǔshēng.

South Pacific (U.S., 1958). Joshua Logan.

Spring in a Small Town (*Xiǎochéng zhī chūn*, China, 1948). Fèi Mù.

A Spring River Flows East (*Yī jiāng chūnshuǐ xiàngdōng liú*, China, 1947–1948). Cài Chǔshēng, Zhèng Jūnlǐ.

Star Trek: The Motion Picture (U.S., 1979). Robert Wise.

A Story from Chikamatsu (*Chikamatsu monogatari*, Japan, 1954). Mizoguchi Kenji.

The Story of a Prostitute (aka *Joy Girls*; *Shunpu-den*, Japan, 1965). Suzuki Seijun.

The Story of the Last Chrysanthemum (*Zangiku monogatari*, Japan, 1939). Mizoguchi Kenji.

Strange Circle (*Guài qúan'r*, PRC, 1986–1987). Wáng Hàowéi.

Street of Joy (*Akasen tamanoi/nukeraremasu,* Japan, 1974). Kumashiro Tatsumi.

The Sun (*Nichirin,* Japan, 1953). Kinugasa Teinosuke.

Sunset Street (*Xīzhào jiē,* PRC, 1982). Wáng Hàowéi.

Superman (U.S., 1978). Richard Donner.

Swansong (*Juéxiǎng,* PRC, 1986). Zhāng Zémíng.

Tampopo (Japan, 1986). Itami Jūzō.

A Taxing Woman (*Marusa no onna,* Japan, 1987–1988). Itami Jūzō.

There Was a Father (*Chichi ariki,* Japan, 1942). Ozu Yasujirō.

The Thick-Walled Room (*Kabe atsuki heya,* Japan, 1953). Kobayashi Masaki.

This Life of Mine (*Wǒ zhèi yībèizi,* PRC, 1950). Shí Huī.

Throne of Blood (*Kumonosujō,* Japan, 1957). Kurosawa Akira.

A Time to Live and a Time to Die (*Tóngnián wǎngshì,* Taiwan [RC], 1985). Hou
   Hsiao-hsien (Hóu Xiàoxián).

Tokyo Drifter (*Tōkyō nagaremono,* Japan, 1966). Suzuki Seijun.

Tokyo Trial (*Tōkyō Saiban,* Japan, 1983). Kobayashi Masaki.

Tora-san Goes to Vienna (*Otoko wa tsurai yo/ Torajirō kokoro no tabiji,* Japan,
   1990). Yamada Yōji.

Twin Sisters (*Zǐmèi huā,* China, 1933). Zhèng Zhèngqiū.

Typhoon Club (*Taifū Kurabu,* Japan, 1986). Somai Shinji.

Ugetsu (*Ugetsu monogatari,* Japan, 1953). Mizoguchi Kenji.

"Un Chien Andalou" (France, 1928). Luis Buñuel and Salvador Dalí.

Under the Cherry Blossoms (*Sakura no mori no mankai no shita,* Japan 1975). Shinoda Masahiro.

Utamaro and His Five Women (*Utamaro o meguru gonin no onna,* Japan, 1946).
   Mizoguchi Kenji.

Victor, Victoria (U.S., 1982). Blake Edwards.

Walk Cheerfully (*Hogaraka ni ayume,* Japan, 1930). Ozu Yasujirō.

The Western Chamber (*Xīxiāng jì,* China, 1939). Zhāng Shíchuān.

Woman of Osaka (*Naniwa onna,* Japan, 1940). Mizoguchi Kenji.

A Worker's Love, or *The Romance of a Fruit Peddler* (*Láogōng zhī àiqíng, huò
   zhiguǒ yuán,* China, 1922). Zhèng Zhèngqiū.

Yamaha Fish Stall (*Yǎmǎhā yúdǎng,* PRC, 1984). Zhāng Liáng.

The Year of Living Dangerously (Australia, 1983). Peter Weir.

Yellow Earth (*Huáng tǔdì,* PRC, 1984). Chén Kǎigē.

Yoshitsune and the Thousand Cherry Trees (*Yoshitsune sembon zakura,* Japan,
   1914).

Young Mr. Lincoln (U.S., 1939). John Ford.

Yumeiji (Japan, 1990). Suzuki Seijun.

Aiken, Edward A. "Reflections on Dada and the Cinema." *Post Script: Essays in Film and the Humanities* 3 (Winter 1984): 5–19.

Anderson, Joseph L., and Donald Richie. *The Japanese Film: Art and Industry.* Expanded ed. Princeton: Princeton University Press, 1982.

Andrew, Dudley. *Film in the Aura of Art.* Princeton: Princeton University Press, 1984.

Arnheim, Rudolf. *Film as Art.* Berkeley: University of California Press, 1957.

Aumont, Jacques. *L'Oeil Interminable: Cinéma et Peinture.* Paris: Librairie Séguier, 1989.

Barmé, Geremie, and John Minford, eds. *Seeds of Fire — Chinese Voices of Conscience.* Hong Kong: Far Eastern Economic Review, 1986.

Barrett, Gregory. *Archetypes in Japanese Film: The Sociopolitical and Religious Significance of the Principal Heroes and Heroines.* Selinsgrove: Susquehanna University Press, 1989.

Barsaq, Leon. *Caligari's Cabinet and Other Grand Illusions: A History of Film Design.* Boston: New York Graphic Society, 1976.

Baudry, Jean-Louis. "Ideological Effects of the Basic Cinematographic Apparatus." *Film Quarterly* 28, no. 2 (1974–1975): 39–47.

Bazin, André. *What Is Cinema?* Translated by Hugh Gray. Berkeley: University of California Press, 1971.

Benjamin, Walter. "The Work of Art in the Age of Mechanical Reproduction." In *Illuminations.* New York: Schocken Books, 1969.

Berger, John. *Ways of Seeing.* London: Pelican Books, 1983.

Berry, Chris. "Chinese Urban Cinema: Hyper-Realism Versus Absurdism," *East-West Film Journal* 3, no. 1 (1988).

———. "Interview with Peng Xiaolian" and "Interview with Hu Mei." In *Camera Obscura* 18 (1989): 26–42.

————, ed. *Perspectives on Chinese Cinema*. 2d. ed. Princeton: Princeton University Press, 1991.

Blouin, Claude. *Dire l'éphémère*. Quebec: Hurtbuise, HMH, 1983.

Bock, Audie. *Japanese Film Directors*. Tokyo: Kodansha, 1978.

Bonitzer, Pascal. *Décadrages: Peinture et cinéma*. Paris: Cahiers du Cinéma/Editions de l'Etoile, 1985.

Bordwell, David. *Ozu and the Poetics of Cinema*. Princeton: Princeton University Press, 1988.

Branigan, Edward. "Color and Cinema: Problems in the Writing of History." *Film Reader* 4 (1979).

Burch, Noël. *To the Distant Observer: Form and Meaning in the Japanese Cinema*. Berkeley: University of California Press, 1979.

Carroll, Noël. *Mystifying Movies: Fads and Fallacies in Contemporary Film Theory*. New York: Columbia University Press, 1988.

Chén Kǎigē and Tony Rayns. *King of the Children and the New Chinese Cinema*. London: Faber and Faber, 1989.

Chén Kǎiyán, ed. *Hēipào shìjiàn — cóng xiǎoshuō dào diànyǐng*. Beijing: Zhōngguó-diànyǐng chūbǎnshè, 1988.

Clark, Paul. *Chinese Cinema: Culture and Politics since 1949*. Cambridge: Cambridge University Press, 1987.

Dalle-Vacche, Angela. "A Painter in Hollywood: Vincente Minelli's *An American in Paris*." *Cinema Journal* 32, no. 1 (Fall 1992): 63–83.

Davis, D. William. "Back to Japan: Militarism and Monumentalism in Prewar Japanese Cinema." *Wide Angle* 11, no. 3 (July 1989): 16–25.

Dayan, Daniel. "The Tutor-Code of Classical Cinema." In Bill Nichols, ed., *Movies and Methods*. Vol. 1. Berkeley: University of California Press, 1976.

Desser, David. *Eros plus Massacre: An Introduction to the Japanese New Wave Cinema*. Bloomington: Indiana University Press, 1988.

————. *The Samurai Films of Akira Kurosawa*. Ann Arbor: UMI Press, 1981.

Dower, John. "Ways of Seeing, Ways of Remembering: The Photography of Prewar Japan." In Japan Photographers' Association, *A Century of Japanese Photography*. New York: Pantheon, 1980, 3–20.

Edgerton, Gary. *Film and the Arts in Symbiosis*. New York: Greenwood, 1988.

Ehrlich, Linda C. "College Course File: East Asian Cinema" (with Ning Ma). *Journal of Film and Video* 42, no. 2 (Summer 1990): 53–70.

————. "Moving Pictures" (review). *Post Script* 8, no. 3 (Summer 1989): 70–72.

Eidsvik, Charles. *Cineliteracy: Films among the Arts*. New York: Random House, 1978.

Eisenstein, Sergei. *The Film Sense*. New York: Harcourt, Brace and Co., 1942.

Fell, John. Review of Gary Edgerton, ed., *Film and the Arts in Symbiosis*. In *Film Quarterly* 42, no. 4 (Summer 1989): 58–59.

Fragola, Anthony. "Art as a Source of Imagistic Generator for Narrative." *Journal of Film and Video* 42, no. 3 (Fall 1990).

Gomrich, E. H. *Art and Illusion*. Princeton: Princeton University Press, 1960.

Hollander, Anne. *Moving Pictures*. New York: Alfred A. Knopf, 1989.

Jones, Elizabeth. "Films That 'Never Transcend the Realm of Art.' " *Post Script* 3 (Winter 1984): 20–33.

Katō Shūichi. *Form, Style, Tradition: Reflections on Japanese Art*. Berkeley: University of California Press, 1979.

Kirby, Lynne. "Painting and Cinema: The Frames of Discourse." (Review of Bonitzer). *Camera Obscura* 18 (1989): 95–105.

Kirihara, Donald. *Patterns of Time: Mizoguchi and the 1930s*. Madison: University of Wisconsin Press, 1992.

Kirkpatrick, Diane. "Editor's Statement: Art History and the Study of Film." *Art Journal* 43, no. 3 (Fall 1983): 221–222.

Lau, Jenny. "A Hermeneutical Reading of *Judou*." *Film Quarterly* 45, no. 2 (Winter 1992): 2–10.

Lawder, Standish D. *The Cubist Cinema*. New York: New York University Press, 1975.

Léger, Fernand. "Painting and Cinema." In *French Film Theory and Criticism 1907–1939*. Edited by Richard Abel. Vol. 1. Princeton: Princeton University Press, 1988.

McDonald, Keiko I. *Cinema East: A Critical Study of Major Japanese Films*. Rutherford, N.J.: Fairleigh Dickinson University Press, 1983.

Marchetti, Gina. "The Blooming of a Revolutionary Aesthetic: *Two Stage Sisters*." *Jump Cut* 34 (1989): 95–106.

Mellen, Joan. *The Waves at Genji's Door*. New York: Pantheon, 1976.

Moholy-Nagy, Laslo. *Painting, Photography, Film*. Cambridge: MIT Press, 1969.

Nilsen, Vladimir. *The Cinema as a Graphic Art*. Translated by Stephen Garry. New York: Hill and Wang, 1937.

Nolletti, Arthur, Jr., and David Desser, eds. *Reframing Japanese Cinema: Authorship, Genre, History*. Bloomington: Indiana University Press, 1992.

Nygren, Scott. "Reconsidering Modernism: Japanese Film and the Postmodern Context." *Wide Angle* 11, no. 3 (July 1989): 6–15.

Paini, Dominique. "Le Cinéma Est la Peinture/Le Cinéma Hait la Peinture: Entretien avec Jacques Aumont." *Cahiers du Cinéma*, June 1989, 421.

Panofsky, Erwin. "Style and Medium in the Motion Picture." *Bulletin of the Department of Art and Archaeology*. Princeton: Princeton University, 1934.

Peterson, James. "A War of Utter Rebellion: Kinugasa's *Page of Madness* and the Japanese Avant-Garde of the 1920s." *Cinema Journal* 29, no. 1 (Fall 1989): 36–53.

Praz, Mario. *Mnemosyne: The Parallel between Literature and the Visual Arts*. Princeton: Princeton University Press, 1970.

Prince, Stephen. *The Warrior's Camera: The Cinema of Akira Kurosawa*. Princeton: Princeton University Press, 1991.

Richie, Donald. *The Films of Akira Kurosawa*. Berkeley: University of California Press, 1970.

————. *Japanese Cinema: An Introduction*. Oxford: Oxford University Press, 1990.

————. *Ozu: His Life and Films*. Berkeley: University of California Press, 1974.

————. "Viewing Japanese Film: Some Considerations." *East-West Film Journal* 1, no. 1 (December 1986): 23–25.

Satō Tadao. *Currents in Japanese Cinema*. Translated by Gregory Barrett. Tokyo: Kodansha, 1982.

———— and Nanbu Kyōichirō. *Nihon eiga hyakusen (One Hundred Selections of Japanese Cinema)*. Tokyo: Akita Shoten, 1973.

Semsel, George, ed. *Chinese Film: The State of the Art in the People's Republic*. New York: Praeger, 1987.

————, Xia Hong, and Hou Jianping, eds. *Chinese Film Theory: A Guide to the New Era*. Translated by Hou Jianping, Li Xiaohong, and Fan Yuan. New York: Praeger, 1990.

Soren, David. *The Rise and Fall of the Horror Film: An Art Historical Approach to Fantasy Cinema*. Columbia, Mo.: Lucas Brothers Publishers, 1977.

Thompson, Kristin. "Notes on the Spatial System of Ozu's Early Films." *Wide Angle* 1, no. 4 (1977): 8–17.

————, and David Bordwell, "Space and Narrative in the Films of Ozu." *Screen* 17, no. 2 (Summer 1976): 41–105.

Tyler, Parker. "The Film Sense and the Painting Sense." *Arts Digest*, February 15, 1954, 10–12, 27–28.

Ueda Makoto. *Literary and Art Theories in Japan*. Cleveland: The Press of Western Reserve University, 1967; Center for Japanese Studies, 1991.

Viatte, Germain, ed. *Peinture, Cinéma, Peinture*. Museum catalogue. Marseille: Centre de la Vieille Charité, 1989.

Weismann, Donald. *The Visual Arts as Human Experience*. Englewood Cliffs, N.J.: Prentice Hall, 1970.

Williams, Alan. Review of Jacques Aumont, *L'Oeil Interminable: Cinéma et Peinture*. *Screen* 32, no. 2 (Summer 1991): 234–243.

Woo, Catherine Yi-Yu Cho. "The Chinese Montage: From Poetry and Painting to the Silver Screen." In *Perspectives on Chinese Cinema*. Edited by Chris Berry, 21–29.

Yau, Esther C. M. "*Yellow Earth*: Western Analysis and a Non-Western Text." *Film Quarterly* 41, no. 2 (1987–1988): 22–33.

Zambrano, A. "*Throne of Blood*: Kurosawa's *Macbeth*." *Literature/Film Quarterly* 2 (1974): 262–274.

ĀN JĬNGFŪ is a lecturer at the Beijing Film Academy. He received his master of arts degree in film studies from the Beijing Film Academy in 1988, and has served as assistant director for several prize-winning Chinese films. He was a visiting instructor in the Department of Film and Video, Columbia College, during the 1992–93 academic year.

DUDLEY ANDREW is Angelo Bertocci Professor of Critical Studies and the Director of the Institute for Cinema and Culture at the University of Iowa. He is the author of, among other books, *Film in the Aura of Art* and (with his brother Paul Andrew) *Kenji Mizoguchi: A Guide to References and Resources.*

CHRIS BERRY teaches Cinema Studies at La Trobe University in Melbourne, Australia. He has worked in the Chinese film industry and edited *Perspectives on Chinese Cinema* (1991). His articles on Chinese cinema have appeared in *Cinema Journal, Camera Obscura, Jump Cut, East-West Film Journal, Cinemaya,* and *Continuum,* among others.

CYNTHIA CONTRERAS, Assistant Professor in the Film Department of Brooklyn College, CUNY, has lectured and written on the works of Kurosawa, Kobayashi, and Shinoda.

D. WILLIAM DAVIS completed his doctorate in film studies from the University of Wisconsin, writing a dissertation on prewar Japanese cinema. He also served as Curator of Film and Video at the Honolulu Academy of Arts.

DAVID DESSER is Professor of Cinema Studies and Speech Communication at the University of Illinois at Urbana-Champaign. He is the author of *The Samurai Films of Akira Kurosawa* (1983) and *Eros plus Massacre: An Introduction to the Japanese New Wave Cinema* (1988).

LINDA C. EHRLICH is Assistant Professor of Japanese and Cinema at the University of Tennessee at Knoxville. Her articles on Asian cinema have appeared in *East-West Film Journal, Cinemaya, Japan Forum*, and *Journal of Film and Video,* among others. She has conducted workshops and lectures at the Cleveland Museum of Art and the University Art Museum, Berkeley, on this topic of the relationship between the visual arts and cinema.

MARY ANN FARQUHAR teaches Chinese literature, film, and language in the Division of Asian and International Studies at Griffith University in Queensland, Australia. Her particular interests are in Chinese popular culture, and she has written a history of children's literature in China.

KATHE GEIST received her Ph.D. in art history from the University of Michigan and has taught at Illinois State University and Koryo International College near Nagoya, Japan. Her articles on Japanese cinema have appeared in *Art Journal, East-West Film Journal, Film Quarterly,* and *Image Forum* (Tokyo), and she is author of *The Cinema of Wim Wenders: From Paris, France, to "Paris, Texas"* (1988).

HǍO DÀZHĒNG is an architect and Associate Professor of Film Theory, China Film Art Research Center, Beijing. Professor Hao translated Dudley Andrew's *Concepts in Film Theory* into Chinese. He now resides in Germany.

JENNY KWOK WAH LAU is Assistant Professor of Film at Ohio University. She has published articles on Chinese cinema in *Wide Angle* and *Film Quarterly,* as well as in Hong Kong journals.

SHERMAN E. LEE is the retired director of the Cleveland Museum of Art and currently Adjunct Professor of Art at the University of North Carolina at Chapel Hill and Duke University. He is author of numerous books on Asian art, including *Eight Dynasties of Chinese Painting* (with W. K. Ho, L. Sideman, and M. Wilson, 1980) and *Reflections of Reality in Japanese Art* (1983).

NÍ ZHÈN, Associate Professor and Director of the theory research section of the Beijing Film Academy, has written extensively on realism in the Chinese cinema and on film theory. A noted screenwriter, his work was seen recently in Zhāng Yìmóu's *Raise the Red Lantern.*

DONALD RICHIE is the award-winning author of many books on the Japanese cinema, including major studies of Kurosawa and Ozu.

THOMAS RIMER is Professor of Japanese Literature and Chair of the Department of East Asian Languages and Literatures at the University of Pittsburgh. He is the author and translator of a variety of books on Japanese literature, art, and culture, including *Pilgrimages: Aspects of Japanese Literature and Culture* (1988).

ANN SHERIF teaches Japanese literature and language at Case Western Reserve University in Cleveland, Ohio. Her translations have appeared in *New Japanese Voices: The Best Contemporary Fiction from Japan* and *N.P.* by Banana Yoshimoto.

SATŌ TADAO is a film critic and historian, and editor of the journal *Eigashi kenkyū*. A collection of his essays has been published in English under the title *Currents in Japanese Cinema*.

DOUGLAS WILKERSON received his Ph.D. from the Department of East Asian Languages and Literatures at Yale University, and teaches Chinese language and literature at The University of Tennessee at Knoxville.

CINEMATIC LANDSCAPES